# Windows NT 4.0
# Workstation

# Windows NT 4.0 Workstation

## Accelerated MCSE Study Guide

Dave Kinnaman
LouAnn Ballew

McGraw-Hill
New York • San Francisco • Washington, D.C. • Auckland
Bogotá • Caracas • Lisbon • London • Madrid • Mexico City
Milan • Montreal • New Delhi • San Juan • Singapore
Sydney • Tokyo • Toronto

**Library of Congress Cataloging-in-Publication Data**

Kinnaman, Dave.
   Accelerated MCSE study guide. Windows NT 4.0 Workstation /  Dave
   Kinnaman, LouAnn Ballew.
      p.    cm.
   Includes index.
   ISBN 0-07-067683-6
   1. Electronic data processing personnel—Certification.
   2. Microsoft software—Examinations—Study guides.   3. Microsoft
   Windows NT.   I. Ballew, LouAnn.
   III. Title.
   QA76.3.K56   1998
   005.4'469—dc21                                                98-39246
                                                                      CIP

# McGraw-Hill

*A Division of The McGraw·Hill Companies*

1 2 3 4 5 6 7 8 9 0   AGM/AGM   9 0 3 2 1 0 9 8

ISBN 0-07-067683-6

The sponsoring editor for this book was Michael Sprague and the production
supervisor was Tina Cameron. It was set by D & G Limited, LLC.

Printed and bound by Quebecor/Martinsburg.

McGraw-Hill books are available at special quantity discounts to use as
premiums and sales promotions, or for use in corporate training programs.
For more information, please write to Director of Special Sales, McGraw-Hill,
11 West 19th Street, New York, NY 10011. Or contact your local bookstore.

This book is printed on recycled, acid-free paper containing a minimum of 50% recycled de-inked fiber.

# Contents

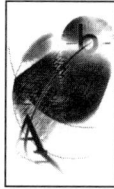

# CHAPTER 1

# Introduction to this Study Guide

So you want to become a Microsoft Certified Systems Engineer —MCSE, do you? Then you've made a good choice in purchasing this book, because it's specifically designed to prepare you for a vital MCSE examination. This chapter is designed to prepare you for planning the whole process of becoming an MCSE by assisting you in outlining the unique process for you to prepare to pass all of your MCSE examinations.

According to Microsoft, "Microsoft Certified Systems Engineers design, install, support, and troubleshoot information systems. MCSEs are network gurus, support technicians, and operating system experts." This is a central information technology role with major responsibilities in today's computer networking world.

## Plan Your MCSE Process

To prepare for such a major role, it takes a solid plan. You must know all your options. So let's begin the planning with a discussion of the components of the objective: The core exams and elective exams that lead toward the MCSE certificate. After identifying the core and elective exams, the remainder of this section is devoted to dispelling several myths about MCSE exams which could derail your plan if you believe them.

## Core and Elective Exams

Two routes toward the MCSE actually exist at this writing. The vast majority of candidates concentrate on the more recent track. The older track is based on Windows NT 3.51, and the newer track is based on Windows NT 4.0. Because the exams for Windows NT 3.51 have been scheduled for retirement, little more will be said about Windows NT 3.51.

### MICROSOFT WINDOWS NT 4.0 TRACK

This track consists of mastering four core and two elective exams. After the core exams, all of the many current elective exams are presented.

*You must choose four core exams from these eight:*

- 70-030: Microsoft Windows 3.1 (retires September 1998)
- 70-048: Microsoft Windows for Workgroups 3.11 (retires September 1998)
- 70-058: Networking Essentials
- 70-064: Implementing and Supporting Microsoft Windows 95
- 70-067: Implementing and Supporting Microsoft Windows NT Server 4.0
- 70-068: Implementing and Supporting Microsoft Windows NT Server 4.0 in the Enterprise
- 70-073: Microsoft Windows NT Workstation 4.0
- 70-098: Implementing and Supporting Microsoft Windows 98

*You must choose two elective exams:*

There are a great number of elective exams available. You can choose to become expert on any two of these ten software products.

1. SNA Server
2. Systems Management Server
3. SQL Server
4. TCP/IP on Microsoft Windows NT
5. Exchange Server
6. Internet Information Server
7. Proxy Server

8. Microsoft Mail for PC Networks

9. Enterprise Site Server, or

10. Explorer 4.0 by Using the Internet Explorer Administration Kit

**CAUTION**
Microsoft allows you to use exams for one, two, or three versions of several software products as electives. Only one exam per product, regardless of version, can be counted toward the two-elective requirement. For example, if you pass both 70-013: Implementing and Supporting Microsoft SNA Server *version 3.0* and 70-085: Implementing and Supporting Microsoft SNA Server *version 4.0*, these two exams only count for one elective. The point is that passing exams on two versions of one product doesn't count as two electives—just one counts as an elective.

With the following options available, MCSE candidates can surely find elective exams to fit their own career and workplace goals.
One of these:

- 70-013: Implementing and Supporting Microsoft SNA Server 3.0
- 70-085: Implementing and Supporting Microsoft SNA Server 4.0

or one of these:

- 70-014: Implementing and Supporting Microsoft Systems Management Server 1.0 (retired)
- 70-018: Implementing and Supporting Microsoft Systems Management Server 1.2
- 70-086: Implementing and Supporting Microsoft Systems Management Server 2.0

or one of these:

- 70-021: Microsoft SQL Server 4.2 Database Implementation
- 70-027: Implementing a Database Design on Microsoft SQL Server 6.5
- 70-029: Implementing a Database Design on Microsoft SQL Server 7.0

or one of these:

- 70-022: Microsoft SQL Server 4.2 Database Administration for Microsoft Windows NT
- 70-026: System Administration for Microsoft SQL Server 6.5
- 70-028: System Administration for Microsoft SQL Server 7.0

or one of these:

- 70-053: Internetworking Microsoft TCP/IP on Microsoft Windows NT (3.5-3.51)
- 70-059: Internetworking with Microsoft TCP/IP on Microsoft Windows NT 4.0

or one of these:

- 70-075: Implementing and Supporting Microsoft Exchange Server 4.0   (retired June 1, 1998)*
- 70-076: Implementing and Supporting Microsoft Exchange Server 5
- 70-081: Implementing and Supporting Microsoft Exchange Server 5.5

or one of these:

- 70-077: Implementing and Supporting Microsoft Internet Information Server 3.0 and Microsoft Index Server 1.1
- 70-087: Implementing and Supporting Microsoft Internet Information Server 4.0

or one of these:

- 70-078: Implementing and Supporting Microsoft Proxy Server 1.0
- 70-088: Implementing and Supporting Microsoft Proxy Server 2.0

or

*Exam 70-075: for Exchange Server 4.0 retired on June 1, 1998. If you have already passed this elective exam, you will be required to take a replacement elective exam on or before September 1, 1999. Replacement exams include all current MCSE electives listed here.

- 70-037: Microsoft Mail for PC Networks 3.2-Enterprise

or

- 70-056: Implementing and Supporting Web Sites Using Microsoft Site Server 3.0

or

- 70-079: Implementing and Supporting Microsoft Internet Explorer 4.0 by Using the Internet Explorer Administration Kit

## Required Software and Hardware

Many current MCSE holders earned their certificates at little or no out-of-pocket expense to themselves because their employers paid the costs for both training and exams. In addition, many of them also did all or almost all of their exam preparation on the clock; so their employers actually paid them to get an MCSE certificate. These fortunate MCSEs didn't even have to pay for software or equipment because their employers also supplied appropriate software and hardware needed to practice all the skills necessary for their MCSE exams. If your employer offers this kind of comprehensive support, that's wonderful. On the other hand, if your employer expects you to pay your own way to the MCSE entirely, here are some thoughts on what you'll need.

### REQUIRED SOFTWARE

In most cases you'll need at least one copy of both the server and the client software because most MCSE exams are about administering networks containing the software in question. You'll need to know how the product works from both the client and administrator points of view, even if the exam is specifically about a client software such as Windows NT 4.0 Workstation. As mentioned, the MCSE exams are usually from the system support and administrator's point of view, rather than the client user's point of view.

Installing a Microsoft client software may, of course, require a pre-existing operating system or a previous version of the client software, depending on the product involved.

Similarly, several Microsoft server operating systems require you to have other server operating systems available on the network or installed and underlying on the server computer. This means that more than one server software program may be required in order for you to use, and become familiar with, all the tested features of the server software required for the exam.

## MINIMUM HARDWARE REQUIREMENTS

One or more Windows NT Workstation computers:

- 12 MB RAM
- VGA video
- Keyboard
- IDE, EIDE, SCSI, or ESDI hard disk
- 486/25 processor or faster
- 124 MB free hard drive space (Recommended minimum: over 300 MB, including a copy of the entire I386 installation directory [223 MB] plus Windows 95 or DOS 6.22). For hard disk controllers using translation mode to address the drive, increase these minimum sizes by 80 MB.
- CD-ROM drive, or a floppy disk drive and an active network connection

One or more Windows NT Server computers:

- 16 MB RAM (32 MB or more recommended)
- VGA video
- Keyboard
- IDE, EIDE, SCSI, or ESDI hard disk
- 486/25 processor (486DX2/50 or better preferred)
- 124 MB free hard drive space (Recommended minimum: over 300 MB, including a copy of the entire I386 installation directory [223 MB] plus Windows 95 or DOS 6.22). For hard disk controllers using translation mode to address the drive, increase these minimum sizes by 80 MB.
- CD-ROM drive (Windows NT compatible recommended) or a floppy disk drive and an active network connection
- Recommended: 28.8 v.34 (or faster) external modem, for remote debugging and troubleshooting

## COSTS TO OBTAIN AN MCSE

As mentioned previously, the costs of an MCSE certificate are invisible to many current certificate holders because the costs are entirely supported by their employers. Because these advanced skills are of great value to the workplace, it's appropriate that employers provide this support in exchange for more efficient and more productive work skills.

Some supportive employers do require a contract, to assure themselves that the newly trained MCSE will not change jobs to another employer shortly after obtaining the MCSE certificate—presumably before the current employer has had time to recoup the costs of the MCSE for their former employee. These contracts typically require the employee to repay MCSE costs on a pro-rated basis depending on how long the MCSE candidate remained with the former employer. Often the new employer picks up the costs of buying out the former employer's training contract as a part of the new, and more advantageous, employment agreement.

Note that MCSE holders are considered more employable, and therefore, more mobile in their employment. The cost efficiency of information technology in workplaces has been hard hit by a mercenary, contract-worker mentality that drains the spirit from workers. In contrast, employers who provide an environment of mutual trust and employment security by fostering loyalty and goodwill in all employees will obtain the best return on their investment in employee MCSE training.

| MCSE Expense Budget | Costs |
|---|---|
| Examinations—$600 (retests at $100 each) | _____ |
| Training, seminars, workshops | _____ |
| Study time | _____ |
| Books and materials | _____ |
| Practice examination software | _____ |
| Network hardware, network analysis equipment | _____ |
| Server and client hardware | _____ |
| Server and client software | _____ |

## MCSE Myth #1—Everyone Must Take Six Exams to Earn the MCSE

### Reality—Some People are Exempt from One Exam

Some networking professionals are exempt from taking the Networking Essentials exam because they already passed a similarly rigorous exam through Novell, Banyan, Sun, or Microsoft. These professionals are already skilled and possess certificates to prove it. Microsoft grants them MCSE certificates after they pass only five additional Microsoft exams.

Specifically, Microsoft automatically grants credit for the Networking Essentials exam once you've passed a Microsoft Certified Professional (MCP) exam and provide evidence that you hold one of these exact certificates:

**NOVELL**

CNE—Certified Novell Engineer

CNI—Certified Novell Instructor

ECNE—Enterprise Certified Novell Engineer

MCNE—Master Certified Novell Engineer

**BANYAN**

CBE—Certified Banyan CBE

CBS—Certified Banyan Specialist

**SUN**

CNA—Sun Certified Network Administrators for Solaris 2.5

CNA—Sun Certified Network Administrators for Solaris 2.6

So if you already hold one of these certificates, just pass one MCP exam and provide proof of your previous networking certificate, and you'll receive credit for two exams for the price of one.

### What's an MCP Exam?

An MCP exam is a Microsoft exam. Passing an MCP exam makes you a Microsoft Certified Professional and automatically enrolls you in the Microsoft MCP program. Not all Microsoft exams are MCP exams, though. Networking Essentials, for instance, is not an MCP exam.

| Microsoft Certified | **MICROSOFT CERTIFIED** |
| Professional | **PROFESSIONALS (MCPs)** |

Microsoft Certified Professionals get their certificates by passing a Microsoft exam based on a Windows server or desktop operating system. Please note: Not all MCP exams contribute to an MCSE certificate! In fact, not many do! When you make your MCSE plans, be sure to check the official Microsoft requirements to assure yourself that requirements have not changed since this study guide was written. Here are all the MCP exams that, as of this writing, can contribute toward an MCSE certification:

## MCP EXAMS IN THE WINDOWS NT 4.0 MCSE TRACK

- 70-030: Microsoft Windows 3.1 (retires September 1998)
- 70-048: Microsoft Windows for Workgroups 3.11-Desktop (retires September 1998)
- 70-064: Implementing and Supporting Microsoft Windows 95
- 70-067 Implementing and Supporting Microsoft Windows NT Server 4.0
- 70-073 Implementing and Supporting Microsoft Windows NT Workstation 4.0

## MCP EXAMS IN THE WINDOWS NT 3.51 MCSE TRACK

- 70-030: Microsoft Windows 3.1 (retires September 1998)
- 70-042: Implementing and Supporting Windows NT Workstation 3.51 (retires as Windows NT Workstation 5.0 exam is released)
- 70-043: Implementing and Supporting Windows NT Server 3.51 (retires as Windows NT Server 5.0 exam is released)
- 70-048: Microsoft Windows for Workgroups 3.11-Desktop (retires September 1998)
- 70-064: Implementing and Supporting Microsoft Windows 95

Every MCSE certificate holder has multiple MCP designations because of the nature of the MCSE requirements.

There is also a "premium" MCP certificate called MCP+Internet available. MCP certificates are considered the basic Microsoft certificate leading to a premium MCP certificate or, in many cases, to MCSE status. MCPs have a private Microsoft Web site, a free magazine, other benefits, and a special logo of their own. Here is the URL for the Microsoft MCP Web site.

Microsoft Certified Professional Web site—Certification Home Page

```
http://www.microsoft.com/mcp
```

By taking an MCP exam early in the MCSE process, you can gain access to the MCP benefits just mentioned. They are valuable to obtaining an MCSE as well.

---

## TWO RETIRED MICROSOFT EXAMS MAY SUBSTITUTE FOR NETWORKING ESSENTIALS

In addition to the networking certificates listed previously from Banyan, Novell, and Sun that can substitute for passing the Networking Essentials exam, there are two more ways to achieve an MCSE with only five (additional) exams. If you happen to have taken and passed one of the following retired Microsoft exams, you can use that previous exam to have the Networking Essentials exam MCSE requirement waived.

Exam 70-046: Networking with Microsoft Windows for Workgroups 3.11 (retired)

*or*

Exam 70-047: Networking with Microsoft Windows 3.1 (retired).

Retired Microsoft exams are explained in detail later in this chapter.

## MCSE Myth #2—Only One Year to Finish

### Reality—Take as Long as You Like to Finish Your MCSE

Take as much time as you need to be prepared for each test. There is no stated time limit for completion of the MCSE certificate. Begin and take examinations when you are ready. Although there is a popular misconception that you have only one year (or two years or *whatever*) to complete your MCSE certificate, there is in fact no time limit. The only limits are your own motivation and the time you have available. Because you are an adult, you can decide for yourself how much more of your life you want to spend working on something other than an MCSE.

So, you should plan to progress at your own deliberate, or expeditious, speed. This depends on your needs, your personal learning style, and the amount of time, money and concentration you can devote to this project. Everyone starts their MCSE studies with different personal backgrounds, different circumstances, and different knowledge. Each reader brings different expectations for this book. Some will want a guide:

- to confirm they already know enough to be certified;

- to accompany a class or even a crash course;

- to study on their own, reading and applying the concepts as they go.

Not having an MCSE time limit is also consistent with good educational design because adults learn best at their own rates and in their own ways. It also keeps Microsoft away from the "bad guy" enforcer role. This way Microsoft never has to say, "Sorry, all your work was for nothing, you're too late—you must start over."

### CAUTION—WHAT IF IT TAKES TOO LONG?
There is a possible down side to extending your MCSE studies. The longer you take, the more likely it is that one of the exams you've already passed will be retired before you finish your MCSE studies. If an exam you've passed is retired while you are still pursuing your MCSE, you'll need to replace the retired exam with a current exam, causing you more work to accomplish the same original goal.

Another reason to move toward your MCSE with all due dispatch is in recognition of your own personal learning style. Many adults learn best if they concentrate heavily on learning, passing exams as a kind of punctuation in their study cycle. Also, each exam has areas of overlap with other exams. What you learn for one exam will help with other exams, as well. Taking Exam B soon after taking Exam A while the learning for Exam A is still fresh in your memory can be ideal for some adult learners. Adjust your exam strategy to accommodate your own learning style.

Establish a timeline for yourself. The longer you take to complete the MCSE track, the less likely you are to finish. Establish a study and examination schedule for yourself and make a serious effort to stick to the schedule and complete the exams in a timely manner.

People generally work better if "the end is in sight," so help yourself by creating a game plan for your certification.

## MCSE Myth #3—Two-week Wait for a Retest

### *Reality—First Retest Anytime, Second Retest After Two Weeks*

Although there have been several changes instituted to improve MCSE exam security, it is still okay to re-take a failed exam as soon as you want. So, if it happens that:

- you fell asleep during the exam;
- you just had a bad day and only missed passing by one question;
- you were coming down with the flu the day of the exam; or
- you otherwise failed an exam in a fluke event that did not represent your true level of mastery of the material;

then you can reschedule the same exam and retest as soon as you please—at full price, of course. If you fail twice, however, you will be required to wait at least two weeks before trying a third time.

### TEST TIP

Many MCSE candidates and MCSE certificate holders are convinced that certain questions appear on more than one exam. It seems to others that one or two questions are pulled from their "mother" exam and placed at random on other exams without a discernible pattern. They claim that questions they expected on the TCP/IP exam turned up on the Windows NT Server or the Enterprise exam, for instance. Building a strong personal foundation of knowledge and experience is the only defense against this sort of random substitution, if it occurs.

It is clear that the exams are at least quasi-hierarchical, in that almost all Windows NT Workstation questions are legitimate fodder for the Windows NT Server exam, and all Windows NT Server exam questions are fair game for the Windows NT Server in the Enterprise exam, for instance. Likewise, all Networking Essentials questions are also fair game on the TCP/IP exam. This is another reason to take the exams in a deliberate, thoughtful order that makes sense with your own experience and knowledge.

## MCSE Myth #4—You Must Pass Exam A Before Exam B

### *Reality—There is No Required Exam Sequence*

### *Which Exam Should You Take First?*

Please understand that there is no required sequence at all. You can take the MCSE exams in any order you please and achieve your certificate with no prejudice based on the order of your exams. However, there are good reasons why you might want to consider a purposeful, rather than random sequence of tests.

Here is a sample study plan. It's based on three assumptions, which may or may not be true for you.

1. You aren't already certifiable in one or more exam areas, and

2. You don't have more extensive experience and knowledge in some exam areas than the others, and

3. You've decided to take these six exams, for example, to satisfy the requirements for the MCSE.

- Example Core Requirements

    70-058 Networking Essentials

    70-067 Implementing and Supporting Microsoft Windows NT Server 4.0

    70-068 Implementing and Supporting Microsoft Windows NT Server 4.0 in the Enterprise

    70-073 Implementing and Supporting Microsoft Windows NT Workstation 4.0

- Example Elective Requirements

    70-059 Internetworking with Microsoft TCP/IP on Windows NT 4.0

    70-077 Implementing and Supporting Microsoft Internet Information Server 3.0 and Microsoft Index Server 1.1

If these exams and givens fit your case, you might want to proceed in one of the exam sequences suggested later. First, check out the sidebar for basic suggestions for sequencing all MCSE exams:

---

### SUGGESTIONS FOR MCSE EXAM SEQUENCING

- **Take the exam(s) you are already better prepared for first, if possible, to get things rolling and to begin your benefits as an MCP. Current Microsoft MCP benefits are summarized in another sidebar.**

- Take the more fundamental exam first, if one exam is a building block for another exam. This allows you to begin laying the conceptual and learning foundation for more complex ideas.
- Take exams with Fair to High overlaps in Table 1-1 in succession, if possible.
- Take exams that will be easiest for you either at the beginning or at the end of the sequence, or as a deliberate break between tougher exams that are more challenging to you.

### Enterprise, Server, Workstation

Table 1.1 estimates the overlap of content and knowledge areas between several popular exams. Of these, the three most closely related exams are

- Windows NT Workstation
- Windows NT Server
- Windows NT Server in the Enterprise

It makes sense to take these three exams in that order (Workstation, Server, and Enterprise) unless you already have an extensive or special expertise in Windows NT Server or Windows NT Server in the Enterprise.

Of the exams listed in Table 1.1, these four are generally considered to be the toughest exams:

- Windows NT Server in the Enterprise
- TCP/IP on Microsoft Windows NT (any version)
- Windows 95 (retired)
- Exchange Server 5.0

As usual, the toughest exam for you will be the one for which you are unprepared.

## Table 1.1

| Perceived<br>Exam<br>Overlaps | Networking<br>Essentials | Windows NT<br>Workstation | Windows<br>NT Server | NT Server<br>in the<br>Enterprise | TCP/IP |
|---|---|---|---|---|---|
| Networking<br>Essentials | | | | | |
| NT Workstation | Low | | | | |
| NT Server | Low | High | | | |
| NT Server /<br>Enterprise | Fair | Low | High | | |
| TCP/IP | High | Low | Low | Low | |
| IIS and Index Server | Low | Low | Fair | Fair | High |
| Windows 95 | Low | Low | Low | Low | Fair |
| Exchange Server 5.0 | Low | Low | Fair | Fair | Fair |

Some exams overlap more than others. The Windows NT Server and the Windows NT Server in the Enterprise Exams have a high degree of overlap.

### TCP/IP, Networking Essentials, IIS and Index Server

The next strongest relationship between the exams is the high degree of overlap between TCP/IP and both the Networking Essentials exam and the IIS and Index Server exam. Networking Essentials is often taken early in the exam sequence because it is considered the foundation of standards and definitions needed for networking concepts used in other exams.

As said, TCP/IP is judged to be one of the more difficult exams, even after the exam was re-designed to moderate the impact of subnetting.

IIS and Index Server is commonly considered one of the most straightforward MCSE exams largely because MCSE candidates are familiar with how to prepare for Microsoft exams by the time they attempt IIS and Index Server. IIS and Index Server also covers a more limited amount of material than the other exams, making it a quicker study.

So, combining all these information sources, here are some acceptable proposed exam sequences:

## EXAM SEQUENCE A

1. Networking Essentials
2. Workstation
3. Server
4. Enterprise
5. TCP/IP
6. IIS and Index Server

## EXAM SEQUENCE B

1. Networking Essentials
2. TCP/IP
3. Workstation
4. Server
5. IIS and Index Server
6. Enterprise

## EXAM SEQUENCE C

1. Workstation
2. Networking Essentials
3. Server
4. Enterprise
5. TCP/IP
6. IIS and Index Server

If you selected other exams for your MCSE rather than the six used in these examples, use these same principles to find your own ideal exam sequence.

### TEST TIP—SOME NETWORKING EXPERTS FIND MICROSOFT EXAMS DIFFICULT

It is not uncommon for networking professionals with years of actual experience to fail the Networking Essentials exam. Likewise, it is often heard that the TCP/IP exam is considered tough by seasoned Internet experts. Why is this so?

The most satisfying explanation is that these professionals already know too much about real-world networking, and they "read into" the exams real-world facts not stated in the question. Many Microsoft exam questions are stated ambiguously, and the resultant vagueness seems to force these professionals to make assumptions. They assume that if the question says X, and they know that X is almost always because of Y, that Z must be true—only to find that Z is not even an available answer!

For their colleagues taking the Networking Essentials or TCP/IP exams from Microsoft, network professionals advise that, nothing from the real-world should be assumed. Read the questions at face value only to avoid reading anything real into the question. Often the questions most troubling to these experts are simply testing their factual knowledge rather than testing their troubleshooting expertise and network design experience.

Therefore, networking professionals with extensive prior experience often postpone these two exams (Networking Essentials and TCP/IP) to the end of their exam sequence hoping to get into the flow of the Microsoft testing manner of thinking before encountering these too familiar topics.

## BETA EXAMS ARE HALF PRICE!

When a new exam is under construction, Microsoft tests the exam questions on folks like you and me. For $50.00, rather than the regular, full price of $100.00, you or I can take, and possibly pass, an exam still in its "beta" stage.

You should expect beta exams to have between 150 and 200 questions because they contain all the questions being considered for all versions of that exam. On a beta exam, you'll have only 3 hours to answer all the questions. This means that on a beta exam you must work at least at the same rapid pace you would use on a regular exam, if not faster.

Although beta exams can save you some money, they can also be frustrating because it takes six to eight weeks to get your scores from Microsoft. Waiting that long can be quite a trauma when you're used to having immediate results as you leave the testing room!

Important—Please Note: Beta Exams are designated with a 71 at the beginning of the exam code number, rather than the regular exam codes which begin with a 70.

To find out if any beta exams are available, check this URL:
MCP Exam Information

```
http://www.microsoft.com/mcp/examinfo/exams.htm
```

Another point should be made about the MCP Exam Information page. The dynamic links on the page jump to the official Microsoft Preparation Guides for each upcoming examination. Notice that the Preparation Guides become available even before the beta exams. This means you can actually be studying for an exam to test your skills at the same time that they're preparing it.

However, to study before the beta exam exists will sometimes require you to have access to the beta software product on which the exam is based. One of the many benefits of obtaining an MCSE certificate is a one-year subscription to the Microsoft Beta Evaluation program—free, monthly CDs containing Microsoft beta software.

As of April, 1998, these exams were expected in beta form soon:
Beta Exam Expected July 1998
*Beta Exam 71-098* Implementing and Supporting Microsoft Windows 98 for Exam 70-098 Implementing and Supporting Microsoft Windows 98
Preparation Guide at:
Exam Preparation Guide for exam 70-098

```
http://www.microsoft.com/mcp/exam/stat/SP70-098.htm
```

Beta Exam Expected Summer 1998
*Beta Exam 71-028* System Administration for Microsoft SQL Server 7.0 for Exam 70-028 System Administration for Microsoft SQL Server 7.0
Preparation Guide at:
Exam 70-028: System Administration for Microsoft SQL Server 7.0 Status Page

```
http://www.microsoft.com/mcp/exam/stat/SP70-028.htm
```

Beta Exam Expected Summer 1998
*Beta Exam 71-055* Developing Solutions with Microsoft FrontPage 98 for Exam 70-055 Developing Solutions with Microsoft FrontPage 98
Preparation Guide at:

Exam 70-055: Developing Solutions with Microsoft FrontPage 98
Status Page

    http://www.microsoft.com/mcp/exam/stat/SP70-055.htm

**Beta Exam Expected Fall 1998**
*Beta Exam 71-086* Implementing and Supporting Microsoft Systems Management Server 2.0 for Exam 70-086 Implementing and Supporting Microsoft Systems Management Server 2.0
Preparation Guide at:
Exam Preparation Guide for exam 70-086

    http://www.microsoft.com/mcp/exam/stat/SP70-086.htm

**Beta Exam Expected Fall 1998**
*Beta Exam 71-029* Implementing a Database Design on Microsoft SQL Server 7.0 for Exam 70-029 Implementing a Database Design on Microsoft SQL Server 7.0
Preparation Guide at:
Exam 70-029: Implementing a Database Design on Microsoft SQL Server 7.0 Status Page

    http://www.microsoft.com/mcp/exam/stat/SP70-029.htm

---

## Old Exams are Eventually Retired

Yes, Microsoft retires old exams. However, they take several specific measures to mollify the effect of obsolete exams on certified professionals—including giving six-months advance warning in writing, and substantially cutting the cost of replacement exams for at least six months after the former exam is retired. Read on for the details.

When an operating system (OS) is no longer commonly in use, supporting the old operating system becomes increasingly expensive. If new and better operating systems are available at reasonable prices, and the migration path for the majority of users is not too burdensome, it stands to reason that the manufacturer would want to withdraw the old OS from support. Similarly, Microsoft examinations are withdrawn and retired when their use has waned, especially when the OS they are based on is becoming obsolete.

In explaining Microsoft's policy on retiring exams, it's useful to know that they value highly the relevance of the skills measured by the exams. If your skills are still good in the marketplace, there will be less reason to retire the exam that certified those skills. Microsoft explains that their exam retirement decisions are based on several factors, including:

- Total number of copies of the product ever sold (the customer base)
- Total number of exams ever taken (the MCP base)
- Ongoing sales of corresponding Microsoft products
- Ongoing sales of corresponding Microsoft courseware

By considering this broad framework, Microsoft can retire only exams that have fallen from use and have truly become obsolete.

Microsoft announces at this URL which exams are being withdrawn and retired:

Microsoft Certified Professional Web site—Retired MCP Exams Information

```
http://www.microsoft.com/mcp/examinfo/retired.htm
```

If your MCSE certificate is based on an exam that is being, or has been retired, you'll probably need to find a replacement exam to prepare for and pass, to position your certificate for renewal.

### WHAT HAPPENS WHEN ONE OF MY EXAMS IS RETIRED?

Although there are no guarantees that these policies will always be the same, here are the current Microsoft policies on exam retirements:

- You'll first be mailed a notification at least six months before your certification is affected.
- You'll be given a deadline date to pass specific replacement exam(s).
- You may take all replacement exams at a 50 percent discount until at least six months after the exam retirement date.

For any questions or comments about Microsoft exam retirements, or if you want to check your certification status or ask about the MCSE program in general, just send e-mail to mcp@msprograms.com or call one of the following regional education centers:

**Microsoft Regional Education Centers**

| | |
|---|---|
| North America | 800-636-7544 |
| Asia and Pacific | 61-2-9870-2250 |
| Europe | 353-1-7038774 |
| Latin America | 801-579-2829 |

There are many more toll-free numbers for Microsoft International Training & Certification Customer Service Centers in several dozen countries worldwide at this URL:

Microsoft Training & Certification Programs—International Training and Certification Customer Service Centers

http://www.microsoft.com/train_cert/resc.htm

One more thought on retiring exams: Because an MCSE certificate is good for life, or until exams are retired, the only way to be sure that MCSE professionals are keeping up with the real world information technology market is for Microsoft to retire exams. For the MCSE to continue to signify the highest level of professional skills, old exams must be retired and replaced with more current exams based on skills currently in demand.

**TEST TIP—EARLY WARNING OF EXAM RETIREMENT**
One of the earliest warnings that an exam you've taken may become obsolete is the announcement of the development of a new exam for the next version of the software, or a beta exam is announced for a new version of the exam. Once beta software or a beta exam has appeared, watch closely for further signs.

Usually there is advance warning many months before the event that an exam is being withdrawn. If you subscribe to the following monthly mailing lists and read the Web pages mentioned, you'll have the longest forewarning so you can choose how you'll prepare for any changes.

- MCP News Flash (monthly)—Includes exam announcements and special promotions
- Training and Certification News (monthly)—About training and certification at Microsoft

To subscribe to either newsletter, visit this Web page, register with Microsoft, and then subscribe:

Personal Information Center

```
http://207.46.130.169/regwiz/forms/PICWhyRegister.htm
```

Don't be caught off guard. Stay in touch with the status of the MCSE exams you've invested in mastering!

## FREE SAMPLE EXAM SOFTWARE CD-ROM

Microsoft will ship a CD containing a dated snapshot of the Microsoft Certified Professional (MCP) Web site and sample examination software called Personal Exam Prep (PEP) exams. This CD is shipped via UPS—United Parcel Service—so an ordinary United States Postal Service post office box address won't work.

By calling Microsoft in the United States or Canada at (800) 636-7544, you can request the most recent CD of the MCP Web site. Ask for the Roadmap CD. They may protest greatly—don't worry. They'll tell you the "Roadmap to Certification CD" is no longer available and that you would be much better off to check the Microsoft Web site for more up-to-date information. However, they'll also still (as of this writing) ship a CD if you insist and if you provide an address other than a post office box.

Of course, if you're in a hurry you can always download the free sample exam software directly from the Microsoft Web site at:

Personal Exam Prep (PEP) Tests

```
http://www.microsoft.com/mcp/examinfo/practice.htm
```

(mspep.exe) (561K)
The free PEP exam download currently covers these Microsoft tests:

- 70-018 Implementing and Supporting Microsoft Systems Management Server 1.2
- 70-026 System Administration of Microsoft SQL Server 6

- 70-058 Networking Essentials
- 70-059 Internetworking with Microsoft TCP/IP on Windows NT 4.0
- 70-063 Implementing and Supporting Microsoft Windows 95 (retired)
- 70-067 Implementing and Supporting Microsoft Windows NT Server 4.0
- 70-068 Implementing and Supporting Microsoft Windows NT Server 4.0 in the Enterprise
- 70-073 Implementing and Supporting Microsoft Windows NT Workstation 4.0
- 70-075 Implementing and Supporting Microsoft Exchange Server 4.0
- 70-077 Implementing and Supporting Microsoft Internet Information Server 3.0 and Microsoft Index Server 1.1
- 70-160 Microsoft Windows Architecture I
- 70-165 Developing Application with Microsoft Visual Basic 5.0

## FREE PERSONAL EXAM PREP (PEP) TEST SOFTWARE

The PEP sample exam software has many values. First, you should take the appropriate PEP exam as the start of your studies for each new exam. This simple act commits you to the course of study for that exam and offers you a valid taste of the depth and breadth of the real exam. Seeing what kind of material is on the exams also allows you to recognize the actual level of detail expected on the exams so that you can avoid studying too much or too little to pass the exam.

Later, by taking the PEP examination from time to time, you can generally gauge your progress through the material. The PEP exam also gives you practice at taking an exam on a computer. Perhaps best of all, it allows you to print the questions and answers for items you may have missed, so that you can concentrate on areas where your understanding is weakest.

Although the PEP tests are written by Self Test Software, they are distributed free by Microsoft to assist MCP candidates in preparing for the real exams. Take advantage of this generous offer.

Several other sources of practice exam software, including several more free samples, are provided in a sidebar later in this chapter.

# Prepare For Each Exam

### FREE TECHNET CD

This offer's value cannot be over-estimated. The free TechNet Trial CD includes the entire Microsoft knowledge base, plus many evaluation and deployment guides, white papers, and all the text from the Microsoft resource kits. This information is straight from the horse's mouth, and is therefore indispensable to your successful studies for the MCSE certificate. And the price can't be beat. Don't delay, get this free TechNet CD today!

Of course Microsoft is hoping you'll actually subscribe to TechNet. Once you have earned the MCSE certificate, you will probably be sure to convince your employer to subscribe, if you don't subscribe yourself. TechNet can help you solve obscure problems more quickly, it can help you keep up to date with fast-paced technology developments inside and outside Microsoft, and it can help you keep your bosses and users happy.

Microsoft TechNet ITHome—Get a Free TechNet Trial Subscription

```
http://204.118.129.122/giftsub/Clt1Form.asp
```

On the same Web page you can also register for ITHome and other free newsletters.

Remember, Microsoft exams generally don't require you to recall obscure information. Common networking situations and ordinary administrative tasks are the real focus. Exam topics include common circumstances, ordinary issues, and popular network problems that networking and operating system experts are confronted with every day.

### USE PRACTICE EXAMS

Taking a practice exam early helps you focus your study on the topics and level of detail appropriate for the exam. As mentioned, taking another practice exam later can help you gauge how well your studies are progressing. Many professionals wait until their practice exam scores are well above the required passing score for that exam, then they take the real exam.

There are many sources of practice exams, and most vendors offer free samples of some kind. Microsoft supplies free sample exams from Self Test Software, and the MCSE mailing lists on the Internet often recommend products from Transcender. Both of these and several other practice exam sources are listed in the sidebar.

## PRACTICE EXAMS AVAILABLE—FREE SAMPLES

BeachFrontQuizzer
**E-Mail:** info@bfq.com
http://www.bfq.com/
Phone: 888/992-3131
A free practice exam for Windows NT 4.0 Workstation is available
for download.

**LearnKey**
http://www.learnkey.com/
Phone: 800/865-0165
Fax: 435/674-9734
1845 W. Sunset Blvd
St. George, UT 84770-6508
MasterExam simulation software—$800 for six exam simulations,
or $150 each.

**NetG**
**E-mail:** info@netg.com **or** support@netg.com
http://www.netg.com/
800/265-1900 (in United States only)
630/369-3000
Fax: 630/983-4518

**NETg International**
**E-mail:** info@uk.netg.com
1 Hogarth Business Park
Burlington Lane
Chiswick, London
England W4 2TJ
Phone: 0181-994-4404
Fax: 0181-994-5611
Supporting Microsoft Windows NT 4.0 Core Technologies—Part
1(course 71410–Unit 1–7.7 MB.) and Microsoft FrontPage Funda-
mentals (course 71101– Unit 2–8.1 MB.) are available as free
sample downloads.

**Prep Technologies, Inc.**
**E-mail:** Sales@mcpprep.com **or** Support@mcpprep.com
http://www.mcpprep.com/

1-888/627-7737 (1-888/MCP-PREP)
1-708/478-8684 (outside US)
CICPreP (Computer Industry Certification Preparation from ITS, Inc.)
A free 135 question practice exam is available for download (5+ MB.).

**Self Test Software**
**E-mail:** feedback@stsware.com
http://www.stsware.com/

**Americas**
Toll-Free: 1-800/244-7330 (Canada and USA)
Elsewhere: 1-770/641-1489
Fax 1-770/641-9719
Self Test Software Inc.
4651 Woodstock Road
Suite 203, M/S 384
Roswell, GA 30075-1686

**Australia/Asia**
**E-mail:** stsau@vue.com
Phone: 61-2-9320-5497
Fax: 61-2-9323-5590

**Sydney, Australia**
**Europe/Africa**
**The Netherlands**
Phone: 31-348-484646
Fax: 31-348-484699
$79 for the first practice exam and $69 for additional practice exams ordered at the same time.
Twelve free practice exams are available for download. These are the same free practice exams that Microsoft distributes by download or CD.

**Transcender**
**Product Questions:** sales@transcender.com
**Technical Support Questions:** support@transcender.com
**Demo download problems:** troubleshooting@transcender.com
http://www.transcender.com/
**Phone** 615/726-8779

Fax  615/726-8884
621 Mainstream Drive Suite 270
Nashville, TN 37228-1229
Fifteen free practice exams are available for download.

**VFX Technologies, Inc**
**E-mail:** sales@vfxtech.com **or** support@vfxtech.com
http://www.vfxtech.com/
Phone  610/265-9222
Fax 610/265-6007
POB 80222
Valley Forge, PA 19484-0222 USA
Twenty-two free practice MCP Endeavor exam preparation modules are available for download.

---

## ORGANIZE BEFORE THE DAY OF EXAM

Make sure you have plenty of time to study before each exam. You know how you work best. Give yourself enough time to both study and get plenty of sleep for at least two days before the exam. Make sure co-workers, family, and friends are aware of the importance of this effort so that they will give you the time and space to devote to your studies.

Once you have the materials and equipment you need, and study times and locations properly selected—discipline yourself to study and practice. Pace yourself so that you complete your study plan on time, and reward yourself when you finish a segment or unit of study.

## SURVEY TESTING CENTERS

Call each testing center in your area to find out what times they offer Microsoft exams. Jot down the center's name, address, and phone number, along with the testing hours and days. Once you've checked the testing hours at all the centers in your local area you're in a position to schedule an exam at "Center B" if "Center A" is already booked for the time you wanted to take your next exam.

The Sylvan technician taking your registration may not easily find all other testing centers near you, so be prepared to suggest alternative testing center names for the technician to locate in the event that your first choice is not available.

After you know when exams are available in your area, plan to take your MCSE exams at times of your own choosing. This puts you in control and allows you to take into account your own life situation and your own style. If you are sharpest in the morning, take the exams in the morning. If you can't get calm enough for an exam until late afternoon, schedule your exams for whatever time of day, or phase of the moon that best suits you. If you really need to have a special time slot, schedule your exam well in advance.

### SAME DAY AND WEEKEND TESTING

You may be able to schedule an exam on the same day that you call to register if you're lucky. This special service requires the test vendor, Sylvan, or VUE to download the exam to or store the exam at the testing site especially for you, and it requires the testing site to have an open slot at a time acceptable to your needs. Sometimes this works out, and sometimes it doesn't. Most testing centers are interested in filling all available exam time slots, so if you get a wild hair to take an exam today, why not give it a try? VUE testing centers can schedule exams for you, and store popular exams onsite, so they are especially well positioned for same day testing.

### SHOP AROUND FOR THE BEST TESTING CENTER AVAILABLE

Shop around your area for the best testing center. Some testing centers are distractingly busy and noisy at all times. Some official testing centers have slow 25 MHz computers, small 12" monitors, cramped seating conditions, or distracting activity outside the windows of the testing rooms. Some centers occasionally even have crabby, uninformed staff. Some centers actually limit testing to certain hours or certain days of the week, rather than allowing testing during all open hours.

Because these MCSE exams are important to your career—you deserve to use the best testing environment available. The best center costs the same $100 than a less pleasant center does. Shop around and find out exactly what's available in your area.

If you are treated improperly, or if appropriate services or accommodations were not available when they should have been, let Sylvan, or VUE, and Microsoft, know by e-mail and telephone.

### CHECK FOR AVIATION TESTING CENTERS

Some of the best testing centers are actually at airports. Aviation training centers, located at all major airports in order to accommodate pilots, are frequently well-equipped and pleasant environments. Aviation training centers participate in Microsoft testing in order to better use their investment in computer testing rooms and to broaden their customer base.

The best thing about aviation training centers is that they are regularly open all day on weekends. The staff at some aviation training centers actually like to work on weekends. One verified example, for instance, of an aviation training center and excellent Microsoft testing center available all day every weekend is Wright Flyers in San Antonio, Texas, telephone: 210/820-3800 or e-mail: Wflyers@Flash.Net.

## OFFICIAL EXAM REGISTRATION AND SCHEDULING

VUE exam scheduling and rescheduling services are available on weekends and evenings; in fact, they're open on the World Wide Web 24 hours 365 days a year. Sylvan's telephone hours are Monday through Friday 7:00 A.M. through 7:00 P.M. Central time, and the new Saturday telephone hours are 7:00 A.M. through 3:00 P.M.

As mentioned, many testing centers are open weekends. If something goes horribly wrong at a Sylvan testing center after 3:00 P.M. on Saturday, or anytime on Sunday—you'll have to wait to talk to Sylvan when they open on Monday morning. As has happened, if a testing center simply fails to open its doors for your scheduled exam while Sylvan is closed for the weekend, you can do nothing until Monday morning.

## INSTALL THE SOFTWARE AND TRY EACH OPTION

Make sure you know the layout of the various options in the software's graphical user interface (GUI), and which popular configuration options are set on each menu. Become "GUI familiar" with each software product required in your next exam by opening and studying each and every option on each and every menu. Also, for whatever they're worth, read the Help files, especially any context-sensitive Help.

Commonly tested, everyday network features like controlling access to sensitive resources, printing over the network, client and server software installation, configuration, troubleshooting, load balancing, fault tolerance, and combinations of these topics (such as security-sensitive printing over the network) are especially important. Remember, the exams are from the network administrator's point of view. Imagine what issues network designers, technical support specialists and network administrators are faced with every day —those are the issues that will be hit hardest on the exams.

MCSE candidates are expected to be proficient at planning, renovating, and operating Microsoft networks that are well integrated with Novell networks, IBM LANs and IBM mainframes, network printers (with their own network interface cards), and other common network services. Microsoft expects you to be able to keep older products, especially older Microsoft products, running as long as possible, to know when they finally must be upgraded, and to know how to accomplish the upgrade or migration with the least pain and expense.

## Pass One Exam at a Time

Microsoft exams are experience-based and require real know-how, not just book learning. Don't be fooled by anyone—you must have real experience with the hardware and software involved to excel on the exams or in the workplace as an MCSE holder.

Passing a Microsoft exam is mostly a statement that you have the experience and knowledge required. There is also an element in passing the exam of knowing how to deal with the exam situation one question at a time. This section describes the various kinds of questions you'll encounter on the MCSE exams and gives you pointers and tips about successful strategies for dealing with each kind of question.

This section then walks you through the process of scheduling an exam, arriving at the test center, and taking the exam. There is also a brief resource list of additional sources of information related to topics in this chapter.

### Choose the Best Answer

These questions are the most popular because they are seemingly simple questions. "Choose the best answer" means one answer, but the fact that there is only one answer doesn't make the question easy—unless you know the material.

First, try to eliminate at least two obviously wrong answers. This narrows the field so you can more easily choose between the remaining options.

**TEST TIP—SOME QUESTIONS INCLUDE EXHIBITS**
Briefly look at the exhibit when you begin to read the question. Note important features in the exhibit then complete a careful reading of the entire question. Return to the exhibit after you've read the entire question to check any relevant details revealed in the question.

Some exhibits have nothing to do with answering the question correctly, so don't waste your time on the exhibit if it has no useful information for finding the solution.

## Choose All That Apply

The most obviously tough questions are those with an uncertain number of multiple choices: "Choose all that apply." Here, you should use the same procedure to eliminate wrong answers first. Select only the items you have confidence in—don't be tempted to take a wild guess. Remember, the Microsoft exams do not allow partial credit for partial answers, so any wrong answer is deadly even if you got the rest of it right!

## Carefully Read the Scenario Questions

There is no better advice for these killer questions. Read the scenario questions carefully and completely. These seemingly complex questions are composed of several parts, generally in this pattern:

1. There are always a few short paragraphs describing the situation, hardware, software, and the organization involved. Sometimes one or two exhibits are included that must be opened, studied, and then minimized or closed again.
2. The required results
3. Two or three optional desired results
4. The proposed solution
5. Four multiple choice answers you must choose between

### "Pay close attention to the number of optional results specified in answer B"

Most scenario questions have an opening screen warning that you should "Pay close attention to the number of optional results specified in answer B." This instruction is to accommodate the fact that there are sometimes two, and sometimes three, optional results and to accommodate occasional proposed solutions that only satisfy the required result and some (but not all) of the optional results.

Often two scenario questions in a row will differ only in their proposed solution. They'll have the same test, the same exhibit, the same results, but different solutions will be proposed. Sometimes some other slight difference might be introduced in the second scenario. Compare those similar questions, noting the differences to see what's missing or what's new in the second question. If the second question satisfies all the required and desired results, that tends to imply that the previous scenario did not satisfy all optional results, at least.

Also, it is common to encounter another scenario question later in the same exam that clarifies the situation in the previous scenario. Some people jot down the question numbers and topics of each scenario so they can return and reconsider a question after reading other, related questions and perhaps having a flash of memory that might help.

**TEST TIP**

The scuttlebutt is that if you just don't have a clue on a complex scenario question, or if you're out of time, you should select answer A (meets all results) or D (meets none), because these are the most frequently correct answers. The recommended method, of course, is to know the material better so that you never need to resort to this kind of superstitious advantage.

For most people, your first priority should be to note the required results. If the proposed solution does not satisfy the required result you're done with the question and you can move on. So there is no need to focus on the optional desired results unless the required result is satisfied.

There can be up to three optional desired results, and each one must be evaluated independently. Usually, if an optional result is satisfied there are specific words in the question that deal with the optional result. Use the practice exams to sharpen your skills at quickly identifying which optional results are satisfied by which words in the question.

Another strategy that works for some people is to focus first on the question and results (both required and optional), writing down all related facts based on the question's wording. This strategy then evaluates the proposed solution based on the previous question analysis. Because some people find the scenario questions to be ambiguously written and vague, this strategy can also lead to time wasted on unimportant or unnecessary analysis, especially if the proposed solution does not meet the required results.

Some people work at exams differently. Aside from intelligence, there are also very different learning and understanding styles among adults. Some people, for instance, find that they deal better with the scenario questions by working backward from the required results and later, if necessary, from the optional results. They break the question into its elements, find their own solutions, and then finally compare notes with the solution proposed by the exam. For example, they might start from the required results, building the case that would be required to create that final required result. Once they have built their own solution that does meet the required result, they then check their solution against the exam's proposed solution. By checking their conclusions against the exam's proposed solution and the givens offered in the question, they then easily decide which required and optional results are achieved. If they know the material, they can answer the scenario questions, they just do it in a way others would call backwards.

It's important for candidates to see the forest and the trees and to know when to see each. In a question about a congested network, the candidate must decide whether the question is trying to ferret out the factual knowledge that FDDI is faster than 802.3 10 Mbps Ethernet or knowledge about the technical standards for installation and configuration details of FDDI. Candidates with extensive networking experience may be tempted to show off and choose the latter when only the simple knowledge that FDDI is faster than Ethernet was required. Don't read information into the question that isn't there.

### EXAM INTERFACE QUIRKS—SYLVAN INTERFACE

The Sylvan exam interface has a peculiar quirk on long questions that can hurt you if you're not careful. This is particularly true if the testing center uses small monitors so that more questions are longer than one screen. On these long questions there is an elevator or scroll bar on the right side of the screen so that you can use the mouse to move down to read the remainder of the question.

When you reach the bottom of the question, but not until you reach the bottom, the left-hand selection box on the outside bottom of the screen changes from "More" to "Next." There is a built-in assumption that if you are not looking at the bottom of the screen when you select your answer you've made a premature answer.

If you have moved back up the screen, to re-read the question for example, and the very bottom of the screen is not visible, and you then check very near but not exactly on your answer, sometimes the box above your selection actually gets selected rather than the box you intended to check. To prevent this you should either be sure you are always looking at the very bottom of the screen before you select the answer, or you should back up from the next question by clicking on the "Previous" question box to double-check your previous selection.

## SELECT THE WRONG ANSWERS

Okay, it sounds nuts. But the best advice around is to begin analysis of each question by selecting the answers that are clearly wrong. Every wrong answer eliminated gets you closer to the correct answer(s). Often there are two answers that can be quickly eliminated leaving you to focus your attention and time on fewer remaining options.

By carefully structuring your time, you can answer more questions correctly during the allotted exam period. Eliminate wrong and distracter answers first to narrow your attention to the more likely correct answers.

## INDIRECT QUESTIONS

Microsoft exams are not straightforward. They often use questions that indirectly test your skill and knowledge without coming straight out and asking you about the facts they are testing. For example, there is no exam question that actually asks "Is the Windows NT 4.0 Emergency Repair Disk bootable?" and there is no question that says "The Windows NT 4.0 Emergency Repair Disk is not bootable, True or False?" But you had better know that the Emergency Repair Disk (ERD) is never bootable. By knowing that the ERD cannot be booted, you can eliminate at least one wrong answer, and therefore come closer to the right answer, on one or more exams. By the way, after you've once had an unfortunate experience that calls for actually using the Windows NT ERD, you'll never again have a doubt about whether you can boot to it—the ERD repair occurs considerably later, well after booting the computer.

After you've taken a Microsoft exam or two, if you think you would be good at composing their kind of indirect question that tests many facets and levels at the same time, check out this URL where you can get information about being a contract test writer for Microsoft:

Microsoft Certified Professional Web site—Become a Contract Writer

http://www.microsoft.com/Train_Cert/Mcp/examinfo/iwrite.htm

## Scheduling an Exam

Register by exam number. Say "I want to register to take Microsoft exam number 70-073." Also know the exact title of the exam, so that it's familiar when the test registrar reads it back to you.

The Microsoft MCSE exams are administered by or through VUE (Virtual University Enterprises, a division of National Computer Systems, Inc.) or Sylvan Prometric. Either Sylvan or VUE can provide MCSE testing. Both VUE and Sylvan have access to records of your previous MCSE tests, and both vendors report your test results directly to Microsoft. Taking an examination through either vendor organization does not obligate you to use the same organization or the same testing center for any other examination.

VUE began testing for Microsoft in May, 1998, after requests for another vendor from throughout the Microsoft professional community. They began by offering exams only in English and largely in North America. VUE projects significant growth during 1998 and 1999, with worldwide coverage available by June 1999.

Call back the day before the exam to confirm your appointment. Anything could have gone wrong, and you want to know before you get to the testing center.

### SYLVAN PROMETRIC

To schedule yourself for an exam through Sylvan, or for information about the Sylvan testing center nearest you, call 800-755-3926 (800-755-exam) or write to Sylvan at:

Sylvan Prometric
Certification Registration
2601 88th Street West
Bloomington, MN  55431

To register online:
Sylvan Prometric (Nav1)
http://www.slspro.com/

Sylvan also offers 16 short, sample online exams, called Assessment Tests, on various Microsoft products. (Although Sylvan has offered online registration for several months, reports have continued that  would-be exam candidates are unable to use the online registration, despite valiant attempts—good luck!)

Phone:  800-755-3926

## VIRTUAL UNIVERSITY ENTERPRISES (VUE)

To schedule yourself for an exam through VUE, or for information about the VUE testing center nearest you, call 888-837-8616 or visit VUE's Web site to register online 24 hours a day, 365 days a year:

Virtual University Enterprises (VUE)

To register online: http://www.vue.com/ms
North America: 888-837-8616 toll-free
5001 W 80th Street Suite 401
Bloomington, MN 55437-1108

VUE is a new kid on the block, but never fear, they are seasoned test people, and their promise to the industry has been new thinking in technology and service, along with higher levels of candidate and testing center service. They have a "we try harder" attitude and back it up with higher standards for testing centers (800×600 video resolution on Windows 95 machines) and an agile, new, 32-bit testing engine. While VUE is in expansion mode, you should expect some growing pains, but also watch for some new thinking and professional amiability.

For instance, VUE immediately found a way to offer live, online, 24-hour, seven days a week exam scheduling and re-scheduling of Microsoft exams for busy professionals. And VUE offers on-site exam scheduling and re-scheduling at testing centers. These conveniences will be tremendously valuable to individual candidates. Because VUE's operation is based on heavy Internet bandwidth, they are able to use secure Java-based system management and site administration software to handle all testing and services. Also, VUE delivers new exams quickly to testing centers over the Internet, rather than by modem and telephone lines as Sylvan does.

## When You Arrive at the Testing Center

Arrive early. It can put you at ease to check in 30 to 60 minutes early. Relax a bit before you actually sit for the exam. Some exam centers won't complete your check-in until the last minute before your scheduled time, and others will get you all signed up and then tell you to let them know when you're ready to begin. Sometimes they'll offer to let you begin early.  Starting a little bit late is also sometimes tolerated, if you want to review your notes one more time—be sure to ask first.

To check in, you'll be asked to provide proof of your identity. Two pieces of identification with your name and signature are required: one must have a photograph of you—a driver's license or passport and a credit card are adequate. There are testing center rules you'll be asked to read, sign, and date. Microsoft has also begun to require on all new exams that the candidate agree to a non-disclosure statement discussed in the next section.

Testing center staff will explain their procedures and show you to the testing computers. This is the time to ask any questions about the testing rules. For instance, find out if you'll be allowed to leave the exam room to visit the restroom (with the clock still running on your exam) if your physical comfort demands a break.

#### CARRY WATER ONLY

Some folks bring bottled water, vitamins, or medications into the exam room, for their own comfort. You should consider what will make you most productive during the 90 minutes of your exam, and prepare accordingly.

Of course, the down side to drinking soda, coffee, or water during or even before the exam occurs when you are nearing the end of the 90-minute exam and really need to visit the restroom.

#### WRITING MATERIAL IN THE EXAM ROOM

This is a touchy area. Testing centers are required to be very picky about cheat notes carried into or out of the exam. There is a story of a candidate who had an ordinary napkin wrapped around a can of soda in the exam room and carried it out for disposal at the end of the exam. The candidate was challenged about the napkin and would probably have been disqualified or worse had the napkin contained any writing.

Always ask for writing implements. Paper and pen are easier to use, but some testing centers will not allow them. Centers that do not allow pen and paper will issue you marking pens and plasticized writing cards that are hard to use.

The marking pens commonly have a wide tip that makes writing difficult, and they dry out very quickly between uses. If they write at all, you must remember to replace the cap or the pen will refuse to write the next time you try. Get the finest tipped pens available. The tips seem to widen with use, so newer pens are better. Ask the testing center to open a new package of pens, and ask for two or three pens in case they go completely dry.

Also ask for another sheet or two of the $8^1/2 \times 10''$ plasticized writing material. If you have a large network drawing in mind, for instance, use the back of the card—two inches of the card's front are already in use by Sylvan Prometric. Don't force yourself to try to use those awkward marking pens in a small space—start another side or another sheet!

### TEST TIP

Don't waste your precious exam time writing down any memorized notes on the exam room writing material. Write down any memorized notes before the exam during the time you could use for taking the how-to-use-this-exam-software tutorial (discussed next). Some exams call for more memorization than others, and some exams have a tremendous amount of minute detail. Use your time wisely by recording any easily forgotten formulae, rules of thumb, and mnemonics before you begin the exam, after you enter the exam room.

The day before the exam, practice writing down all those notes you've decided will help you on your exam. Force yourself to write from memory only to prove you can remember it long enough to write it down in the exam room.

### ONLINE TUTORIAL

There is an optional exam tutorial available before each MCSE exam. The tutorial is designed to show you how the computer-administered exam software works and to help you become familiar with how the exam will proceed before the clock starts on your real exam. Don't get confused by the presence of the tutorial—if the clock in the upper right corner is ticking, you are taking the real exam, not the tutorial.

### TEST TIP—NERVOUS?

If you happen to be nervous before an exam, it might help reduce your anxiety to take some off-the-clock time with the optional tutorial to breathe deeply and calm yourself down and get into the right mood for passing the exam. Even if you've already seen the tutorial, and know exactly how to run the exam software, the tutorial can be a safety valve to give you a little time to adjust your attitude. Controlling your own use of time around the exam can give you just the boost you need!

### REQUIRED NON-DISCLOSURE AGREEMENT

Microsoft requires certification candidates to accept a Non-Disclosure Agreement before taking some exams. If you take an exam first released after February, 1998, you'll be required to provide an affirmation that you accept the terms of a brief, formal, non-disclosure agreement. This policy will eventually cover all MCSE exams. Microsoft says this policy will help maintain the integrity of the MCP program. The text of the agreement is provided in the sidebar and is also available at this URL:

Microsoft Certified Professional Web site—Certification Non-Disclosure Agreement for MCP Exams

```
http://www.microsoft.com/mcp/articles/nda.htm
```

---

**NON-DISCLOSURE AGREEMENT AND GENERAL TERMS OF USE FOR EXAMS DEVELOPED FOR THE MICROSOFT CERTIFIED PROFESSIONAL PROGRAM**

This exam is Microsoft confidential and is protected by trade secret law. It is made available to you, the examinee, solely for the purpose of becoming certified in the technical area referenced in the title of this exam. You are expressly prohibited from disclosing, publishing, reproducing, or transmitting this exam, in whole or in part, in any form or by any means, verbal or written, electronic or mechanical, for any purpose, without the prior express written permission of Microsoft Corporation.

Click the Yes button to symbolize your signature and to accept these terms. Click the No button if you do not accept these terms. You must click Yes to continue with the exam.

---

### Mandatory Demographic Survey

Microsoft says they appreciate your participation in the mandatory demographic survey before each exam. For years the survey was optional—now it is mandatory. Microsoft estimates the survey will take most candidates less than five minutes. Of course, the survey time does not count against your clocked exam period.

To motivate you to furnish sincere and valid answers on the mandatory survey, Microsoft stresses that the survey results are vital to the program and useful for setting the passing score of each exam, validating new exam questions, and in developing training materials for MCSE candidates. Microsoft says "By providing accurate and complete information on this survey, you will help

Microsoft improve both the quality of MCP exams and the value of your certification."

The mandatory demographic survey collects information tied to your Social Security Number about your work experience, your work environment, the software tested by the exam, and information about your exam preparation methods. The survey has three components. One portion is common to all exams, another is keyed to the exam track, and the third portion is specific to that one exam. Carefully note the wording of any promises of confidentiality, data cross-matching, or disclosure of your personal information.

## CHECK THE EXAM NUMBER AND EXAM TITLE

Although it is unlikely, there have been stories about the wrong test being loaded for an exam candidate. The first task of taking a Microsoft exam is to be sure you are beginning the exam you intended to take. By double-checking the exam number and exam title you might save yourself and the testing center hours of difficulty if somehow the wrong exam showed up for you. So be sure you check the exam title before you begin the clock on the exam—checking the exam title doesn't need to be part of your timed exam.

## ITEM REVIEW STRATEGIES

In the upper, right-hand corner, there is a small square box with the word "Mark" next to it. This little box is your key to another method for better managing your time during MCSE exams. When you encounter a question that stumps you, or leaves you feeling like you didn't study the right material at all, check an answer with the best guess you can quickly make, check the "Mark" box and move on to the next question. At the end of the exam there is an item review option that enables you to revisit only the questions you marked.

When you reach the end of the questions, a page summarizing your answers to all the questions is shown. It has red marks where you have not yet completed the question or skipped it entirely. Try to fill in at least a best guess as you go through the exam the first time—you can't get a question right that was left blank or incomplete!

The end-of-exam summary page also shows which items you marked for later review. If you click on the box for "Item Review," you will be taken back through your marked questions from the beginning of the exam, without needing to see the other, non-marked questions intervening. Or, if you double-click on any answer on the summary page, you'll be taken to that question, marked or not.

After you're quite comfortable with the testing process, you might want to consider this advanced strategy for dealing with marked questions. As you go through the exam, remember to jot down topics that are in the "stumper" questions you've marked. If a later question includes that same topic, make a note of what the question number is, right next to your 'tough topics' list. This way, when it comes time for you to review the questions you marked, you'll have the numbers of informative or "clue-filled" questions to review on that same topic. Although the final summary screen allows you to access any question, unless you've recorded the question number as you go along it may be too time consuming to find that informative question during item review.

## SOURCES OF ADDITIONAL INFORMATION

Microsoft maintains a large staff to handle your questions about the MCSE certificate. Give them a call at:

Microsoft MCP Program: 800/636-7544

If you have a CompuServe account, you can access the Microsoft area with this command:

```
GO MSEDCERT
```

### Microsoft Newsgroups

By pointing your Internet news-reading software to the NNTP news server at Microsoft, you can read ongoing news, questions, answers, and comments on dozens of topics close to Microsoft products.
Microsoft Public NNTP server: `msnews.microsoft.com`
Two typical hierarchies for your attention are these:

```
microsoft.public.windowsnt
microsoft.public.inetexplorer
```

### The Saluki E-mail Mailing List

Saluki is a very active majordomo Internet e-mail mailing list. Some days have 50 to 100 messages about MCSE studies and related topics. To subscribe send an e-mail message to:

```
majordomo@saluki.com
```

In the body of the message write:

subscribe mcse Yourfirstname Lastname

For example:

subscribe mcse Scott Armstrong

You may use an alias if you wish.
For further information about Saluki, write to Scott Armstrong at
saluki@gate.net or Dean Klug at deano@gate.net.

### The Windows NT 4.0 Workstation Exam

The Windows NT 4.0 Workstation exam is a core exam, and it is from the administrators point of view, even though it is about a client software, rather than a server software. Windows NT Workstation is usually taken early in the exam sequence, and by definition the Windows NT Workstation exam has a high degree of overlap with the Windows NT Server exam.

The Windows NT Workstation exam is heavy on particular details of everyday support for Windows NT networks, such as installing, configuring, and removing hardware components, and using Control Panel applications to configure the Windows NT. The Workstation exam covers installing and configuring printers, handling various file systems, sharing and securing resources, controlling groups, unattended operating system installations, dual-booting, and uninstalling Windows NT Workstation. The exam also includes ample helpings of dial-up networking, RAS, NetWare, monitoring, optimization, and troubleshooting. This is quite a plateful. The cure, of course, is to gain solid experience in administering Windows NT Workstation in preparation for the exam.

### Exam Room Notes

For the Windows NT Workstation exam, here are typical items to memorize and write down as soon as you enter the exam room before the clock starts:

- Networked HP printer or Jet Direct—DLC protocol
- Minimum hardware requirements—120MB disk, 12MB RAM (I386), 16MB RAM (RISC), and 486-DX33
- Peer Web Services—FTP, Gopher, WWW
- will not boot—last known good
- TCP/IP—IP, mask (gateway), automatic—DHCP

- /u—setup.inf, unattended.txt, UDF, SYSDIFF, windiff and setup.inf wrong

- MRS.

 M—Move
 R—Retain
 S—Same (partition)

 This is the only time permissions or attributes are retained. All other files inherit the target folder's (not target partition's) permissions and attributes.

- Winnt32—3.51 upgrade, Winnt-new install

- Regedt32—security, Regedit—search keys and branches

- Novell 3.x user —password change setpass

- Novell 4.x NDS—password change ALT+CTRL+DEL

- Extra page after print—Add Form feed in CSNW

- Alert print job—Notify when printed in CSNW

- Separate jobs—Print Banner

**CHAPTER 2**

# Hardware Hunger

This chapter explains how the Windows NT Workstation exam covers these hardware topics:

- Minimum computer hardware requirements
- Popular hardware options
- Disk sets
- The Windows NT Hardware Compatibility List

The goal of this chapter is to begin to prepare you for and to review the many hardware-related concepts and questions on this exam. Chapter 14, "Printers and Print Devices," provides the main coverage of many concepts introduced in this chapter.

## Minimum Hardware Requirements

For the exam, you should know the hardware requirements for each Windows NT Workstation computer. They are:

## Windows NT Workstation computers:

- 12 MB RAM
- VGA video
- Keyboard
- IDE, EIDE, SCSI, or ESDI hard disk
- 486/25 processor or faster
- 124 MB free hard drive space (Recommended minimum: over 300 MB, including a copy of the entire I386 installation directory [223 MB] plus Windows 95 or DOS 6.22). For hard disk controllers using translation mode to address the drive, increase these minimum sizes by 80 MB.
- CD-ROM drive or a floppy disk drive and an active network connection

## Windows NT Server computers:

- 16 MB RAM (32 MB or more recommended)
- VGA video
- Keyboard
- IDE, EIDE, SCSI, or ESDI hard disk
- 486/25 processor (486DX2/50 or better preferred)
- 124 MB free hard drive space (Recommended minimum: over 300 MB, including a copy of the entire I386 installation directory [223 MB] plus Windows 95 or DOS 6.22). For hard disk controllers using translation mode to address the drive, increase these minimum sizes by 80 MB.
- CD-ROM drive (Windows NT compatible recommended) or a floppy disk drive and an active network connection
- Recommended: 28.8 v.34 (or faster) external modem, for remote debugging and troubleshooting

### IT AIN'T NECESSARILY SO

According to the Microsoft Web site, the current hardware requirements in the real world are slightly different, so don't memorize the next set of information in *italic* for the exam. Use only the hardware requirements mentioned previously to study for the exam. Microsoft's position has changed (shown in italics) but the exam has not!

### Frequently Asked Questions
http://www.microsoft.com/ntworkstation/ntwnew/info/ntfaq.htm

*"The minimum system requirements for Windows NT Workstation 4.0 are: Pentium or faster processor, 16 MB of RAM, and 110 MB of available hard disk space. RISC-based systems require a workstation with an Alpha AXP, MIPS K4x00, or Power PC processor, as well as 32 MB of RAM, and 110 MB of available hard disk space."* This quote is as of the following date: Last Modified: Thursday, April 16, 1998 22:33:10 GMT.

Similarly, as of May, 1998, the requirements for Windows NT Server, from the Microsoft site URL shown next, are as follows.

### System Requirements
http://www.microsoft.com/NTServer/Basics/SystemReqs.asp

Microsoft Windows NT Server 4.0 Operating System, Intel and compatible systems:

486/33 MHz or higher, or Pentium or Pentium PRO processor 125 MB of available hard disk space, minimum 16 MB of RAM, CD-ROM drive, VGA, Super VGA, or video graphics adapter compatible with Windows NT Server 4.0

RISC-based systems: RISC processor compatible with Windows NT Server version 4.0, 160 MB of available hard disk space, 16 MB of RAM, CD-ROM drive, VGA, Super VGA, or video graphics adapter compatible with Windows NT Server 4.0

Any Windows NT network administrator can tell you that the more RAM you give Windows NT, the happier the operating system (OS) and the user will be. The authors have not used Windows NT on a computer with less than 32 Megabytes of RAM, and 64 is certainly preferred. Similarly, reserving an entire gigabyte of available disk drive storage space on the system boot is more practical with today's piggy applications.

MCSE candidates should be aware of the Microsoft Windows NT Hardware Compatibility List covered later in this chapter as another important source of hardware information.

### Migration from Windows 95 to Windows NT

An additional, useful site, for preparation for the Windows NT Workstation exam, is:

Migration from Windows 95 to Windows NT Workstation 4.0

```
http://www.microsoft.com/ntworkstation/info/ntmigration.htm
```

The exam expects you to understand the advantages and disadvantages of each operating system and how Windows NT networks deal with each OS. Administrators are expected to know how to plan for and conduct successful migrations from other OSs to Windows NT. Generally, Windows 95 is able to accommodate more legacy hardware than Windows NT, is more end-user friendly, and has more well-developed plug-and-play features. Just because you've been running Windows 95 on your network computers does not mean that it's a good idea to try to move to Windows NT—look before you leap.

## Popular Hardware Options on the Exam

Of the many computer peripherals and computer hardware options, here are a few that come up on the Microsoft exams more often than others. As you should expect by now, these options are important to the daily administration and support of Windows NT Workstation network computers. You should study these hardware installation, configuration, and security options in particular.

This section provides a condensed version of several hardware-relevant exam questions and answers. Each portion of this section also refers you to later chapters for more background and details on that topic. Seek out opportunities to have real world experience with these hardware devices. Consider actually removing (from the software configuration) and then replacing them on a test computer so you know all the options faced while installing them.

Be "GUI familiar" with each of their Control Panel applets—pull down every menu, read and understand every option, including any online and context-sensitive help.

- Backup tape systems

- Network adapter installation

- Printing over the network (and printers with their own NICs)

- HP "Jet Direct," Lexmark, and other network printers with their own NICs

- Macintosh printers
- NetWare print options
- TCP/IP printers
- UNIX printers
- SCSI disk drives
- UPS (uninterruptible power supplies)

### Backup Tape Systems

Backup tape systems are commonly covered on the Windows NT Workstation exam by requiring you to demonstrate that you have some idea of how to install tape device drivers, and/or that you have some idea of how to back up the registry.

**TIP**

Open the SCSI Adapters applet in Control Panel. Does it allow you to configure any SCSI devices other than the SCSI adapter(s)? No.

SCSI
Adapters

Even if your server does not have a SCSI adapter, you can see what a SCSI adapter looks like in Figures 2.1 and 2.2. SCSI devices on the SCSI bus are visible, but cannot be configured from the SCSI Adapter applet. Only the SCSI adapter itself can be configured from the SCSI Adapters applet.

So, even if you have a SCSI tape drive, can you possibly configure it in the SCSI Adapters applet? No. Use the Tape Devices applet to configure tape device drivers, as shown in Figure 2.3.

All devices on the SCSI bus are displayed in the SCSI Adapters applet in Control Panel. However, only the SCSI adapter itself can be

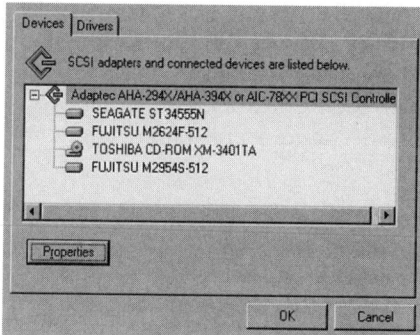

**Figure 2.1** The SCSI Adapters applet displays all devices on the SCSI bus but only allows configuration of the SCSI Adapters.

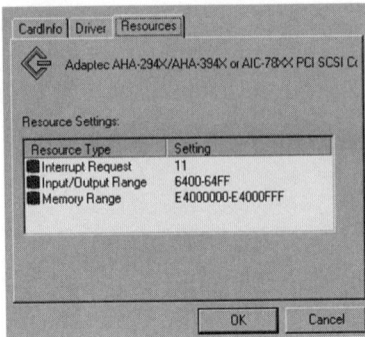

**Figure 2.2**   The SCSI Adapters applet resource tab allows configuration of the SCSI adapter(s).

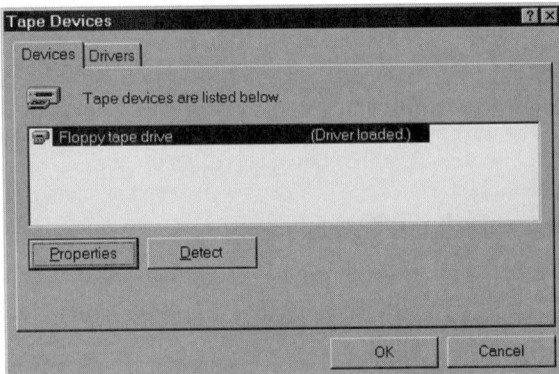

**Figure 2.3**   Use the Tape Devices applet to detect and configure all tape devices and drivers.

configured in the applet. You can check the properties for each SCSI device, but you cannot change or configure anything about the SCSI devices, other than the SCSI adapter.

Instead, use the built in Tape Devices applet in the Control Panel to configure tape device drivers.

The Tape Devices applet detects and configures many Windows NT compatible tape devices.

In order for the Windows NT Backup program (on the Administrative Tools menu) to be allowed to back up the registry, at least one other file on the same partition must be backed up at the same time. Someone with permission to access and back up the registry must be logged in, of course, for Backup to perform this operation.

### Network Adapter Installation

There is a frequently recurring question about installing the Windows NT OS, and in particular the communication protocols needed to participate in a network without the network adapter being physically available. The adapter is expected to be available for later installation. The question challenges you to solve this dilemma—how do you install communication protocols when the computer isn't even connected to the network?

Windows NT comes with a built-in software solution to this problem. When you install a network adapter on Windows NT, among the long list of available network adapter drivers you'll find one called the MS Loopback Adapter. Network adapters, including the MS Loopback Adapter, are installed during the overall installation of the OS and can be removed or installed later using the Control Panel Network applet Adapters tab.

Incidentally, this trick, installing the MS Loopback Adapter, will not work for the real-world installation of a backup domain controller because backup domain controller installation requires network access to security information on the primary domain controller.

### Printing over the network and printers with their own NICs

This section reviews the printer problems and solutions typically encountered on the NT Workstation Exam. These printer problems are often about:

- HP "Jet Direct," Lexmark and other network printers with their own NICs
- Macintosh printers
- NetWare print options
- TCP/IP printers
- UNIX printers

Table 2.1 shows the typical printing topics on the left, and the usual exam solution on the right.

At the top of Table 2.1, notice that HP printers, sometimes called "Jet Direct" printers, are steadily referred to on the exam. Newer exams refer to this sort of printer instead as a networked printer or a printer with its own network adapter—probably because Lexmark (formerly IBM) and other printer manufacturers also make this sort of equipment. Giving HP sole mention is probably unfair.

**Table 2.1**
Understand these printer solutions for the exam.

| Printing Challenge | Exam Solution |
|---|---|
| Network printers with their own NICs: HP "Jet Direct," Lexmark and other printers | Add DLC protocol |
| Macintosh printers | Add AppleTalk protocol |
| NetWare printing | |
| 1. Disable blank page at the end of job? | 1. "Add Form Feed" |
| 2. Stop a print notice from being displayed on your Windows NT computer | 2. "Notify When Printed" |
| 3. Stop a banner page from being printed before each print job. In Client Services for NetWare (CSNW), deselect | 3. "Print Banner" |
| TCP/IP printers | TCP/IP, IP address and printer name |
| UNIX printers | Use UNIX LPR command |

Chapter 14, provides the details you'll need to understand and remember Table 2.1 for the exam.

## SCSI Disk Drives

SCSI devices are commonly brought up on the Windows NT Workstation exam in two ways.

As mentioned earlier in this chapter in connection with the SCSI Adapters applet not  being used to install tape device drivers, especially not IDE tape device drivers.

As an irrelevant background fact in a question about optimum placement of the page file and/or optimizing network access by adjusting protocol binding order.

The question goes something like this: *A computer has four SCSI hard disk drives. Each drive has total capacity of two gigabytes. All drives are formatted as FAT rather than NTFS. The page file is on the system/ boot partition. The computer has 32 MB of RAM. Blah, blah, blah. If Mary is promoted to management in Atlanta, when will the train get to Chicago?*

Almost none of the setup information is required to answer this question correctly, because the proposed solution does not meet the required result. The setup information is relevant to the optional results. The optional results of faster paging and faster network access, however, are not relevant to getting the question answered right. This question is an especially clear example of the type of question for which you should not bother wasting time figuring out the optional results because the proposed solution quickly fails.

As to the proposed solution, later in this chapter, we tell you why, but for now just understand that volume sets do not improve computer performance. Stripe sets and disk duplexing can improve performance (computer speed), but volume sets never improve performance.

Another feature of how Windows NT deals with SCSI drives is the ARC naming conventions used in the boot.ini file so that Windows NT knows where to find important files. Various ARC naming rules are essential to life as an MCSE, and are discussed in Chapter 3.

## Uninterruptible Power Supply (UPS)

UPSs are computer peripheral hardware that provide limited fault tolerance protection from electrical power failures and other electrical power anomalies. UPSs are covered in the Windows NT Workstation exam by expecting you to be able to identify the two steps needed to install them. To install an UPS so that Windows NT knows it has UPS protection, perform these steps.

1. Power up to charge the UPS battery, start the UPS and use the proper, manufacturer's specified, serial cable to connect the UPS to an available software communications port through a working, hardware serial port receptacle on the computer.
2. Use the Control Panel UPS applet to configure the UPS.

Figure 2.4 shows you the UPS configuration options available from the Control Panel UPS applet. Notice that in some cases you may be expected to configure positive or negative voltages.

The exam question also refers to the Windows NT Hardware Compatibility List (HCL) covered later in this chapter. The fact that the UPS in the question is on the HCL is good because it assures you that the UPS can be installed using the two-step procedure just mentioned.

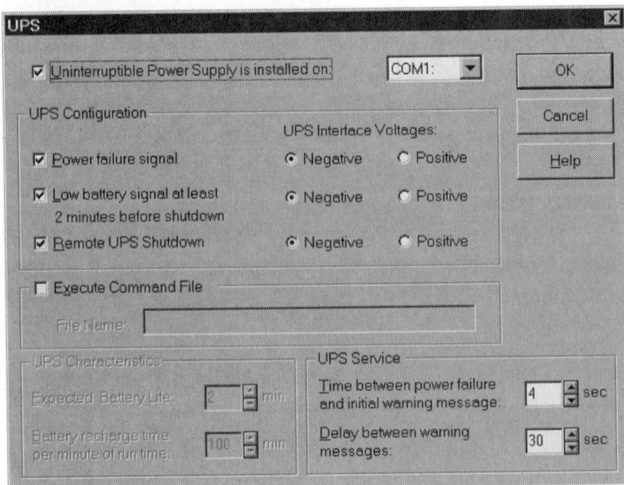

**Figure 2.4**   Use the UPS applet to configure the UPSs.

Don't be distracted by parallel cables. Only serial cables are used with HCL approved UPSs. And don't be fooled by the Devices applet in the Control Panel—the Devices applet cannot be used to configure a UPS. (Open it, and you'll see—the Devices applet is used to start or stop various devices and to manage different hardware profiles.)

## Disk Sets

Windows NT Workstation has two non-fault-tolerant disk sets—stripe sets and volume sets. Each of these kinds of disk storage set configuration offers one or more advantages, other than fault tolerance, that you should remember. Table 2.2 also points out some disadvantages of these various storage sets.

**Table 2.2** The exam requires you to be GUI familiar with Disk Administrator and all it can do. The stripe set with parity option is not available on Windows NT 4.0 Workstations.

| Disk Set Type | Minimum Number of Drives in Set | Maximum Number of Drives in Set | Limitations |
|---|---|---|---|
| Stripe Set with parity (fault tolerant) | 3 | 32 | Loss of storage space to parity information, loss of CPU performance for calculation of parity data, loss of read/write performance to handle additional (parity) information. |
| Stripe Set without parity | 2 | 32 | Cannot be expanded. Not fault tolerant. |
| Volume Set | 1 | 32 | NTFS volume sets can be expanded. Not fault tolerant. |

**TIP**
Read each question on the exam very carefully. If the question involves a stripe set, never assume that the stripe set is one with parity unless it is stated in the question. Some questions might lead you to believe from the context that the situation involves a stripe set with parity, but without the words "with parity," a stripe set is not fault tolerant.

### Stripe Sets Without Parity

Windows NT Workstation can create non-parity stripe sets— remember that a stripe set must have parity to be fault tolerant. Another term used for non-parity stripe sets is RAID 0 (disk striping), although the stripe set data is neither redundant nor fault tolerant. Disk striping is very fast because data can be read from or written to two or more drives simultaneously. Disk striping is not fault tolerant.

A stripe set combines 2 to 32 sections of space from separate physical disks to create one logical partition. Data is written sequentially in 64K chunks across the disks. The advantage to this arrangement is faster read and write access to your drives. Stripe sets are the fastest and most economical way to store data.

Stripe sets cannot be extended or expanded after they are established. Stripe sets without parity have no need to store parity information on a different drive, so stripe sets without parity allow use of proportionately more of the drive space to store mission critical data (rather than parity data). If you use stripe sets without parity for their performance improvement, there is, of course, an increased need for serious attention to backup systems to restore data when a drive fails.

### Volume Sets

Volume sets are also available on Windows NT Workstation. Volume sets are available in Windows NT as a convenient but less efficient way of aggregating available drive space on one or more disk drives. Volume sets gather all the small pieces of different drives into a single administrative volume, so that two or more pieces of available disk space appear to the file system as a single drive volume. Volume sets are even less efficient than ordinary storage drives because the many pieces of drive space are read in order rather than simultaneously in parallel like a stripe set. Therefore, the lesson to be remembered is that volume sets do not improve disk performance; and, of course, volume sets are simply not fault tolerant.

### NTFS Volume Sets

NTFS volume sets can be expanded even after they are established, making them more flexible than ordinary FAT volume sets. Disk Administrator is the tool to use to expand an existing NTFS volume set. This special case is something Microsoft is proud of, so you can expect to see it on the exam even though it is not fault tolerant.

## RECOVERY FROM HARDWARE FAILURE

Microsoft is immanently practical in that they expect MCSE candidates to have enough familiarity with Windows NT to serenely handle various types of hardware failures. Table 2.3 shows two possible hardware failures and the steps you would take to recover from them.

**Table 2.3** Recovery from hardware failure is a common theme on MCSE exams.

| Disk Set Type | Failure | Recovery Step 1 | Recovery Step 2 |
| --- | --- | --- | --- |
| Stripe Set without parity | One or More Disk Drives | Replace failed disk drive(s) | Restore from backup* |
| Volume Set | One or More Disk Drives | Replace failed disk drive(s) | Restore from backup* |

*Notice that "restore from backup" is indicated for both items in Table 2.3. This represents a total loss, and starting over "almost from scratch" based on your most recent backup data set. Most real-world, mission-critical production systems would not be deliberately designed with such a total reliance on the most recent backup, and Microsoft expects you to recognize these "restore from backup" situations as serious, potential disasters.

## The Famous NT Hardware Compatibility List

The NT Hardware Compatibility List can tell you, prior to a hardware purchase, whether a given device will play nice with Windows NT. This is important because Microsoft does not support Windows NT unless it's running on hardware listed on the HCL.

Even if you get it to work, non-HCL hardware can backfire on you later by disallowing Microsoft support just when you need it most. By using Windows NT as your workstation and network OS, you are wedding yourself to the hardware vendors that work well with Microsoft.

There are several levels of compatibility noted in the list, including levels akin to these: "we know some people have made it work, but it didn't pass *all* our tests," "it works in all our tests," or "it works in all our tests and we think it will meet our future standards," as well as whether the device is expected to also work with Windows 95.

As just mentioned, compatibility is an issue that has many shades of gray. Some hardware manufactures and vendors place Windows NT logos or statements of compatibility on their equipment, in order to indicate that the hardware is compatible with Windows NT. Some of the equipment is also on the HCL, and some is not. Microsoft will support their software only if the equipment is on the HCL.

However, Microsoft does everything possible to make this important resource impossible to find. Once you find it, don't be fooled into bookmarking it. There is an enduring, widespread belief that the URL moves periodically without forwarding pointers. If you aren't using the most recent version of the Microsoft or Netscape browser, or if you have cookies turned off, you will probably be unable to access the Hardware Compatibility List (HCL) even if you have the correct URL.

It is therefore with some trepidation that we offer you this URL for the Windows NT Hardware Compatibility List:

Windows NT Hardware Compatibility List

```
http://www.microsoft.com/isapi/hwtest/hcl.idc
```

The on-site Microsoft search engine, which uses Microsoft Index Server, is also usually unable to find the HCL list in non-premium parts of the site. Now, why would this be? Try your hand at the search, and see for yourself.

## For Review

- Windows NT Workstation requires at least 486/25, 12 MB RAM, 124 MB drive space.

- Windows NT Server requires at least 486/25, 16 MB RAM, 124 MB drive space.

- Configure tape backup systems with the Tape Devices applet in Control Panel.

- Use the MS Loopback Adapter to install communication protocols on a computer without a network interface card.

- In NetWare printing, to stop a blank page from being printed at the end of each job, uncheck the "Add Form Feed" option in Client Services for NetWare (CSNW).

- Use the appropriate serial cable to connect a UPS to an available communications port through a serial port receptacle on the computer, and then configure the UPS using the Control Panel UPS applet.

- Without parity explicitly mentioned, Stripe Sets are fast and not fault tolerant.

- Volume Sets are less efficient and do not improve performance.

- Only NTFS Volume Sets can be expanded after creation.

- Microsoft supports software running on certain approved, compatible hardware, and does not support software running on hardware unless the hardware appears on the HCL.

## From Here

Printing over the network and various other printing topics are covered in Chapter 14.

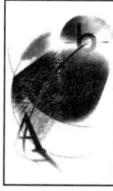

**CHAPTER 3**

# The Windows NT File System

Windows NT Workstation computers have two kinds of file systems:

- FAT
- NTFS

Windows NT 4.0 does not support the HPFS file system that comes with OS/2. A procedure for upgrading Windows NT 3.51 installations of HPFS to Windows NT 4.0 NTFS is given in Chapter 7, "Upgrade Installations."

Disk management, Disk Administrator, boot.ini, and ARC names are also covered in this chapter.

## SUPPORTED AND NONSUPPORTED FILE SYSTEMS

The New Technologies File System (NTFS) uses the Master File Table (MFT) as the basis for the volume structure. The MFT contains at least one record for each file, giving NTFS the appearance of a relational database. Compact Disk File System (CDFS) is used to allow access to compact disks. The File Allocation Table (FAT) file system is compatible with DOS, Windows 3.1, Windows 95/98 and many other operating systems. Table 3.1 shows file systems that are supported or not supported with Windows NT 4.0 Workstation:

**Table 3.1**
Windows NT is compatible with FAT, NTFS, and CDFS.

| File System | Supported | Unsupported |
| --- | --- | --- |
| CDFS | X | |
| FAT | X | |
| NTFS | X | |
| FAT32 | | X |
| HPFS | | X |
| Macintosh | (Server only) | X |

The High Performance File System (HPFS) that comes with OS/2 is no longer supported and cannot be read by Windows NT 4.0. Windows NT also does not support the Windows 95/98 FAT32 file system.

Windows NT Workstation does not support Macintosh file system translation even on a Windows NT Workstation NTFS partition. Only Windows NT Server has the ability to support Macintosh file system translations and only on NTFS partitions.

## File Systems

Windows NT Workstation supports both NTFS and FAT file systems. When selecting a file system there are several things to take into consideration. These include whether you will run your computer as a dual-boot system and your need for security. NTFS has several features not available in FAT including support for security and compression on a per file basis, as well as the ability to audit file access.

Both FAT and NTFS support long filenames. In FAT, each 8.3 filename takes up 32 bytes. If long filenames are used, an additional entry is created for each 13 characters in the long filename. Filenames may be up to 256 characters and contain spaces and periods. To maintain compatibility with other operating systems, Windows NT automatically generates an 8.3 filename for all files.

**TIP**
To display both long and short filenames type dir /x at a command prompt.

Because of its low overhead on small disks, the FAT file system is best suited for disks of 400 MB or less. However, on larger disks, the overhead of using FAT becomes prohibitive—making NTFS a more efficient choice.

**TIP**
On a RISC-based computer, you must have a 2 MB FAT system partition.

However, if you elect to format your partition with NTFS it will not be accessible from other operating systems such as Windows 95 or MS-DOS. FAT supports file sizes up to 4 GB while NTFS can handle files up to 64 GB depending on the cluster size. Cluster size is variable under NTFS and can be up to 64 K.

NTFS also has the ability to detect on the fly defective sectors on a SCSI drive. If a sector is found faulty, then the data is recovered, moved to a safe location, and the sector marked as unusable. This is referred to as *sector sparing*.

**TIP**
Windows NT no longer supports HPFS. If you wish to install NT on a partition formatted with HPFS, then you will need to re-format the drive as either FAT or NTFS. See Chapter 7.

## Disk Management

A basic part of planning the installation of Windows NT Workstation is planning how to partition your hard disk or disks. Not only is the size of the partition important, but the type of files to be placed there is vital to the decision process.

The system partition is the partition that contains the files necessary to initialize the operating system, that is, to boot. The boot partition also helps start the operating system. The boot partition contains the operating system files. The system partition must be on a primary partition; however, the boot partition may be a primary or logical partition. System and boot files may, in fact, be placed on the same or different partitions.

## DISK ADMINISTRATOR

Disk Administrator is a graphical tool for administrating disk resources. It allows you to create or delete partitions and replaces DOS `fdisk`. In addition, your disk properties may be changed using this tool, including changing drive letter assignments, changing a volume label, and formatting partitions. Windows NT Workstation Disk Administrator can also create and manage disk configurations including stripe sets and volume sets.

Two additional kinds of partitions available on Windows NT Workstation are the volume set and the stripe set. Volume sets formatted with NTFS allow expansion of the partition on the fly but do not provide any fault tolerance. Stripe sets can improve performance dramatically but do not provide any fault tolerance.

## VOLUME SETS

A volume set gives you the option of extending a full partition on the fly. A volume set can be composed of 2–32 sections of disk space and may span from 1–32 physical drives. Each of these pieces may be a different size. The resulting combination appears as one logical drive.

### CAUTION

Although a volume set can provide needed space immediately, it does not provide fault tolerance. If any disk containing a portion of the volume set fails, the entire volume set is lost. The only way to recover the data if this occurs is to restore from backup.

Create a volume set by selecting two or more areas of free space. Select Partition from the Disk Administrator menu, and select Create Volume Set, as shown in Figure 3.1. Then type in the size of the volume set as shown in Figure 3.2, and click on the OK button. The partition must then formatted before it can be used.

**Figure 3.1** When portions of free space from different physical drives are selected, Disk Administrator offers to make a volume set or a stripe set.

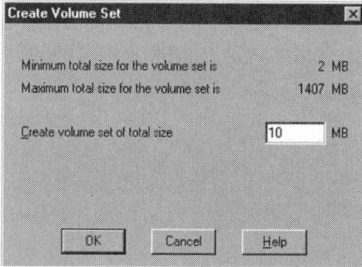

**Figure 3.2**   You must type in the total size of the set you intend to create for either a stripe set or a volume set.

Neither system nor boot files can be placed on a volume set. A volume set may be formatted as either FAT or NTFS. If you want to later extend a volume set, however, it must be formatted as NTFS. Figure 3.3 shows how Disk Administrator displays a volume set.

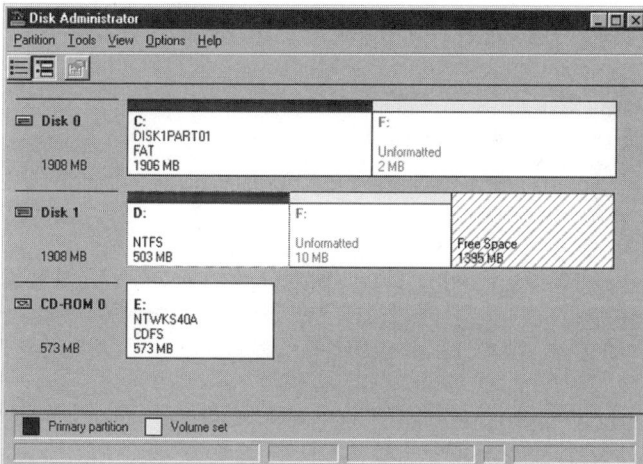

**Figure 3.3**   A volume set has been created, and additional space is available on Disk 1.

### Extending an NTFS Volume Set

An NTFS volume set can be extended either with additional free space on the same hard drive or by incorporating free space from a separate hard drive. To extend a volume set, select the volume set you wish to extend, then, while holding down the control key, select additional area(s) of free space. Remember, a volume set has to

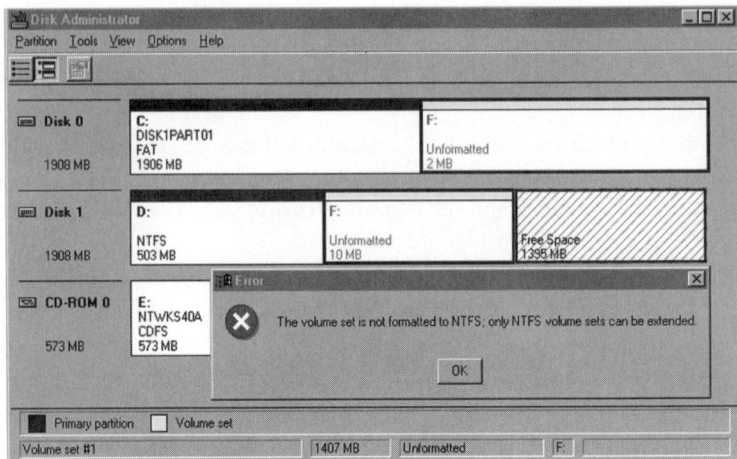

**Figure 3.4**   To be later extended, volume sets must be formatted NTFS.

be formatted as NTFS in order to be extended. If the volume set is not formatted as NTFS, the error message in Figure 3.4 appears.

> **TIP**
> A volume set is read sequentially making it the least efficient way to organize your disks. Only consider using a volume set when you need additional space immediately.

Volume sets do not improve performance. To improve performance, use stripe sets, which are covered next.

## STRIPE SETS

A stripe set combines 2–32 sections of space from separate physical disks to create one logical partition. Data is written sequentially in 64K chunks across the disks. The advantage to this arrangement is faster read and write access to your drives. This makes the stripe set the fastest and most economical way to store data. However, after a stripe set is created, it cannot be extended.

> **CAUTION**
> Stripe sets do not provide any fault tolerance. Therefore, in the case of a disk crash you must replace the failed disk, recreate the stripe set, and restore the data from backup.

Use the Disk Administrator to create a stripe set. Select the first area of free space, then, while holding down the Control key, select 1–31 additional areas of free space, each of which must be on a separate physical disk.

On the Partition Menu in Disk Administrator, select Create Stripe Set. Next, Disk Administrator displays the minimum and maximum sizes for the stripe set you are creating based on the amount of free space (similar to Figure 3.2).

**TIP**
Each section of free space comprising a stripe set must be the same size. To calculate the maximum size of available space, multiply the size of the smallest section by the total number of sections selected.

When asked for the largest size stripe set, be sure to consider all the different combinations. Don't be taken in by the urge to use space from all available disks. The smallest portion on any drive limits the overall size of the set. Larger portions of fewer drives might result in a larger stripe set.

Type in the total size of the stripe set you want to create and click OK. These changes are not saved until you commit the changes. After creating the stripe set and committing the changes, you will need to format the new logical partition in either FAT or NTFS.

The Disk Administrator display of a small, unformatted, two-disk stripe set is shown in Figure 3.5.

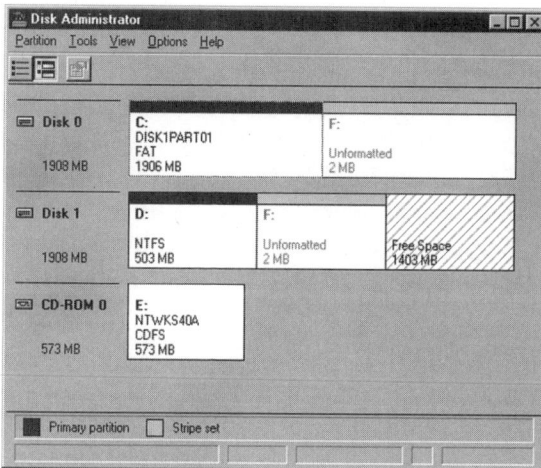

**Figure 3.5** Stripe sets must have the same amount of space on each disk drive.

### Boot.ini and ARC Names

The system partition contains the files required to boot the Windows NT operating system. These files include:

- Boot.ini—controls boot options, including dual booting
- Bootsect.dos—used to boot to an operating system other than Windows NT
- NTLDR—loads the operating system and controls startup
- NTDetect.com—gathers information on hardware support
- NTBootdd.sys—required only if using a SCSI drive without BIOS enabled

The boot.ini file contains an ARC pathname describing where Windows NT's boot partition is located. For each Windows NT installation there is an associated ARC pathname. During the boot process, the boot.ini file offers a screen allowing the user to choose which installation to boot. To edit the boot.ini file, open a DOS box and change to drive C:, change the boot.ini file attributes with the command `attrib 2r 2s 2h boot.ini`, and after editing, add the attributes with the command `attrib 1r 1s 1h boot.ini`. While its attributes are down, edit the file with the DOS edit command or another text editor that will not add formatting.

The ARC pathname has two forms:

- MULTI( )
- SCSI( )

Either form can be used on Intel computers. Only the SCSI form can be used on RISC computers. The discussion below focuses on using these forms with Intel computers.

### Multi( ) ARC Name

A Multi( ) ARC name can be used with IDE, EIDE, ESDI, and SCSI adapters with the BIOS enabled. A Multi( ) ARC name has the form

```
multi(0)disk(0)rdisk(0)partition(1)\WINNT=" Windows NT
Workstation Version 4.00"
```

where

- `multi(0)`—the ordinal of the adapter and for `multi()` always 0
- `disk(0)`—only used with a scsi( ) ARC name; always 0 for `multi()`

- `rdisk(0)`—the ordinal of the disk on the adapter; 0-3

- `partition(1)`—counting starts at 1; represents the partition number

### SCSI( ) ARC Name

A SCSI( ) ARC name is used with SCSI adapters with the BIOS disabled and requires the driver `NTBootdd.sys`. A SCSI( ) ARC name provides the form

```
scsi(0)disk(0)rdisk(0)partition(1)\WINNT=" Windows NT
Workstation Version 4.00"
```

where

- `scsi(0)`—the ordinal of the adapter and counting starts at 0

- `disk(0)`—the SCSI ID of the target disk

- `rdisk(0)`—the logical unit number; almost always 0

- `partition(1)`—counting starts at 1; represents the partition number

   Planning the organization of your hard disk(s) is a very important part of administering a Windows NT computer. As such, it is a topic covered on the certification exams, so you should understand and remember each of the concepts presented in this chapter.

## For Review

- Windows NT 4.0 does not support HPFS or FAT32

- Only NTFS volume sets can be expanded

- Volume sets do not improve performance

- Stripe sets improve performance

- These files are required to boot:

    - `Boot.ini`—controls boot options, including dual booting

    - `Bootsect.dos`—used to boot to an operating system other than Windows NT

    - `NTLDR`—loads the operating system and controls startup

    - `NTDetect.com`—gathers information on hardware support

    - `NTBootdd.sys` (optional, if SCSI BIOS is disabled)

# From Here

Installation and configuration of the Windows NT 4.0 operating system is covered in Chapter 6, "Installation Overview," Chapter 7, "Upgrade Installations," and Chapter 8 "Installation Methods." Installation and configuration of hardware and peripherals is covered in Chapter 9 "Installing and Configuring Hardware," and in Chapter 14 "Printers and Print Devices."

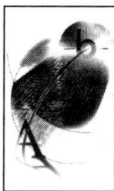

# CHAPTER 4

# Keeping Everything Secure

Windows NT Workstation has many inherent security features. Windows NT Workstation bases its strongest security model on granting access to users who have individual accounts on the workstation. With this security model, centralized control can be maintained for an individual user's access to the network and to each network resource.

For a user to access the workstation and the network, a corresponding user account must already exist and appropriate permissions and rights must be assigned to the account.

This chapter covers these issues to consider when planning security:

- Logon Security
- Account (Password) Policies
- User-level Security
- Shares and permissions
- Auditing
- Printer Security

## Logon Security

Windows NT Workstation has a secure logon dialog so that programs such as trojan horse cracking programs cannot simulate the Windows NT logon screen to capture user names and passwords.

To logon to a Windows NT Workstation, a user must give an account name (and password) that has already been created on the network. This is unlike Windows 95, which allows a user to log on to the computer without a pre-existing account. Windows NT security is tighter. Even if the user specifies a "guest" account, the guest account itself must exist, must have specific access rights, and must be enabled. By default, the guest account in Windows NT is disabled.

For those times when a user does not log off the network, but will be away from the workstation, a degree of security can be implemented by using a screen saver with a password. To set up a screen saver with password go to Control Panel | Display | Screen Saver (as shown in Figure 4.1). The screen saver is initiated by setting the wait time and password. Select Password Protected to enable the feature. One minute is the shortest wait available, but users find that one minute waits, while quite secure, do require them to enter their screensaver password frequently. The default wait before the screen saver activates is 15 minutes.

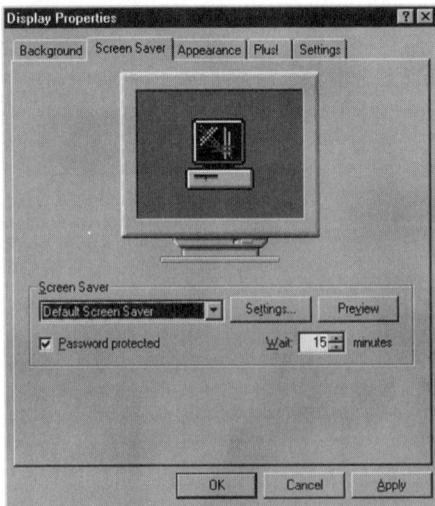

**Figure 4.1**  Use the Display applet to enable a password protected screen saver.

## Account (Password) Policies

Perhaps no other feature has greater value and greater risk than the way that passwords are used on a network. For full control, the administrator determines all passwords. For no control, the administrator turns over control to the user. In Windows NT, the password policy can be one, the other, or a complex combination of the two.

By default, the only password rule in effect is User Must Change Password at Next Logon. There are no required password rules. Planning is crucial in determining the account password policy for your network. In addressing security requirements, the password policy can be as unique as the organization. The Account Policy dialog box, shown in Figure 4.2, is used to set password policy for the network.

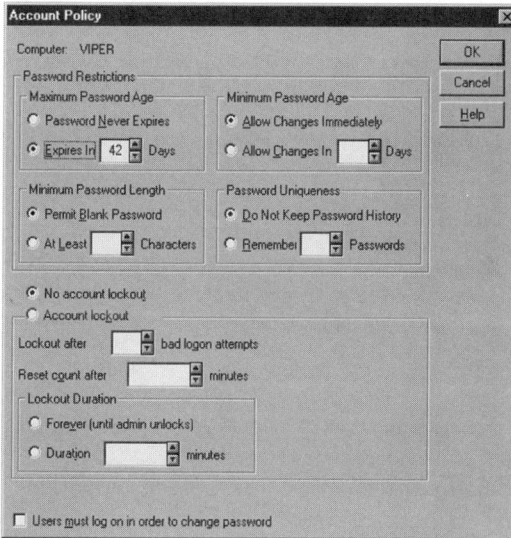

**Figure 4.2**  Use the Account Policy dialog box to create your password policy.

### ADMINISTRATOR OR USER CONTROLLED?

Configuring the Account Policy determines who creates the password. The first consideration in setting Account Policy is determining who creates the password—user or administrator. For the administrator, this can be a time-consuming process. Every password must be recorded and kept in a safe place. Although time consuming and cumbersome, this sort of centralized, powerful security role is important to some organizations. However, it is much simpler, and probably more secure, to allow the users to create their passwords. When the user forgets their password, the administrator can still change the password through User Manager.

The Account Lockout option is a good way to maintain a secure network. When so many password attempts are unsuccessful, Account Lockout locks that account from the whole network. Crackers are discouraged from gaining unauthorized access to the network and network resources by using Account Lockout.

Other password enforcement options that can be set include:

- Maximum password age
- Minimum password age
- Minimum password length
- Password uniqueness

More information about Account Policies can be found in Chapter 11, "Users."

## User-Level Security

User-level security is based on access permissions assigned to users and to group accounts. Security is centralized with each user having only one unique username and password. Permission to access each specific network resource is granted to individual users or, preferably, groups of users. User-level security provides ease of use, administration, and security—fewer people have actual administrative authority over resources, and network resources are not accessed though passwords. Instead, user-level security allows only accounts with appropriate permissions access to any network resource.

When a user or a group account is first created, the new entity is issued a security identifier (SID). Each SID is a unique machine-generated number created using information based on the user, time, date, and the domain identifying the user or group account on that network. To determine the level of access to resources for a user or group, Windows NT uses the group's SID in place of a user or group's name. Each time a user attempts to access a resource, Windows NT verifies that the user's SID has permission to access that resource at the level requested.

User-level security access control is advantageous because it does not require a user to remember a separate password for each resource on the network. Network security and access to resources can be centrally administered and is not dependent on the vagaries of memory in individual computer users.

User-level security is discussed in more detail in Chapter 13, "Share and NTFS Permissions."

## Shares and Permissions

### FAT PARTITIONS

On a FAT partition the only way to provide network access to a folder is through sharing. If a user tries to access over the network a folder located on a FAT partition and the folder has not been shared, the user will not have access to the folder.

On a Windows NT Workstation, only a member of the Administrators or Power Users groups can share folders.

Keep in mind that sharing only applies to network access to resources. If a user logs directly onto a computer to which they have the "Log on Locally" user right, the shares and share permissions on that computer do not apply. Share permissions apply over the network, not locally.

To share a folder, permissions are assigned to the folder, or share. How users or groups access a folder can be controlled by assigning shared folder permissions.

Permissions can be very tricky. Users can be assigned permissions as an individual user and/or as a member of one or more defined groups, each of which may have different levels of access assigned for any one network resource. Because of this complex combination, network administration can become quite intricate. The job is not to just restrict access, but also to ensure that users are able to access files and resources they actually need!

### NTFS PARTITIONS

NTFS creates deeper levels of security than a share by complexly securing files as well as folders. Also, NTFS permissions do apply locally as well as remotely, unlike a share on a FAT partition.

Administering access security on NTFS partitions is more complicated than FAT shares, and allows file and folder permissions to be combined. In an effort to alleviate some of the complications, Windows NT created Standard Permissions for folders, which apply to files within the folders.

Chapter 13 discusses assigning access to resources in more detail.

## Auditing

Auditing is an important security consideration for any organization. Planning for security audits is crucial. The needs of the organization determine the auditing, if any, that must be performed.

Establishing an audit policy is the responsibility of an administrator. The administrator can initiate an audit policy and the Administrators group is the only group authorized to view the auditing logs.

Although setting up an audit policy is discussed in Chapter 11, a few key points to remember are:

- Only NTFS partitions can be audited.
- Auditing is not automatic—it must be initiated.
- Only administrators can start auditing.
- You must setup auditing on the computer that has events you want to audit.
- Auditing is a great way to see what's working, what's not, and who's doing it.
- Auditing can create huge logs of network activity.

## Printer Security

Access to printers and tracking printer use can also be controlled using Windows NT security features.

Although, initially, all shared printers are available to all network users, permissions can be set for each printer. To set printer permissions, access Printer | Properties | Security | Permissions. Figure 4.3 shows the Printer Permissions dialog box where the type of access for user and group accounts can be set.

There are four levels of access permission that apply to shared network printers:

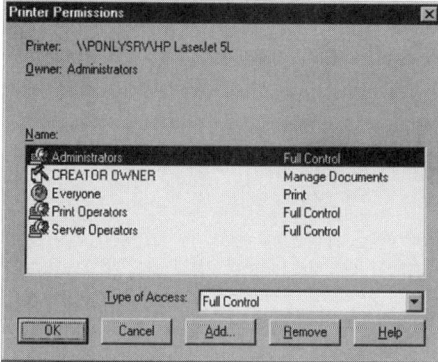

**Figure 4.3**   Set the type of access for users and groups using the Printer Permissions dialog box.

- No Access
- Print
- Manage Documents
- Full Control

By default, on a Windows NT Workstation, Administrators and Power Users have Full Control.

The Ownership button provides information on who owns the printer. The dialog box also provides a Take Ownership option, as shown in Figure 4.4. A user with Full Control of the printer can take ownership of the printer. A user who owns the printer can set permissions for that printer.

Auditing access to a printer and printer use is discussed in Chapter 11.

**Figure 4.4**   Ownership of a printer can be taken by a user with Full Control of the printer.

# For Review

- A user account must exist on Windows NT Workstation before a user can access the computer.

- A screen saver with password can be used to provide a degree of security when the user will be away from the workstation.

- Accounts can be locked out after a number of unsuccessful login attempts.

- User-level security provides a means of centralizing administration of access to resources.

- Members of the Administrators and Power Users groups can share folders on a Windows NT Workstation.

- Audit information, stored in the Event Viewer's security log can only be viewed by a member of the Administrators group.

- Permissions can be set for each printer on the network.

# From Here

Chapter 11 discusses the Account Policy and the Audit Policy. User-level security and assigning access to resources are discussed in more detail in Chapter 13.

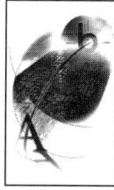

**CHAPTER 5**

# Keeping It All Running

This chapter is about little-known Windows NT secrets: Windows NT Service Packs and the RegClean 4.1 utility. Neither of these topics are assured to be on your exam, and both programs are to be used at your own risk, if at all.

After Windows NT 4.0 was released, a number of annoying bugs were discovered, documented, and fixed. The way to implement these fixes is to apply the current service pack to your computer's operating system. Any improvements and enhancements to the operating system may also be distributed in a service pack. However, you should understand that Microsoft does not promise that application of a Service Pack is risk free, or that it will fix whatever might be wrong.

**CAUTION**
If the computer you are considering applying a service pack to contains proprietary hardware or multiple processors, proceed with the utmost caution. Check with your computer hardware vendor to be sure any proprietary hardware is compatible with the service pack. Carefully follow the alternate instructions for multiple CPU computers if your computer has two or more CPUs.

## SERVICE PACKS ARE FREE

Microsoft supplies service packs free, with the proviso that nothing that goes wrong involving the Service Pack is their fault. Most people find that Service Pack 3 for Windows NT is beneficial, or at least neutral, to their computer's operation, so Service Pack 3 is the example used here.

Microsoft service packs are cumulative. There is no reason to apply Service Pack 1 or 2 if you are about to apply Service Pack 3. Service Pack 3 contains all the good stuff from Service Pack 1 and 2 carried forward and included in Service Pack 3.

Hot fixes, which are released between the service packs, are specific to one problem area and are not cumulative. It takes a serious problem or a courageous (or desperate) system administrator to experiment with hot fixes. Hot fixes are something you should know about, but they are not recommended here.

## Applying Service Pack 3

As shown in Figure 5.1, before and after applying a service pack you should run `rdisk /s` to create an Emergency Repair Disk (ERD). Also, make a complete backup of all data on the computer before you install a service pack. Applying a service pack is roughly tantamount to installing an operating system—you are tinkering with the operating system when you apply a service pack.

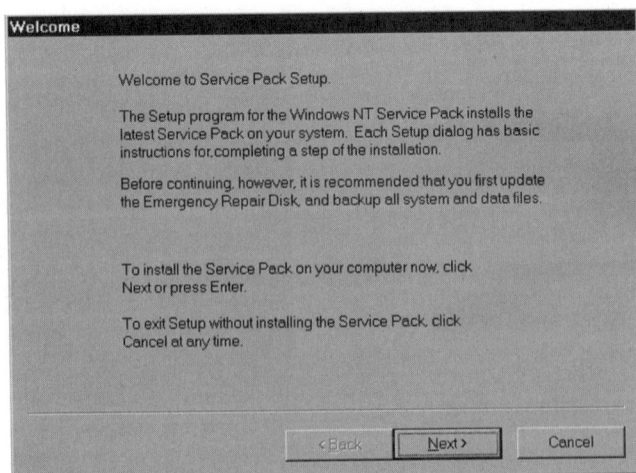

**Figure 5.1** Make an ERD and a 100% backup before applying a service pack!

Service Pack 3 is over 18 MB, and when it runs it insists on un-packing itself on the C: drive. Therefore, to use Service Pack 3 the computer must have lots of free space on C:. Before unpacking itself into a temporary directory, Service Pack 3 first verifies itself to be sure it has not become corrupted, as seen in Figure 5.2.

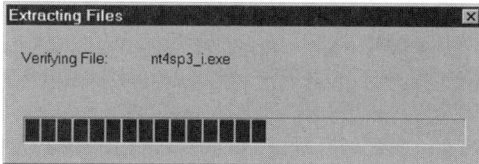

**Figure 5.2**   Service Pack 3 first checks its own integrity.

After it passes its own verification test, Service Pack 3 unpacks it-self onto the C: drive, as shown in Figure 5.3.

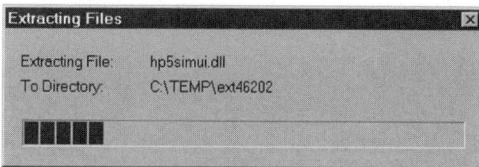

**Figure 5.3**   Service Pack 3 then extracts files onto your C: drive.

Next, Service Pack Setup offers to uninstall a previous installation of Service Pack, or to proceed with the current Service Pack. After you select the option to proceed, Setup offers the choice to create an uninstall directory, as shown in Figure 5.4.

After everything is ready, setup asks one more time if you want to continue or cancel the operation. Next, you'll see the "Please wait . . . " screen shown in Figure 5.5.

After the service pack has inspected and has detected your com-puter, it finally decides to replace old (bad) files with newer (better) files. As shown in Figure 5.6, if it encounters a file that has a newer date than its own, it politely asks if you want to replace the newer file—no, you don't want to replace newer files in most cases.

When Service Pack 3 has finished grooming your operating sys-tem files, it warns you that it's going to reboot. This message also re-minds you, as seen in Figure 5.7, that from now on if you change or add any components to the computer, you should re-apply the service pack.

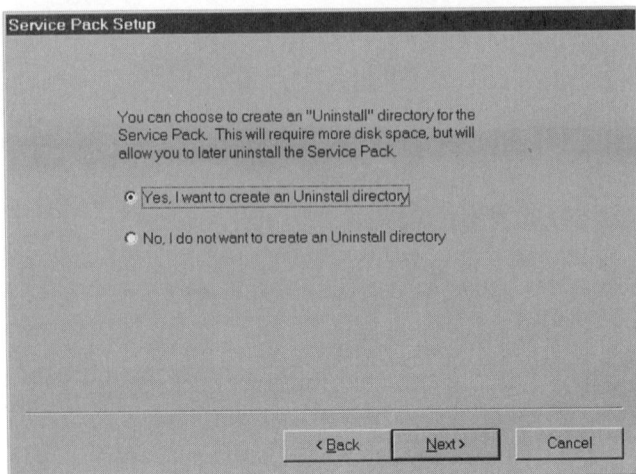

**Figure 5.4** Service Pack 3 offers to install an uninstall directory.

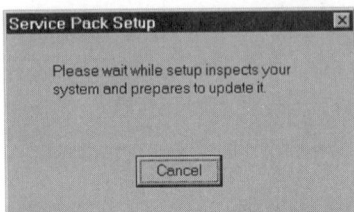

**Figure 5.5** This is the time to cross your fingers.

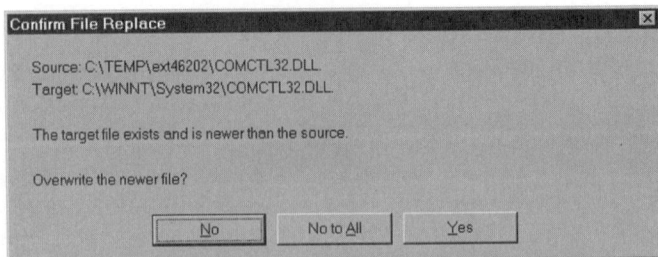

**Figure 5.6** Service Pack 3 asks before replacing newer files.

While many experts believe that only major changes to the operating system itself or major changes to the hardware configuration of a computer would cause them to re-apply a service pack,

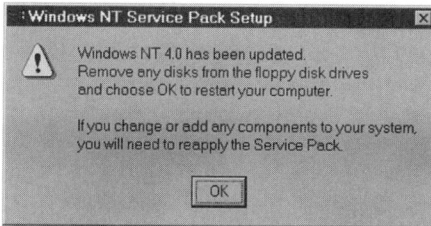

**Figure 5.7** If anything changes on this computer, re-apply the service pack.

others contend that cranky applications, and even newly installed applications, sometimes mysteriously behave better after a follow-up service pack installation. "You pays your money and takes your chances."

## RegClean 4.1

If you've ever deleted an application, or uninstalled an application and had the uninstall fail, or if you've changed browsers back and forth from Netscape to something else and back again, or if you've fiddled with Control Panel applets to add or remove software or hardware, then the registry on that computer probably has some junk in it that is no longer needed, or perhaps is even detrimental. RegClean tries to straighten that out for you, for free.

Older versions of RegClean were not so successful, but RegClean 4.1 seems to be stable and tidy enough. Microsoft RegClean 4.1 is a Windows NT registry analysis and correction utility, as shown in Figure 5.8.

Why would one want to let Microsoft fiddle with the inner sanctum of the Windows NT operating system—the registry? Good question! Most people don't get down into the registry even to look unless they are forced to. But you're going to be an MCSE, and you are the one that those other folks are going to come to when things go wrong. You need to appear to walk with no fear—even through the registry. So, here's one way to become more familiar with the dreaded registry.

RegClean creates easy-to-implement undo files, and stores them in the same folder where you keep RegClean. If you run it two or three times, eventually it will find all the stuff it's going to find, and it stops making changes. To see what was changed, just open the undo files with a text editor.

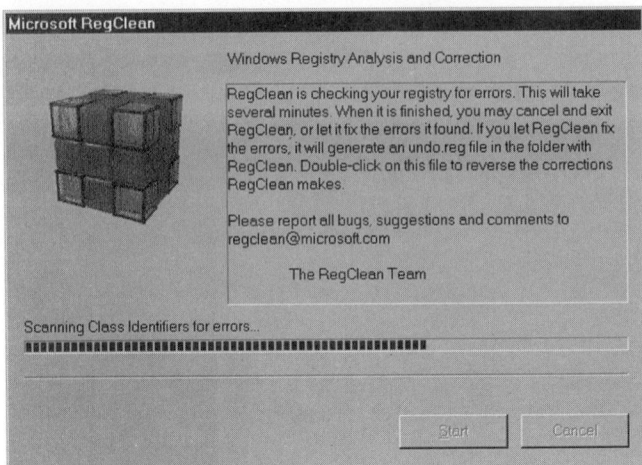

**Figure 5.8** RegClean 4.1 first loads several sets of data, and then scans them for errors.

**CAUTION**
Don't double click on the undo files from Windows Explorer unless you actually intend to reverse the changes made by RegClean!

Here is a RegClean undo file that didn't change anything:

```
REGEDIT4
;    Double click on this file from Explorer to automatically
;    undo these deletions or modifications and return the
     values to the registry.

;    - Modified or removed by RegClean 4.1 (97.71) from
     computer: PONLYNTSERVER
;      on Thursday, February 05, 1998 20:30:50
```

As mentioned, do not use previous versions of RegClean, or your mileage may vary wildly.

Applying Service Packs and adjusting registry entries are the stuff of network support and administration. Decisions about these weighty topics will become more than commonplace for you once you begin work as an MCSE.

# For Review

- Service Packs bring your operating system up to speed with Microsoft's latest changes and bug fixes.
- RegClean 4.1 is free, tidy and painless to use.

# From Here

Next, Chapter 6, "Installation Overview," Chapter 7, "Upgrade Installations," and Chapter 8 "Installation Methods," get you ready to install Windows NT 4.0 Workstations all around your network. Then Chapter 9, "Installing and Configuring Hardware," familiarizes you with the many Control Panel applets.

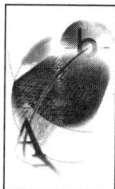

**CHAPTER 6**

# Installation Overview

The Windows NT 4.0 Workstation exam content for operating system installation requires you to know about the computer hardware and the network configuration. Microsoft goes to great pains to ensure you understand the importance of planning the installation. Here are the topics covered in this chapter:

- Hardware Compatibility List
- NT Hardware Qualifier (NTHQ)
- Minimum Hardware Requirements
- Installation Phases
- Dual Booting
- Removing Windows NT Workstation

Chapter 7, "Upgrade Installations," discusses when an upgrade is an option. Chapter 8, "Installation Methods," discusses the different methods for performing the actual installation of Windows NT 4.0 Workstation.

## Hardware Compatibility List (HCL)

Before beginning any installation, it is crucial you check the current HCL at the Microsoft web site. Because the HCL location is subject to change, go to www.microsoft.com and search for it.

This web site list is updated periodically and there may be references to the HCL on the MCSE test. Microsoft only supports the installation of Windows NT 4.0 Workstation on hardware on the list. Therefore, hardware not listed is not guaranteed.

## NT Hardware Qualifier, or NTHQ

Included on the Windows NT installation CD is the NTHQ, or NT Hardware Qualifier. The NTHQ tool can only be used on Intel-based computers, however. NTHQ, found on the Windows NT Workstation Setup CD-ROM in the \SUPPORT\HQTOOL\ folder, creates an MS-DOS floppy. Before installation of Windows NT this floppy is used to boot the system and will detect all hardware, helping to diagnose potential problems before installing Windows NT.

## Minimum Hardware Requirements

For the exam, know the minimum hardware requirements for Windows NT Workstation. Table 6.1 shows the minimum requirements.

**Table 6.1** Windows NT Workstation requires at least 12 MB of RAM memory.

| NT Workstation 4.0 Requirements | INTEL-based | RISC |
| --- | --- | --- |
| CPU | 486/25 MHz or higher | RISC processor Alpha, MIPS or PowerPC |
| Memory | 12 MB RAM minimum | 16 MB RAM minimum |

**Table 6.1** *(cont.)*

| Hard Disk Space | 120 MB on a single disk | 148 MB on a single disk |
|---|---|---|
| Display Monitor | VGA or higher | VGA or higher |
| Mouse | Pointing device | Pointing device |
| Drive Requirements | HD 3.5" floppy & CD-ROM Or 3.5" floppy with network connection** | CD-ROM drive* |

*RISC—must initiate installation from the CD ROM.

** Intel-based systems can install Windows NT without the CD ROM using a network connection, however a 3.5" floppy drive is still required.

Note: The faster the processor and the more RAM the better Windows NT Workstation will perform.

On the MCSE exam, there are sometimes long, involved questions that conclude by asking about installing Windows NT 4.0 on a 386 machine. You must know the minimum requirements to get the answers correct. You cannot install 4.0 on a 386.

Also, keep the distinctions between Windows NT Server and Windows NT Workstation clear. Specifically, Workstation requires aminimum of 12 MB RAM and Server requires 16 MB. The differences are slight, but important to know. You can learn Workstation at 12, but you can't drive a Server until you're 16.

## Installation Phases

Without a doubt, you must know the four phases to the Windows NT installation.

### 1. INITIALIZING INSTALLATION

During this phase, setup determines whether there is a previous version of Windows NT installed and will ask if you want to upgrade or install the new version of Windows NT without upgrading.

Hardware detection also takes place during this phase. Finally, Setup will ask you where to install the Windows NT files as well as what type of file system to use and verify partition information.

## FILE SYSTEMS

When beginning your installation, you may find yourself dealing with three or more file systems, depending on which, if any, operating system was installed already. The three most popular are: FAT, FAT32, and NTFS. Table 6.2 will help organize your understanding of which operating systems supports which file system:

**Table 6.2** Windows 95 can handle FAT32, Windows NT can't. Windows NT can handle NTFS, Windows 95 can't.

| Windows95 | Windows NT* |
|-----------|-------------|
| FAT | FAT |
| FAT32 | NTFS |

*Note: HPFS is no longer supported in Windows NT 4.0. See Chapter 7, for applicable procedures.

Let's say you configured your local computer with a dual boot of Windows 95 and Windows NT. Assume you have three partitions. If each partition is configured with different file systems, as shown in Table 6.3, here is how each operating system will or will not recognize the file systems:

**Table 6.3** In this example Windows NT can read drives C and E. Windows 95 can read Drives C and D.

| Partition | File System | Windows 95 | Windows NT |
|-----------|-------------|------------|------------|
| DriveC | FAT | Yes | Yes |
| DriveD | FAT32 | Yes | No |
| DriveE | NTFS | No | Yes |

In this instance, Drive D cannot serve as the boot partition for the Windows NT file system because FAT32 is an unrecognized file system to Windows NT 4.0. To work as a dual boot, install Windows NT to Drive C or E. This can become a complex arrangement, so it is understandable that Microsoft does not recommend a dual boot configuration.

When selecting a file system for a dual-boot system, the prime consideration is which operating system needs to access data files. That is, if in the above situation only Windows 95 needs to access information on Drive D, then FAT32 is acceptable. On the other hand, if Windows 95 needs to access data from Drive E, the file system would have to be converted.

To avoid this situation on a dual-boot system, each partition or drive should be configured with the FAT file system. However, this may not be ideal because many of the advanced features available in FAT32 and NTFS are lost.

## FAT FILE SYSTEM

As a great, all-around file system, FAT can be accessed by all Windows operating systems, including MS-DOS and OS/2. Microsoft does not recommend using the FAT file system for Windows NT installations except when required by a dual-boot situation.

In addition to the variety of access the FAT file system allows, FAT also provides less security; that can be a plus or a minus depending on your needs. There is more about this subject in Chapter 13, "Share and NTFS Permissions."

## NTFS FILE SYSTEM

NTFS, or New Technology File System, is a new file system created by Microsoft for Windows NT. Consequently, Windows NT is the only operating system that can work with NTFS. Windows NT can also recognize FAT (but not FAT32). In a configuration booting with Windows NT only, this will be fine. A dual boot, however, requires more planning.

NTFS was designed by Microsoft to create a more secure file system environment than was possible in the FAT system. Unfortunately, the re-design created incompatibilities with the other file systems. Nevertheless, NTFS provides more features and should be used whenever possible. Among the enhancements are:

- File-level security
- File Compression
- Extended Volumes
- Maintains permissions during a NetWare Migration
- Macintosh file-sharing support

Table 6.4 is a quick comparison of the features available in the two file systems. You should be aware of these for the exam.

**Table 6.4** A comparison of the features available using FAT or NTFS.

|  | FAT | NTFS |
|---|---|---|
| Allows Shared Folders | Yes | Yes |
| File/Folder Level Security | No | Yes |
| Share Level Security | Yes | Yes |
| Auditing | No | Yes |
| MAC support on the server | No | Yes |
| MAC support on workstation | No | No |
| POSIX support | Yes | Yes |
| Long File Names | Yes | Yes |
| File Compression | No | Yes |

If you're not sure which file system to use during installation, choose FAT. You can convert FAT to NTFS at any time, however, you cannot convert NTFS to FAT. Converting FAT to NTFS is performed at a C:> prompt, and the command is `Convert.exe`. If you need help with the utility, type `help convert` at a command prompt. Windows NT Setup defaults to the FAT file system.

## PARTITIONING THE DISKS

Windows NT Setup can create partitions during the setup process. You will be prompted during installation for this option. Partitions are logical units on the hard disk distinguished by sequential drive letters.

You may also partition the disk before installation by using the DOS `fdisk` command at a command prompt. After installation, use Disk Administrator to create, delete and format partitions. Keep in mind partitioning disks removes all data on the disk area in question.

## SYSTEM AND BOOT PARTITIONS

For the exam, it is important to have an understanding of the differences between these two partitions.

Windows NT requires both a system partition and a boot partition. The system partition contains the files necessary to boot Windows NT. The boot partition is wherever the Windows NT operating system files are installed. Got that?

On an Intel-based computer, the active partition is the system partition. This is usually Drive C, but not always. Table 6.5 may help you understand this.

**Table 6.5** The operating system files are on the boot partition. Guess where files needed to boot the computer are?

| System Partition | Boot Partition |
|---|---|
| For the hardware-specific files needed to boot Windows NT (`boot.ini`, `bootsect.dos`, `NTLDR`, `NTDetect.com`, **possibly** `Ntbootdd.sys`). | For the Windows NT operating system files, the **Winnt folder** `%systemroot%\system32`. |

If the Windows NT operating system files are on the same partition with the system partition, that partition also becomes the boot partition. See Chapter 3, "Windows NT File System," for more information on managing partitions.

> For instance, take a case in which there are two partitions on the hard disk, Drives C and D. The Winnt folder can be on Drive D while the system partition containing the boot files can be on Drive C. This is a common configuration in a dual-boot situation.

---

When this phase is completed, Setup presents a screen with the following message:

```
Press ENTER to restart your computer.
When your computer restarts, Setup will continue.
```

If you forgot to check the HCL and are installing from a CD-ROM that is not supported by Windows NT, you may encounter the following message:

```
NONCRITICAL ERROR

The external library procedure, CopySingleFile, reported the following
error:  Unable to do the specified file copy operation.
```

In order to continue the installation, copy the required drivers to the hard disk drive from the \DRVLIB folder on the Windows NT Workstation CD-ROM before executing the WINNT command.

If, following a successful installation of Windows NT Workstation, you receive the previous message after installing a device driver, it may be that a file with the same name already exists on the hard drive and is being used by the operating system.

## 2. GATHERING INFORMATION ABOUT YOUR COMPUTER

Setup initializes this portion of the installation using the Windows NT Setup wizard. During this phase, you will be asked:

- The kind of Setup

Typical

Portable

Compact

Custom

- What password would you like to use for the Administrator Account?
- Would you like to create an Emergency Repair Disk?

## EMERGENCY REPAIR DISK (ERD)

The Emergency Repair Disk Utility (RDISK.EXE) creates an Emergency Repair Disk.

The initial ERD is created during Setup. A new ERD should be created at least every time the system configuration changes.

The ERD includes information on the boot sector, startup environment, and the registry.

The ERD created during setup also includes information from the SAM and Security databases. To include the SAM and Security database information on subsequent ERDs, use the command rdisk /s.

---

The ERD is not bootable. To use the ERD, you must have created the three setup disks during setup. The setup disks will (eventually) offer an option to repair and then present these four selections:

- Inspect registry files
- Inspect startup environment
- Verify Windows NT system files
- Inspect Boot Sector

When prompted, insert the ERD.

---

If, for example, the user account database is lost because of a system crash, the ERD can be used to restore the account and security information if the /s switch was used when the rdisk command was run.

Remember—with or without the /s switch, when using the ERD, the system will revert back to the configuration current when the ERD was created.

## 3. INSTALLING WINDOWS NT NETWORKING

This portion of Setup will ask you several important questions. The first question will be about your network configuration, specifically, whether you are wired to the network or accessing the network via a dial up connection.

**NOTE**
If you answer "none" when asked about your network configuration, setup will end and go to finishing setup. Otherwise, setup continues with this section.

Among other responses you will be prompted for are:

- Information about your network adapter card—You will be given the option to allow setup to automatically detect and install the hardware. However, because Windows NT is not yet fully plug-n-play, you must verify the information obtained through automatic detection.

If, for some reason, you have not installed a network adapter card and want to install network communication protocols during Setup, you can tell Setup that your network adapter is the MS Loopback Adapter.

- Protocols to install and any necessary protocol or network configuration parameters
- Additional Network Services to install
- Joining a Workgroup or Domain

In order to have the Windows NT Workstation join a domain during the installation process, the installer must provide the name of an account with Administrator rights and the corresponding account password.

## 4. FINISHING SETUP

At this point, you have installed Windows NT Server. In the final stage you set the time zone for your system and configure your video monitor.

If the screen goes blank when testing the monitor type, the refresh frequency could be set incorrectly.

## Dual Booting

Windows NT Workstation 4.0 can dual boot with other operating systems such as:

- DOS
- OS/2
- Windows 95/98
- Windows NT Server 3.x or 4.0
- Windows NT Workstation 3.x or 4.0

One significant drawback to a dual boot configuration is that applications must be installed twice—once for each operating system. Hardware devices must also be installed twice on a computer with a dual boot.

Existing applications and devices must be re-installed from Windows NT Workstation 4.0 because the Windows NT registry is different and settings may be stored in different locations on Windows NT Workstation and the other operating system.

FYI: It is often possible to install the application files in one place for each operating system and access them from each operating system. However, the application must be installed once from each operating system.

If you create a computer with a dual-boot configuration, it is required that each operating system be installed in a separate folder.

## Removing Windows NT Workstation

Just as important as installing Windows NT is knowing how to remove it. The test does contain questions about this special process. Here are the steps you'll need to take to remove Windows NT from a computer.

1. Create a boot disk for the alternative operating system and copy the `sys.com` utility to the boot disk. Be sure and test the boot disk before going any further.

2. Get rid of any NTFS partitions. This can be done in one of three ways.

- Disk Administrator
- Run the Windows NT setup disks
- Run `fdisk` from MS-DOS 6.x

3. Delete the WINNT folder, its contents, and subfolders (`deltree` is quicker if you have a copy of DOS 6.2).
4. Delete the following files:

- `Ntldr`
- `Ntdetect.com`
- `Boot.ini`
- `Ntbootdd.sys`
- `Bootsect.dos`
- `Pagefile.sys`

5. Reboot the computer using the boot disk created in Step 1.
6. Type SYS C: (this places the necessary boot files back on the C: drive boot track).
7. When you reboot your computer, Windows NT will be gone and you will have reverted to the alternative operating system.

## For Review

- HCL (Hardware Compatibility List)—This list defines what is compatible with Windows NT.
- NTHQ (NT Hardware Qualifier)—This can be created from the Windows NT setup disk.
- Windows NT Workstation minimum requirements: 486/25 microprocessor or higher, 12 MB RAM, VGA Display Monitor, and a 120 MB Hard Drive

- The boot and system partitions can be the same or different partitions.

- The boot partition is wherever the Windows NT operating system files are installed.

- The system partition contains the files necessary to boot Windows NT.

- A CopySingleFile Noncritical Error can occur when:

The CD-ROM is not supported by Windows NT.

A file with the same name already exists on the hard drive and is being used by the operating system.

- The Emergency Repair Disk (ERD) is not bootable. The three setup disks are required to use the ERD.

- Rdisk creates an ERD. A new ERD should be created after each change in the system configuration.

- Rdisk /s places account and security database information on the ERD.

- Remember that with or without the /s switch, when using the ERD the system will revert back to the configuration when the ERD was created.

- If for some reason you have not installed a network adapter card and want to install networking protocols during setup, you can use the MS Loopback Adapter.

- In order to have the Windows NT Workstation join a domain during the installation process, the installer must provide the name of an account with Administrator rights and the corresponding account password.

- If the screen goes blank when testing the monitor type, the refresh frequency is set incorrectly.

- Windows NT Workstation 4.0 can dual boot with other operating systems.

- If you create a computer with a dual boot configuration, it is required that each operating system be installed in separate folders.

- When removing Windows NT and returning to a different operating system always remove the NTFS partition after you create the boot disk for the other operating system.

- When uninstalling Windows NT, use the `sys.com` utility to place necessary DOS boot files back on the C: Drive boot track.

## From Here

See Chapter 3, "Windows NT File System," for more information on managing partitions. Chapter 7, "Upgrade Installations," discusses when an upgrade is an option. Chapter 8, "Installation Methods," discusses the different ways to install Windows NT Workstation. Chapter 13, "Share and NTFS Permissions" discusses the different security available on FAT and NTFS partitions.

# Upgrade Installations

This chapter discusses upgrading Windows NT 3.51 to Windows NT 4.0, and why a Windows 95/98 operating system cannot be upgraded to Windows NT 4.0. For more information on installation, see:

- Chapter 6, "Installation Overview," discusses hardware requirements, installation phases, file systems, disk partitions, and removing Windows NT Workstation.

- Chapter 8, "Installation Methods," discusses different methods of installing Windows NT Workstation.

## Upgrading from Windows NT 3.51 to Windows NT 4.0

Setup detects previous versions of Windows NT and gives you the option of upgrading to the newer version.

During the upgrade process from Windows NT 3.51, the Registry, network settings, and all accounts are preserved in Windows NT 4.0.

Remember to check the Windows NT 3.51 computer's hardware. If the Windows NT 3.51 operating system is running on a 386 computer, Windows NT Workstation 4.0 cannot be upgraded or installed.

### WINDOWS NT 3.51 ON A HPFS PARTITION

Windows NT 4.0 does not support the HPFS file system. So when the Windows NT 3.51 operating system is located on an HPFS partition, the HPFS partition must be converted to an NTFS partition before the upgrade.

In order to upgrade Windows NT 3.51 on an HPFS partition to Windows NT 4.0, proceed as follows.

- Convert the HPFS partition to an NTFS partition by using the convert.exe utility

- Upgrade the operating system using the command winnt32.exe

Installing Windows NT 4.0 as a dual-boot option with Windows NT 3.51 is discussed in Chapter 6.

## An Upgrade from Windows 95/98 To Windows NT 4.0 is not Available

Windows 95/98 cannot be upgraded to Windows NT Workstation 4.0, because there is no upgrade procedure from Windows 95/98 to Windows NT Workstation 4.0. If the exam asks you about upgrading from Windows 95/98 to Windows NT 4.0, don't fall for it!

The Windows 95/98 registry is not compatible with the Windows NT 4.0 registry. Windows NT 4.0 must be installed, not upgraded, on a Windows 95/98 computer. All applications are then reinstalled.

See Chapter 8 for information on installing Windows NT 4.0 on a Windows 95/98 computer.

### FOR REVIEW

- Windows NT can be installed as an upgrade or a fresh install over previous versions of Windows NT.

- When upgrading from Windows NT 3.51, the Registry, network settings, and all accounts are preserved in Windows NT 4.0 when installing to an NTFS partition.

- Before upgrading, check the hardware on the Windows NT 3.51 computer.

- Convert the HPFS partition to an NTFS partition before upgrading Windows NT 3.51 to Windows NT 4.0.

- Use `winnt32.exe` when upgrading from Windows NT 3.51.

- Windows 95/98 cannot be upgraded to Windows NT 4.0.

**FROM HERE**

Chapter 6, discusses basic installation information, and Chapter 8 discusses the different methods for installing Windows NT Workstation.

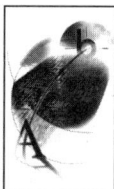

# Installation Methods

This chapter discusses different methods of installing Windows NT Workstation 4.0, including:

- Fresh Installation
- Server-Based Installation
- Unattended Installation

For more information on installation, see:

- Chapter 6, "Installation Overview," discusses hardware requirements, installation phases, file systems, disk partitions, dual booting, and removing Windows NT Workstation.
- Chapter 7, "Upgrade Installation," discusses upgrading a Windows NT Workstation 3.51 to Windows NT Workstation 4.0.

## Fresh Install of Windows NT Workstation

If no previous operating system exists, Windows NT Workstation uses three floppy disks to begin the setup process. The disks install on the hard drive a condensed version of Windows NT Workstation that allows the CD-ROM to be accessed for continuing the installation. Begin your Windows NT Workstation installation by using the winnt.exe command.

If you are doing an over-the-network install, consider using winnt.exe /b. The /b switch copies all installation files directly to the hard drive and does not create the setup disks.

### IF A WINDOWS 95 OR DOS CD-ROM DRIVE IS NOT SUPPORTED BY WINDOWS NT

If the current Windows 95 or DOS CD-ROM does not appear on the HCL, this is not necessarily a hopeless situation. Begin the Windows NT installation by booting to Windows 95 or DOS and following this procedure:

1. Start the operating system that supports the CD-ROM

2. Connect to a network share, or

3. Copy the installation files to the hard drive

4. Start the installation from either the network share or the hard drive copy of the installation files.

## Server-Based Install from the Installation Files

Setting up Windows NT Workstation to install over a network is simple. Over-the-network installation is an excellent way for sites with multiple-client computers to install Windows NT Workstation. It is also faster because installation is from files on the server and doesn't always require reading from a CD or floppies.

There are two methods for distributing the installation files over the network.

### SHARING THE CD ROM

- Share the server's CD-ROM and insert the Windows NT Workstation CD.

- Change the share permissions on the server CD-ROM from Everyone Full Control to Everyone Read.

## USING THE XCOPY COMMAND

- Create a folder on the server for the files. Share the folder.

- Use the XCOPY /s command to copy the appropriate folder and subfolders based on the type of processor.

Note: Using /s is crucial to ensure the installation subfolders are copied.

Using XCOPY requires more room on the server; however, using the CD-ROM slows down installation.

## Unattended Installation

The test covers unattended installation, also known as a scripted installation, in detail. If you want to do additional research, the best Microsoft materials to consult are the Windows NT Workstation Resource Kit and TechNet.

Ordinarily only two files are required for an unattended installation.

- Unattend.txt
- Uniqueness Database File (UDF)

When applications that are not supported by a scripted installation need to be installed, the sysdiff.exe utility is also used in addition to unattend.txt and UDF.

### UNATTEND.TXT

Answers to setup questions posed during installation are in unattend.txt. During a single installation of Windows NT Workstation, you would typically answer these questions while sitting in front of the computer. In an Unattended Installation, the questions are answered automatically, eliminating the need for user input.

Creating an answer file is easy. The Windows NT Workstation installation CD-ROM includes the SETUPMGR.EXE program shown in Figure 8.1 and located in the \SUPPORT\DEPTOOLS\ folder. This program will help you create the custom replies you need for your answer file.

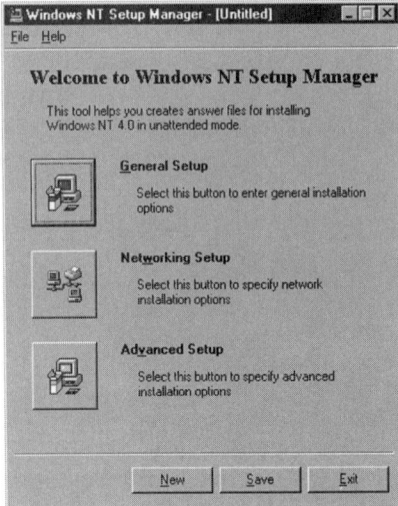

**Figure 8.1.**  Windows NT Setup Manager helps create answer files for installing Windows NT Workstation 4.0 in unattended mode.

The command for an unattended installation is:

```
winnt.exe /u:unattend.txt
```

or

```
winnt32.exe /u:unattend.txt (for Windows NT upgrades)
```

The /u switch specified in the above command indicates this is an unattended installation.

An answer file (unattend.txt) is required for each hardware platform on which Windows NT Workstation 4.0 will be installed. For example, if Windows NT Workstation 4.0 is to be installed on both desktop computers and laptop computers, two answer files will have to be created.

## THE UNIQUENESS DATABASE FILE (UDF)

For the exam, it is necessary for you to understand that you can use both an Answer File and a UDF. While the Answer File, or unattend.txt, creates a global installation with default settings for all computers, the UDF provides specific information for individual computers.

Let's say you need to specify the user name and computer name for some computers during installation. The UDF does that by overriding the %username% and %computername% section of the answer file.

A UDF can have a number of uniqueness IDs, and each uniqueness ID can specify a different configuration. When a uniqueness ID is included in the winnt(32).exe command, the UDF values override the unattend.txt values.

Even if multiple answer files are required because of different hardware configurations, only one UDF is necessary because the UDF contains uniqueness IDs.

When using a UDF, the install command would be written as follows:

```
winnt(32).exe /u:unattend.txt /udf:ID[filename]
```

## SYSDIFF.EXE

The sysdiff.exe utility is used to install software applications that don't support scripted installations. For this exam, sysdiff.exe has three switches of interest.

- SNAP–records a snapshot of a computer's registry, files, and folders.
- DIFF–records the difference between the SNAP configuration and after the desired applications have been installed.

- APPLY–the method of applying the DIFF configurations recorded.

The procedure for using the sysdiff utility is as follows:

1. After installing Windows NT Workstation on a computer, run sysdiff /snap snapshot_file where snapshot_file is a filename you create. This creates a model of your source computer.

2. Next, configure the source computer exactly as you will eventually configure the destination computers, remembering

   ■ Microprocessors of the source and destination computers must be identical.

   ■ The system root folder, or WINNT folder, must be located identically on source and destination computers.

3. Run

   ```
   sysdiff /diff snapshot_file difference_file
   ```

   where `snapshot_file` is the file created in the first step and `difference_file` is a filename you create. This difference file designates the distinctions between the beginning model and ending model of the source computer.

4. The last step is to run

   ```
   sysdiff /apply difference_file
   ```

   on the target computer.

Be careful to not confuse the `sysdiff.exe` utility with the `windiff.exe` utility. `windiff.exe` is a utility that compares the differences between registry entries before and after an upgrade.

**FOR REVIEW**

■ If the CD-ROM does not appear on the HCL, boot to the operating system that supports the CD-ROM, connect to a network share or copy the installation files to a hard drive, and then begin the installation.

■ Three files are required for an unattended installation:

■ `unattend.txt`

■ `UDF`

■ `sysdiff.exe`

■ Setup questions posed during installation are answerd in `unattend.txt`.

■ An answer file (`unattend.txt`) is required for each hardware platform on which Windows NT Workstation 4.0 will be installed.

■ The Answer File, or `unattend.txt`, provides default settings for all computers, and the UDF provides specific information for individual computers.

■ A UDF can have a number of uniqueness IDs. Each uniqueness ID can specify a different configuration.

■ Even if multiple answer files are required because of different hardware configurations, only one UDF is necessary because the UDF contains uniqueness IDs.

■ The `sysdiff.exe` utility is used to install software applications that don't support scripted installations. For this exam, `sysdiff.exe` has three switches of interest.

  ■ SNAP–records a snapshot of a computer's registry, files, and folders.

  ■ DIFF–records difference between the SNAP configuration and after the desired applications have been installed.

  ■ APPLY–the method of applying the DIFF configurations recorded.

**FROM HERE**

Chapter 6, discusses basic installation information. Chapter 7, discusses how to upgrade a Windows NT 3.51 to Windows NT Workstation 4.0.

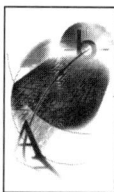

# CHAPTER 9

# Installing and Configuring Hardware

The applets in the Control Panel provide Windows NT users with safer and simpler ways to edit the registry. These applications are the tools to use to configure Windows NT Workstation to provide a better working environment. Because of the importance of these applets, expect to see several questions on the test about how to use them. Figure 9.1 shows a Windows NT Workstation Control Panel.

Some of these applets change system settings while others configure settings specific to individual users.

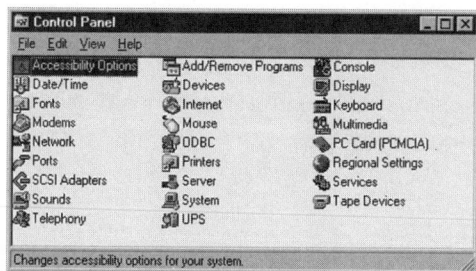

| Control Panel | | |
|---|---|---|
| File Edit View Help | | |
| Accessibility Options | Add/Remove Programs | Console |
| Date/Time | Devices | Display |
| Fonts | Internet | Keyboard |
| Modems | Mouse | Multimedia |
| Network | ODBC | PC Card (PCMCIA) |
| Ports | Printers | Regional Settings |
| SCSI Adapters | Server | Services |
| Sounds | System | Tape Devices |
| Telephony | UPS | |

Changes accessibility options for your system.

**Figure 9–1.** Use Control Panel to select the appropriate applet for installing and configuring a specific device.

The applets that change system settings are:

- Add/Remove Programs
- Date/Time
- Devices
- Fonts
- Internet
- Modems
- Multimedia
- Network
- ODBC
- PC Card (PCMCIA)
- Ports
- Printers
- SCSI Adapters
- Server
- Services
- System
- Tape Devices
- Telephony
- UPS

The applets that change user settings are:

- Accessibility Options
- Console
- Display (with the exception of changing the display driver)
- Keyboard (with the exception of changing the keyboard driver)
- Mouse (with the exception of changing the mouse driver)
- Regional Settings
- Sounds

## System Settings

### ADD/REMOVE PROGRAMS

The Add/Remove Programs property dialog box has two functions:

Install or uninstall programs

Change Windows NT setup parameters

The Install/Uninstall Tab is used to add new programs and to modify or remove programs that have registered their uninstall procedure during installation.

The applet's Windows NT Setup tab can be used to add or remove Windows components. This same list of components was available during installation. In order to add or remove components, you may be required to provide the Windows NT CD or have access to shared installation files.

### DATE/TIME

Use the Date/Time applet to set the date and time for your system. Of greater importance, it is also used to select the correct time zone. If the time zone is not correct, it can cause problems with applications, especially mail and scheduling programs.

### DEVICES

The Devices applet provides you with information on the status of devices installed on your computer. With the Devices applet you can:

Stop or start a device

Configure the desired status of each device driver at startup

Enable or disable various devices for different hardware profiles

### FONTS

The Fonts applet is used to add or remove fonts from your system. Each font can be individually viewed, and a sheet showing the font can be printed, but only one font shows at a time. You can also use the View menu of this applet to find fonts that are similar.

## INTERNET

This applet is used to configure properties for Microsoft Internet Explorer including Dial on Demand and whether to use a proxy server to access the Internet. The appearance of this applet and the options available are dependent on what version of Internet Explorer is installed.

*Internet*

## MODEMS

*Modems*

The Modems applet is used to install, modify, or remove modems. It can also be used to access and modify the Dialing Properties used on your computer. The Modems applet dialog box is shown in Figure 9.2.

## MULTIMEDIA

*Multimedia*

The Multimedia applet opens the Multimedia Properties dialog box that has five pages. They are:

- Audio
- Video

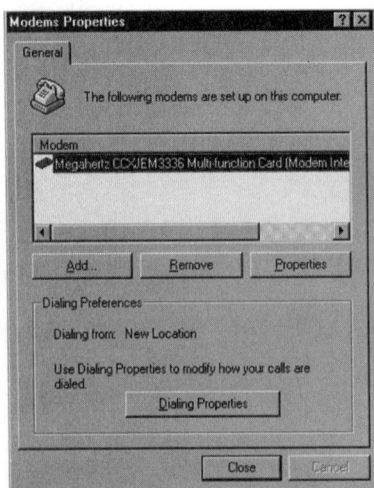

**Figure 9.2**  Use the Modems Applet in Control Panel to install and configure a modem.

- MIDI
- CD Music
- Devices

Use the Multimedia applet to configure various multi-media devices such as your sound card, video display, the CD player volume, and MIDI devices.

The Device page displays all the multimedia devices, which ones are installed, and the status of each. The Device page in the Multimedia applet is used to install the necessary drivers for various multimedia devices as shown in Figure 9.3.

## NETWORK

The Network applet displays the Network Properties dialog box. This dialog box enables you to install and configure services, protocols, and adapters. There are five pages displayed in the Network Properties dialog box. They are:

- Identification
- Services

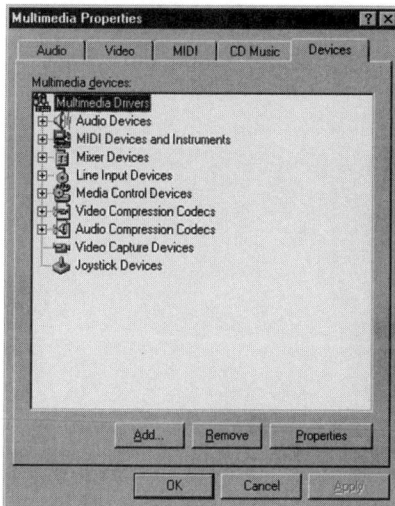

**Figure 9.3.** Use the Multimedia applet in Control Panel to install and configure MIDI devices.

- Protocols
- Adapters
- Bindings

### Identification

The Identification page displays the name of the computer and the workgroup or domain of which it is a member. The Identification Changes page, shown in Figure 9.4, is used to change the name of the computer. The workgroup or domain can also be changed from this page.

### Services

The Services tab is used to add, remove, or modify network services that are installed on the computer. These include default services such as the Workstation Service and the Server Service.

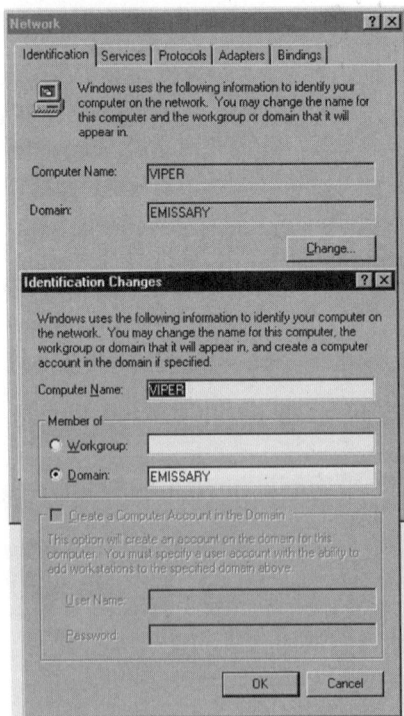

**Figure 9.4** Use the Change button available from the Identification tab in the Network applet to join a different domain.

### Protocols

By default, when Windows NT Workstation is installed TCP/IP is selected to be installed. Other protocols you can add include Net-BEUI, NWLink, DLC, and PPTP (Point-to-Point Tunneling Protocol). These are covered in detail in Chapter 17, "Available Protocols."

These protocols' properties are configured from here and may be modified if need be. However, only an administrator or a user who is a member of the Administrator group can add, delete or modify protocols.

### Adapters

The Adapters page is where you add, modify, or delete adapters. The update button allows you to install a new device driver for adapters already installed.

### Bindings

Bindings refer to the connections between the hardware (network card) and the software (protocols and services). The Bindings tab allows you to enable or disable the binding of protocols to services or adapters as well as change their order. See Chapter 18, "Binding Order," for more detailed information on configuring bindings.

### ODBC

The ODBC applet opens the ODBC Data Source Administrator dialog box. Use this dialog box to install and configure any ODBC drivers needed by the applications you are running.

### PC CARD (PCMCIA)

The PC Card (PCMCIA) applet is used to add or remove drivers. It is also used to configure installed adapters. This applet displays the status of installed PC Card devices. Resource settings for a PC Card may be configured manually or automatically.

### PORTS

The Ports applet is used to add and remove serial ports from your computer.

This applet is also used to change resource settings such as the IRQ, Base I/O address, and COM Port Number. Communication settings such as speed, error checking, and data flow are also configured here. Only administrators can make changes to COM ports.

## PRINTERS

The Printers applet is used to install or remove printers. In addition, it is used to configure printer options. See Chapter 14, "Printers and Print Devices," for detailed information on managing printers and documents.

## SCSI ADAPTERS

The SCSI Adapters applet, shown in Figure 9.5, has two pages, Devices and Drivers. The SCSI Adapters applet is used to install or remove SCSI adapter drivers. It displays the installed SCSI adapters, installed drivers, and properties of the devices. This applet also displays any IDE or EIDE adapters installed on your computer.

## SERVER

The Server applet has five buttons at the bottom. It is used to display:

Any users connected to shared resources

What shared resources are on the local computer

What resources are open

How directory replication is configured on this computer

Who receives administrative alerts

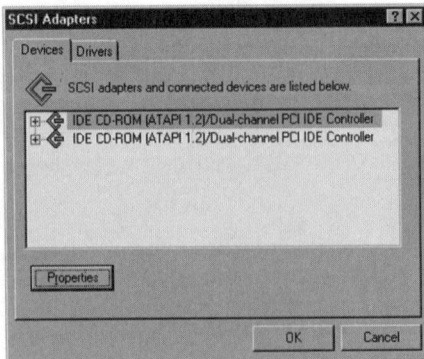

**Figure 9.5** Install SCSI adapters using the SCSI Adapters applet in Control Panel.

## SERVICES

The Services applet:

Displays the status of services installed on your computer

Can start or stop a service
Can be used to configure startup options for each service, as shown in Figure 9.6

Can assign services to different hardware profiles with different startup configurations

## SYSTEM

The System applet brings up the System Properties dialog box that has six tabs or pages. They are:

- General
- Performance
- Environment
- Startup/Shutdown
- Hardware Profiles
- User Profiles

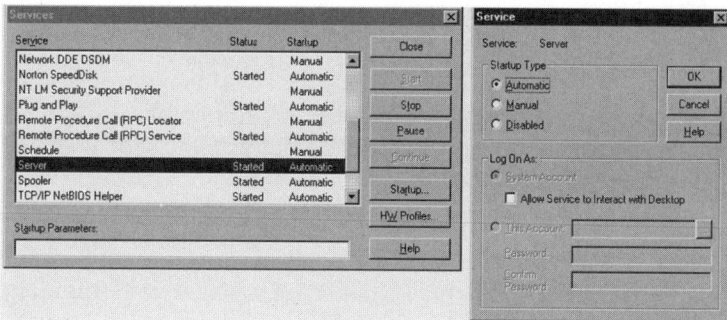

**Figure 9.6** Use the Startup option from the Services applet in Control Panel to configure startup options for a specific service.

### General

The General tab provides information on the version and build of the operating system, the registered owner, and an overview of the computer's configuration including the type of processor and the amount of RAM installed.

### Performance

The Performance tab is used for two purposes:

- Configuring application performance
- Managing virtual memory

### Application Performance

The slide bar sets the relative responsiveness of the foreground application in relation to any background applications. Application Performance is discussed in detail in Chapter 23, "Setting Application Priority."

### Virtual Memory

The Performance tab is also used for configuring Virtual Memory. The total of all pagefiles is displayed on this tab. To configure the Virtual Memory, click on the Change button.

The Virtual Memory dialog box as shown in Figure 9.7 shows in the top section each drive and any configured pagefile it may contain. Use the next section to change the pagefile on an individual disk. If the pagefile is relocated or the size is changed, reboot the computer for the changes to take effect.

To improve performance, place your pagefile on a hard disk drive other than the drive containing the system partition.

### Environment

Environment variables are used by Windows NT to control how applications behave. Figure 9.8 shows the Environment tab of the System Properties dialog box. It shows System Variables (top box) and User Variables (second box).

When Windows NT boots, it parses the autoexec.bat (if one exists) and sets any environment variables found there. For example, the PATH statement from the autoexec.bat will be appended to the system path statement.

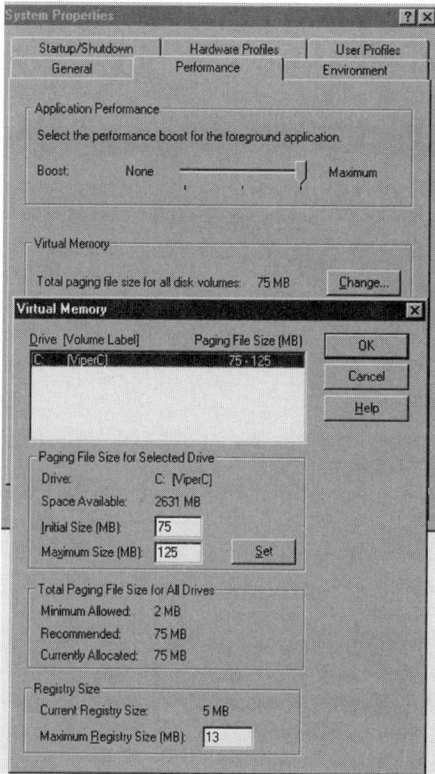

**Figure 9.7**  Use the Virtual Memory dialog box to configure the size and location of the pagefiles(s).

The order that variables are set are:

- autoexec.bat variables
- system environment variables
- user environment variables

This means that if a variable is set in autoexec.bat, such as `SET TEMP=C:\` and a user variable exists, such as `SET TEMP = C:\TEMP` the user variable will override. That is, the TEMP variable will be equal to C:\TEMP.

### Startup/Shutdown
There are two sections to the Startup/Shutdown page of the System Properties dialog box.

■ System Startup

■ Recovery

### System Startup

System Startup, shown in Figure 9.9, edits the boot.ini file. It is used to select which operating system you want to be the default selection and to set the length of time the boot.ini menu is displayed before the default operating system is started.

### Recovery

Options available in the Recovery section, shown in Figure 9.9, include:

Write an event to the system log

Send an administrative alert

Write debugging information to:

Automatically Reboot

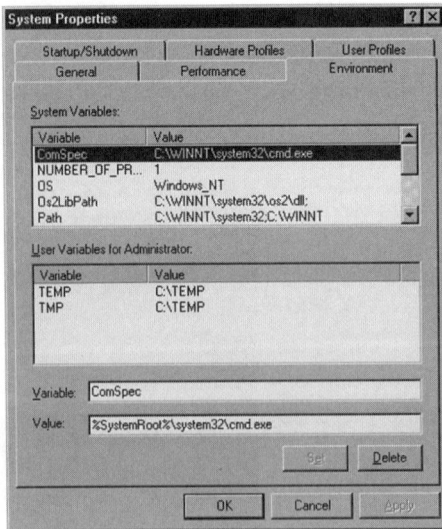

**Figure 9.8** Set or delete system and user variables with the Environment tab from the System Properties applet in Control Panel.

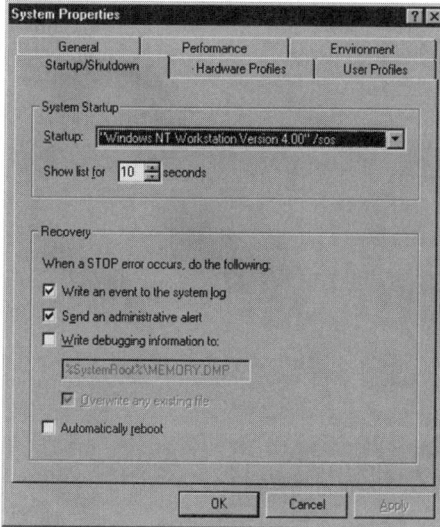

**Figure 9.9**   Use the Starup/Shutdown dialog box to configure system startup and recovery options.

By specifying *Write debugging information to:*, the work station will write a memory dump file if it should crash.

## STOP ERRORS AND APPLICATION ERRORS

STOP Errors

STOP errors accompany a Windows NT Workstation operating system "Blue Screen" (also known as a blue screen of death or BSOD, for short). Use system recovery options, including a `memory` dump file, to troubleshoot STOP errors.

Application Errors

Application errors are generated when applications go astray. When an application error occurs, Dr. Watson starts automatically. To configure Dr. Watson, go to Start | Run and type drwtsn32. As shown in Figure 9.10, creating a `crash` dump file is one of the options available for configuring Dr. Watson.

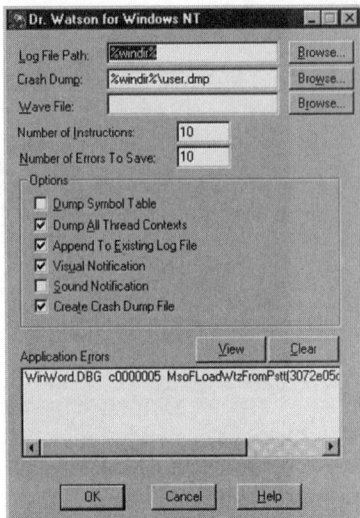

**Figure 9.10**  Configure a crash dump file for Dr. Watson when an application error occurs.

### Hardware Profiles

The Hardware Profiles page, shown in Figure 9.11, allows you to configure multiple hardware profiles, each of which have different devices loaded when you start your computer. Once you create the second profile, an additional menu appears during the boot process that allows you to select the profile you wish to use. You can configure which is your default profile and how long the system should wait for a selection before loading the default profile.

If you have a laptop with a docking station, you get an error message when you boot it without being in the docking station because the hardware that is part of the docking station (such as network adapter) is not there. In order to prevent this, create two hardware profiles: one for when docked and the other when not docked.

### User Profiles

The User Profiles page of the System Properties dialog box, shown in Figure 9.12, allows you to delete, modify, or copy user profiles located on your local machine.

Managing user profiles is covered in detail in Chapter 12, "Profiles."

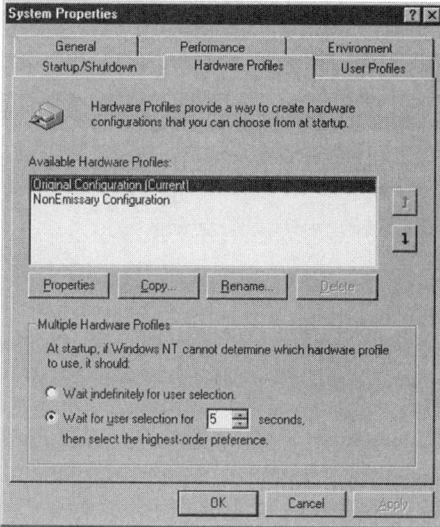

**Figure 9.11** Create additional hardware profiles for different configuration requirements.

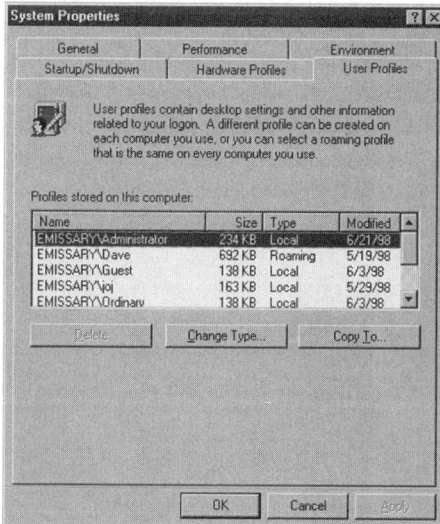

**Figure 9.12** The User Profiles dialog box in the System Properties applet can be used to delete, modify, or copy user profiles.

## TAPE DEVICES

The Tape Devices applet shown in Figure 9.13 displays tape devices (and their drivers) installed on the computer. The Tape Devices applet is also used to detect a tape drive when installing a new device and to install the appropriate driver.

Windows NT Backup, on the Administrative Tools menu, cannot be used unless a tape device of some kind is installed.

## TELEPHONY

The Telephony applet has two tabs for setting Dialing Properties.

- My Locations
- Telephony Drivers

## UPS

Use the UPS applet shown in Figure 9.14 to configure an uninterruptable power supply (UPS) connected to a serial port on the Workstation. During a power outage, the UPS communicates with the computer through a serial port using a special UPS cable.

The UPS service first stops the server service in order to prevent users from establishing new connections. Next it

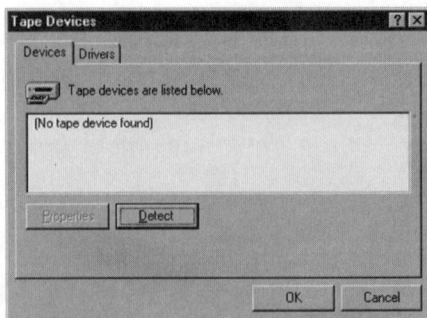

**Figure 9.13**   Use the Tape Devices applet in Control Panel to detect and install tape devices.

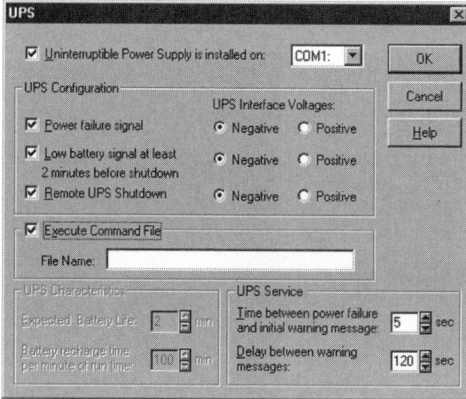

**Figure 9.14** Use the UPS applet in Control Panel to configure the various UPS options.

sends a message to all users that a power outage has occurred and that they should log off. If the power is not restored during the configured time, the UPS service performs a system shutdown. Once power has been restored, a message is sent to users notifying them of the return of power.

## User Settings

### ACCESSIBILITY OPTIONS

Use this applet to configure keyboard, sound, and mouse behavior for users with impairments. Keyboard options include sticky keys, filter keys, and toggle keys that allow in dividuals with limited mobility to use the keyboard more efficiently. The mouse page enables the use of the arrow keys to replace the mouse.

For hearing impaired individuals, the Sound page allows configuration of visual alerts for system sounds or to generate captions for speech. The General page can configure an idle time out to turn off the accessibility features. It is also used to enable and configure the use of SerialKey devices.

## CONSOLE

Use the Console applet to configure the default appearance of the DOS command window. Options that can be configured include fonts, color, and size. It is also used to set up the buffer size and command history.

## DISPLAY

The Display Properties applet has five pages.

- Background
- Screen saver
- Appearance
- Plus!
- Settings

This applet is used to change the desktop appearance such as the background, wallpaper, colors, and font size. In addition, screen savers can be selected and configured. This applet is also used to install or update the video adapter device driver.

In order to secure your computer after a period of inactivity, configure a password protected screen saver, as shown in Figure 9.15.

## KEYBOARD

The Keyboard applet has three pages.

- Speed
- Input Locale
- General

The Speed page is used to modify the behavior of the keyboard such as the repeat rate and delay, as well as the cursor blink rate. The Input Locale page allows configuring the keyboard for foreign languages.

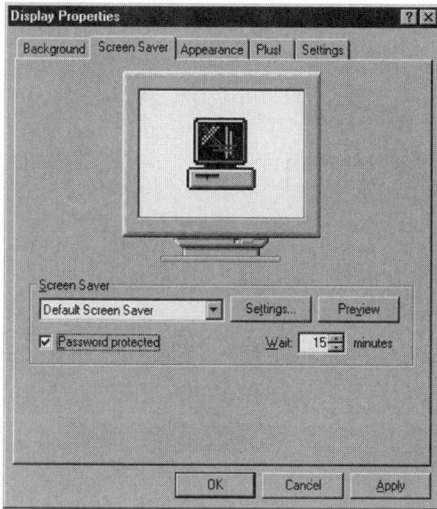

**Figure 9.15**  Set a password protected screen saver from the Screen Saver dialog box in Display Properties.

The General page displays the presently installed keyboard driver. It also allows you to install a different keyboard driver to be able to use a special keyboard.

## MOUSE

The settings available via the Mouse applet are dependent on the installed mouse driver. Settings include active mouse button selection, double-click sensitivity, and tracking speed. In addition, other options may be available such as turning on mouse trails and having the pointer snap to the default button of a dialog box.

This applet allows you to change the appearance of your cursor including installing animated cursors. You also use this applet to change the device driver used for your pointing device.

## REGIONAL SETTINGS

Use the Regional Settings to change how numbers, dates, times, and currency are displayed. Different Input Locales can also be configured here and the default locate selected.

## SOUNDS

The Sounds applet opens the Sounds Properties dialog box. This dialog box provides the interface necessary to assign certain sounds to system events. This requires that a sound card and speakers be installed.

## FOR REVIEW

- The Modems applet is used to install, modify or remove modems.

- Use the Multimedia applet to configure various multimedia devices such as your sound card, video display, CD player volume control, and MIDI devices.

- The name of the computer, or the workgroup or domain to participate in can be changed from the Identification tab of the Network applet.

- The SCSI Adapters applet is used to install or remove SCSI adapter drivers.

- The Services applet

  - Displays the status of the services installed on your computer

  - Can start or stop a service

  - Can be used to configure startup options for each service

  - Can assign services to different hardware profiles with different startup configurations

- Use the Virtual Memory section of the Performance tab on the System applet to change the pagefile on an individual disk.

- To improve performance, place your pagefile on the disk containing your data rather than the disk on which the Windows NT Workstation system files are located.

- Environment variables are used by Windows NT to control how applications behave.

- Use the System Startup section of the Startup/Shutdown tab on the System applet to select which operating system you want to be the default selection and to set the length of time that the boot.ini menu is displayed before the default operating system is started.

- By specifying *Write debugging information to:* in the Recovery section of the Startup/Shutdown tab on the System applet, the workstation will write a memory dump file if it crashes.

- STOP errors accompany a Windows NT Workstation operating system "Blue Screen." Use system recovery options, including a *memory* dump file, to troubleshoot STOP errors.

- Application errors are generated when applications go astray. When an application error occurs, Dr. Watson starts automatically. Configure Dr. Watson to create a crash dump file by using `Start | Run | drwtsn32`.

- The Hardware Profiles page of the System applet allows you to configure multiple hardware profiles, each of which have different devices loaded when you start your computer.

- Use the Tape Devices applet in Control Panel to detect and install tape devices.

- Use the UPS applet to configure an uninterruptable power supply (UPS), connected to a serial port on the Workstation.

- Set a password-protected screen saver from the Screen Saver dialog box in Display Properties.

**FROM HERE**

Managing user profiles is covered in detail in Chapter 12, "Profiles." See Chapter 14, "Printers and Print Devices," for detailed information on managing printers and documents. Protocols are covered in detail in Chapter 17, "Available Protocols." Chapter 18, "Binding Order," provides more information on configuring bindings. Application Performance is discussed in detail in Chapter 23, "Setting Application Priority."

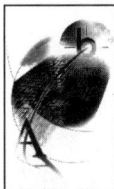

# CHAPTER 10

# Configuring and Using Software Services

Although the Windows NT Workstation exam is about client software, you should not assume that the perspective is from the client's point of view. Instead, the exam looks at how the server installs, configures, administers, and supports Windows NT Workstation computers and other client computers. Additionally, some questions focus on the server-based utilities, which can be installed and administered through the Windows NT Workstation.

This chapter introduces several built-in software services available to Windows NT Workstation. The services enable administrators to remotely administer the server from the workstation. Additionally, you will review some of the more frequently used services. They include the following:

- Backup
- File and directory sharing
- Policy editor
- Regedit
- Regedt32
- Services applet in Control Panel
- Windows Explorer enhanced with Administrative Tools

# Backup

Microsoft Windows NT backup programs have a few shortcomings. Therefore, most system administrators, with Microsoft's blessing, have relied on third-party vendors to create the backup programs that most system administrators use on their networks, such as UltraBac at http://www.ultrabac.com/new/default.htm.

Backup is an enhanced feature of Windows Explorer. On a workstation, logged on as the administrator, you can perform backups of any computer on the network.

Before proceeding with any backups, you will want to plan and create a strategy to enable as short and as smooth a backup process as possible. You often can do this by storing most of the data that needs backing up in a centralized location. Review other sections of this book about methods such as home folders to use to fine-tune your backup process.

The limitations of the Backup utility also can be your ally, helping to focus your review on the minimum amount of information you need to know for the MCSE exams. The most important thing to remember about Windows NT Backup is that Windows NT Backup supports tape drives only.

If you start the backup program without a tape drive, you will see the error messages shown in Figure 10.1.

Recall the Hardware Compatibility List (HCL) from Chapter 6. The same information applies to the tape drive. The drive must be NT compatible. You should check the compatibility by using the HCL on the Microsoft web site.

Windows NT will prompt you for the tape drive after you see the error message shown in Figure 10.1. You cannot proceed past this point if you do not have a tape drive attached. Please note that you can configure a new tape drive during the initial stages of the backup process.

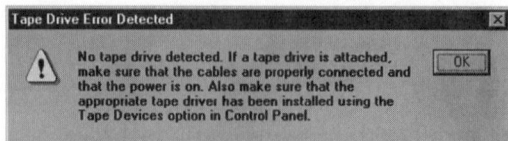

**Figure 10.1** Windows NT does backups only to tape devices.

To do a backup to floppies, you still must use the following:

- Xcopy
- DOS backup

The following backup rule applies to individual users: Any user with read permissions to a file can perform backups on that file.

This rule is a limitation because the user's permission is restricted to specific files, rather than to entire folders.

For all the MCSE exams, remember that backup and restore are different rights. The right to back up does not automatically give someone the right to restore data from a backup. The right to restore is assigned by default to only three groups:

- Administrators
- Backup Operators
- Server Operators*

**TIP**
Server Operators are not one of the built-in groups enabled to do backups when working from a Windows NT Workstation computer, backing up that workstation or other workstations. If an exam question asks about backing up from a workstation, Server Operators might be used as a distracter (wrong) answer.

No other group (other than Administrators, Backup Operators, and Server Operators) or user can restore from backup unless the administrator gives them that right. Also keep in mind that being a member of one of these groups doesn't give the person the right to backup/restore in another domain unless the user is a member of a group in that domain with appropriate rights.

A good restoration policy is one in which you actually perform a test restoration periodically, whether you need to or not. You should do this to ensure the integrity of your backups.

The best feature of the Windows NT 4.0 backup utility is that it can be automatic or manual. For the exam, you need to know that the automatic backups are configured using the AT.exe, or AT command, which enables backups to be started at a certain time.

---

*By default, the Server Operators group is not available on Windows NT Workstation.

Windows NT enables you to create batch files to start the automatic backup and perform the backup unattended.

You can configure numerous commands and options for the batch file. However, for the MCSE exams you should remember the following:

- /b—This switch, when included in the batch file, backs up the Registry.

- The restoration of a Registry requires that the tape drive be attached to the computer on which the Registry is being restored.

**NOTE**

Install the tape drive on the computer being backed up. You must do this if you want to back up the Registry on that computer. For example, if you are backing up the workstation at which you are working, and you want the Registry backed up, then you must have the tape drive attached. If you choose to back up another workstation remotely from your workstation, you must attach the tape drive to the other workstation if you need the Registry backed up.

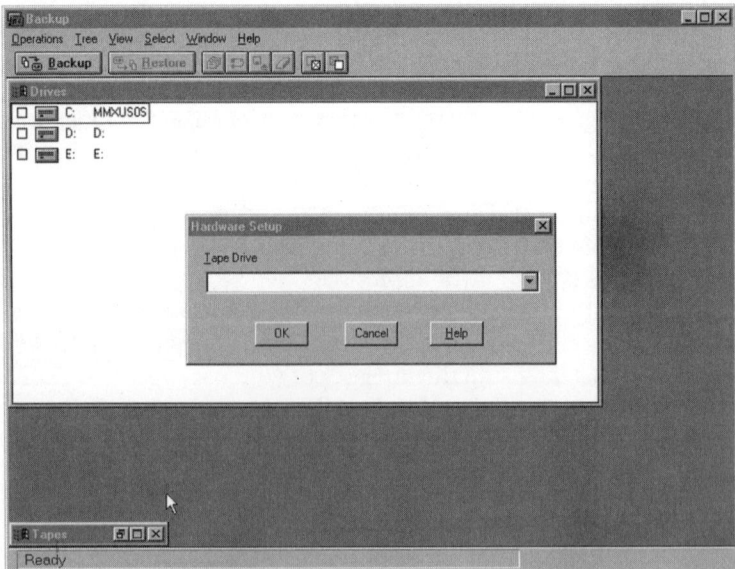

**Figure 10.2**  Backup enables you to select drives and files for backup and to select alternate tape drives.

■ `net use`—This command enables you to connect and disconnect remotely to do a backup. You must include these statements, in this order in the batch file:

At the beginning, to connect: `net use drive:`

At the end, to disconnect: `net use drive: /delete`

When you start backing up, you have the option of selecting which drive(s) you want to back up. Also, by clicking on the drive letter, you can select individual files or folders, which is useful if you choose not to back up entire volumes.

## Backup Types

Every time a Normal or Incremental backup is performed, a marker is placed in the files. The marker determines where the next backup will begin. For the MCSE tests, remember that the Copy and Differential backup types do not use a marker.

The exams ask you about backups. Specifically, the questions are scenarios about the backup types. They focus on the following:

■ Setting up a backup

■ How a backup is performed

■ How to recover from a crash using the restore function

■ What files are retrievable, depending on backup types

Table 10.1 lists various backup types. For the exam, know all of them, especially the last three.

---

**Table 10.1**
Normal, Differential, and Incremental Backups

|  | Backs up if changed | Backs up if selected | Time Required* | Security Provided** | Marker Placed? |
|---|---|---|---|---|---|
| Copy |  | Yes | 1 | Excellent | no |
| Daily Copy | Yes |  | 1 | Best | no |

*continues*

**Table 10.1**
Normal, Differential, and Incremental Backups

| | Backs up if changed | Backs up if selected | Time Required* | Security Provided** | Marker Placed? |
|---|---|---|---|---|---|
| Differential | Yes | | 3 | Good | no |
| Normal | | Yes | 1 | Excellent | yes |
| Incremental | Yes | | 3 | Good | yes |

*Time Required—With 1 being the most time or longest backup time and 5 being the shortest time.

**Security Provided—When you back up more data, your risk in the event of a system crash and data loss is lower.

By looking at Table 10.1, you can make three conclusions:

1. Incremental backups take the least time. Because they place a marker, the backup starts at the marker and proceeds forward.

2. Differential backup time is variable. When you do a differential backup, the program looks for the last marker. Backup time depends on how the last backup was performed: with a marker, Normal, or Incremental. Backup time also depends on how much change has occurred since the last backup was performed.

3. Normal backups take the longest because they back up everything, regardless of markers.

It is generally recommended to combine backup types to save time and protect data. Never assume, however, that saving time is the most important consideration. If there is ever a need to restore files, your backup strategy comes under scrutiny. If you do only a normal backup every Sunday, what happens if the system crashes on Wednesday, and you lose the files and changes from Monday though Wednesday? Planning a backup strategy is crucial.

## Some Rules of Thumb

- More backup time; more backed up; restore time reduced

  If time is a major consideration, one strategy is to do a normal backup weekly and do differential backups throughout the week.

- Less backup time; less backed up; restore time increased

  If this is your strategy, consider a weekly normal backup and incremental backups throughout the week.

The backup process creates catalogs. Here is what's created on a backup catalog:

- Tape catalogs—Display all the backup sets on a tape.

- Backup set catalog—Displays an overview of everything in a backup set.

- Backup set—Contains the actual backed up files from a single backup session.

As part of your backup strategy, always keep a copy of your backups in a secure location off site.

## File and Directory Sharing

You can share files and directories in Windows NT Workstation. Additionally, you can configure shares and permissions on NTFS and FAT volumes.

The Windows NT Workstation provides a unique group not found on the server: Power Users.

Some Microsoft exams mention the Power Users group. On the tests are references to the Power User group's rights to administer workstation utilities like an administrator. The key difference is that a power user cannot administer the network or workstation as fully as the administrator account. Review Table 10.2 to understand the difference.

**Table 10.2** Power Users may not assign rights to other users.

|  | Power User | Administrator |
| --- | :---: | :---: |
| Share printers | X | X |
| Administer shares | X | X |
| Administer groups | X | X |
| Administer users | X | X |
| Assign user rights |  | X |

This table is only a synopsis of the rights of the two groups. Notice that they both have powerful capabilities on the workstation. The assign user rights function, however, is reserved for the Administrators. Ultimately, the Administrator group acts as the checks and balances for the network. You can see why you should alter default user rights cautiously.

Both Power Users and Administrators can share workstation resources. The only stipulation is that the Server Service must be running on the workstation (in addition to the Workstation service).

As your first step in this process, select a resource to be shared by using Windows Explorer, Network Neighborhood, or My Computer, as in the following example.

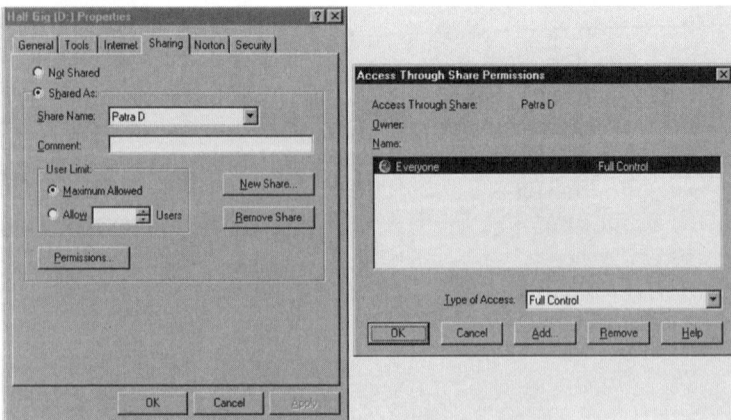

**Figure 10.3** Create a new share by naming the share.

When you create a share name keep these points in mind:

- A share name is required when you select Shared As. Remember, DOS and Windows 3.1 can read only 8.3 file names. Keep this in mind when filling in the Share Name field. Also, don't make the name difficult to remember.

- The $ is used to designate a hidden share and a hidden folder. The system root folder automatically is shared as C$ (if C is the drive root). This becomes a hidden ADMIN share. Because it is hidden, the share does not appear in Network Neighborhood, etc.

- FAT partitions allow shares on folders only while NTFS partitions allow both shares on folders and permissions on individual files.

- Full Control is the default permission assigned to the Everyone group. To change permissions, click the button Permissions on the Properties page. To remove Full Control, go to the Access through Share Permissions, select the permission, and click Remove. You can add permissions by selecting the Type of Access drop-down menu, select the permission to add, and click ADD.

- NT Workstation limits shares to a maximum of 10 users allowed simultaneously. You can allow from 1–10 users by configuring the Properties page as shown in the preceding example.

Remember that the Everyone group with Full Control is assigned to any NTFS partition when it is created. Because this permission is assigned to the entire partition, every thing on that partition is given the same permission by default.

If you have files on the partition, for maximum security always remove the Everyone group. Leave the Full Control permission if you want.

In the example in Figure 10.4, working from your Administrator's workstation, you are sharing the Replication folder on the server. As the administrator, you commonly will do your administrative work from a Windows NT Workstation. Administering your network from the workstation does not limit you. Remember that your administrative rights follow you whenever you log on as the Administrator account.

It's as simple as that. You can configure the share, changing the permissions as needed. Finally, remember that you should consider the users who need access to the folders.

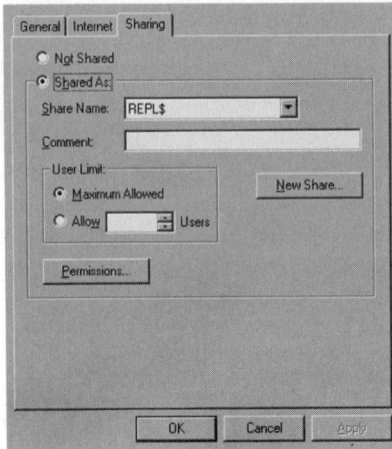

**Figure 10.4** Share the replication folder from this dialog box.

# Policy Editor

System Policy Editor is not automatically part of NT Workstation. It is one of the Network Administration tools you can install from the NT Server Setup disk. Like other administrative functions usually done on the server, placing Policy Editor on the Workstation enables the Administrator to work from a computer other than the server. This is often preferable to working directly on the server.

Some of the other Network Administration tools that can be added to a workstation to assist in administering a domain and/or network are as follows:

- DHCP Manager
- Server Manager
- User Manager for Domains
- Remote Access Manager
- WINS Manager
- DNS Manager

For the Windows NT Workstation test, remember that you are still administering the server. You are adding server utilities to a

Windows NT Workstation. The difference is that you are working from the workstation. Adding these utilities, of course, does not change the workstation into a server.

For example, when editing the system policy files from a workstation, the actual files remain on the domain controllers. The difference is that you are working from the workstation, logged on as the administrator with full administrative rights.

Using the System Policy Editor on the workstation, you access the policy files on the server, make the changes, and save the changes to the server, the domain controller. In other words, nothing changes except where you do your work.

Figure 10.5 is an example of opening the policy file on the server. To find this folder, select the Look In option shown, which would enable you to browse the network, including the server, for the policy files shown.

Policies are useful in every organization, but especially so in larger organizations. Implementing policies enable administrators to control the computer work areas and to maintain consistency.

In Figure 10.6, System Policy Editor, two default policies are created when NT Server is installed. They are the Default Computer and Default User.

Both of these policies may be sufficient for setting policies for any organization. You can tailor these two policies to the needs of the organization. You also can create entirely new system policy

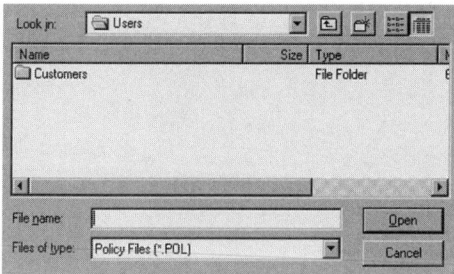

**Figure 10.5** Open policies from the File menu in System Policy Editor.

configurations. Regardless, it is important to remember for the test that a policy can apply to the whole domain or to as few as one or two users.

To configure the default policies for users, double-click on the icon. You then see the screen that appears, enabling you to configure each default property.

As you can see from the example, several default system policies exist. You can administer all these policies from the workstation. Here are a few of the more common default policies:

- Control Panel—Controls the display by enabling user input. You also can forbid or limit user access to the Control Panel.

- Desktop—For configuring colors and wallpapers.

- Shell—Control of what appears on the screen.

- System—For configuring user access to the Registry and Registry Editor.

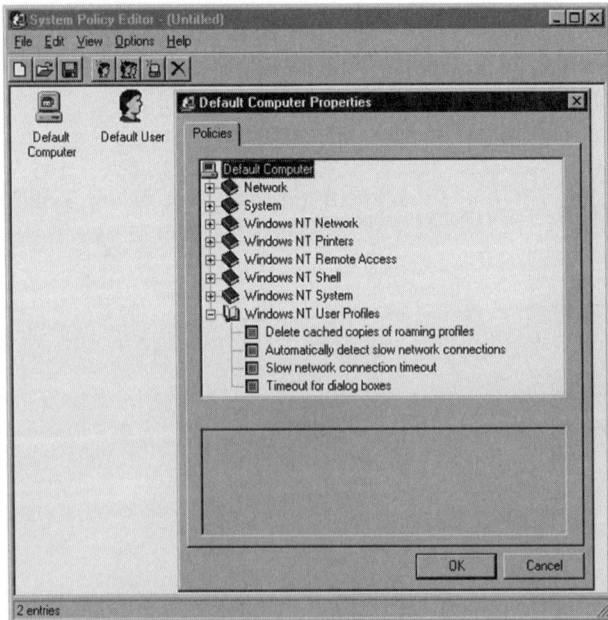

**Figure 10.6** Two default policies are created in System Policy Editor.

- Windows NT Shell—For configuring desktop shortcuts.

- Windows NT System—For creating an environment comprised of various system variables.

Assume that you want to change the Desktop configuration for a user or group of users. Using System Policy Editor from your workstation, perform the following steps:

1. Select user or group of users
2. Select Policies
3. Select the Windows NT User Profiles (as shown in the preceding example)
4. Select Desktop
5. Change the profile by checking or unchecking the options shown. These options are diverse, ranging from the wallpaper used, mouse configurations, timeout options, etc.
6. Close the profiles by selecting OK.

The MCSE exam covers the subject of policies by including it in the scope of the other questions. To prepare yourself for this, know the following:

- Workstation-based System Policy Editor. Policies are managed through the server. Even if you're doing your administrative work on a Workstation, you do it through the server.

- Use System Policy Editor to create system profiles. Using the System Policy Editor, new policies can be created at any time.

- Use System Policy Editor to manage the default system profiles. Default profiles are modified to suit the needs of the organization, or kept as is.

- By default, policy files on the server are saved in this folder:

```
\winnt\system32\repl\imports\scripts\ntconfig.pol
```

Remember that the alias for NTCONFIG.POL is NETLOGON.
Some questions on the test refer to this file and its location on the server.

■ Changes made to policies go into effect only after logoff/logon. This concept is important to remember. Users must log off and back on to the system before any new policies go into effect.

■ Because system policies can apply to individuals and groups, they exist for all computers. Nonsystem policies, or user policies, are created for local computers. You can create a local profile for a workstation that administers the network. The difference is that the local profile is stored on the computer you are sitting at; system profiles are stored on the domain controllers.

If you decide not to use the default users, Figure 10.7 shows how to add a new user.

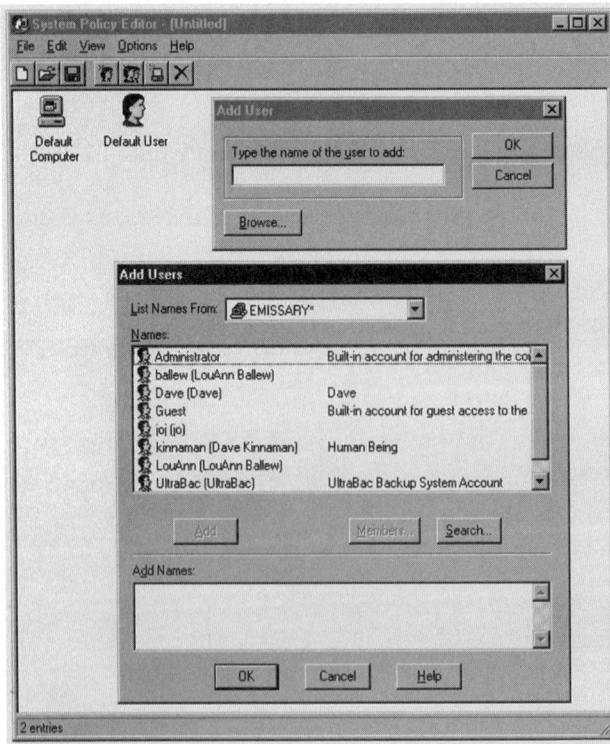

**Figure 10.7** Browse from the Add New User screen to see current users.

1. Select the File menu and select the Add User option.

2. From the Add User dialog box (middle of Figure 10.7), perform either of the following:

   - Type the user's computer name to add it.
   - Browse the domain to select the user name.

3. Looking at Figure 10.7, the Add Users box lists names from a domain. This process is a convenient way to create users because:

   - You can add multiple users at one time. After highlighting a user, select Add. Do this as often as you like.
   - You can select users from multiple domains. Click the List Names From dialog box and select the domain from the drop-down menu that appears.

4. When finished adding names, select OK to finish.

5. From that point, configure each user's policies as you want.

You also can configure group policies from the Workstation system policy editor as well as add groups.

Figure 10.8 is an example of adding a group to the system policy file.

1. Select the File menu and select the Add Group option.

2. From the Add Group dialog box (middle of the figure), do one of the following:

   - Type the group name to add it.
   - Browse the domain to select the group.

3. In the figure, the Add Groups box will list names from a domain. Continue the process you used when adding users.

   - You can add multiple groups at one time. After highlighting a user, select Add. You can do this as often as you like.
   - You can select Groups from multiple domains. Click the List Names From dialog box and select the domain from the drop-down menu that appears.

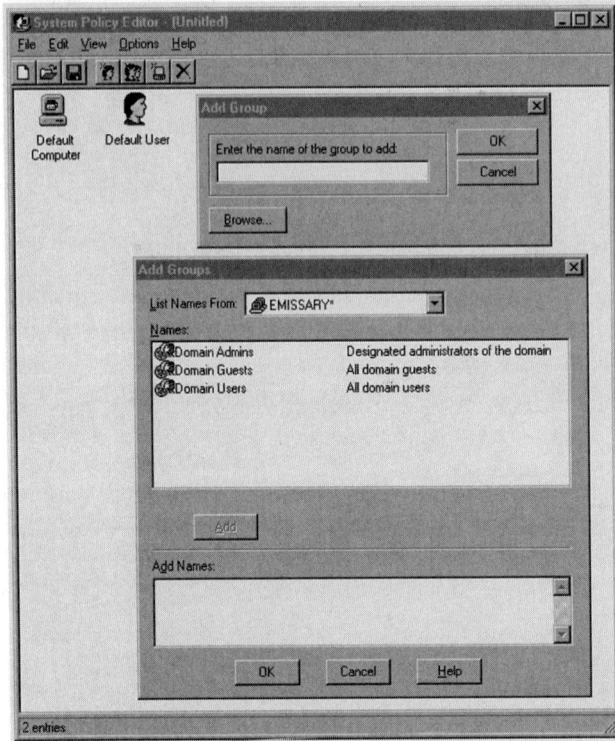

**Figure 10.8** Add a group to the system policy file.

4. When finished adding groups, select OK to finish.

5. From that point, configure each group's policies as you want.

   Microsoft provides the Microsoft Zero Administration Kit to help you administer the network system policies from a Windows NT Workstation. This kit comes complete with preconfigured settings that can be copied into place. Check it out at their Web site, www.microsoft.com.

## Regedit

Previously, you worked with the System Policy Editor, a tool that creates and modifies entries in the Windows NT Registry. A more direct way to edit the Registry is called Regedit.

By typing Regedit at the Run command, you bring up a screen like Figure 10.9.

Editing the Registry using Regedit may not be a great idea unless you know what you're doing. If you have to do so, however, make a backup of the Registry, so you can restore it in case of any problems. In almost all cases, you'll be better off to edit the Registry through the Control Panel applets or System Policy Editor.

The Registry stores just about every important piece of information essential to the operating system and system configuration.

For the MCSE exam, you should know the five Registry subtrees:

- Local_Machine—All the devices, software, and services running on the local computer.

- HKey_Users—Stores the SIDs of the current users.

- HKey_Current_User—Stores the profiles of the current users.

- HKey_Classes_Root—Stores additional data about software.

- Hkey_Current_Config—Stores the current hardware profiles.

You also should know that Regedit provides a better search capability than Regedt32. Regedit can search for values, strings, and keys, but Regedt32 cannot. However, Regedt32 (see the next section), actually provides a larger menu selection with limited search capabilities. Using Regedt32, you can search for keys and subkeys. Regedit, on the other hand, can search for value entries and values as well as keys and subkeys.

Remember that Regedit is available in Windows 95, and Regedt32 is not. Table 10.3 helps depict these differences.

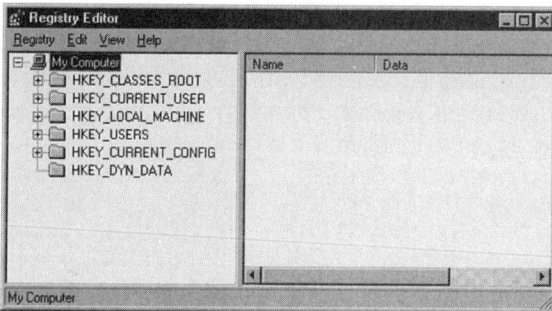

**Figure 10.9** Use Regedit to inspect and edit the Registry.

**Table 10.3**
Regedit and Regedt32 Both Edit the Registry

|  | Regedit | Regedt32 |
| --- | :---: | :---: |
| Search with values, strings, keys, subkeys | X |  |
| Limited search capabilities |  | X |
| More menu selections |  | X |
| Available on Windows 95 | X |  |

# Regedt32

Earlier, you reviewed System Policy Editor. If this utility were not available on NT Workstation, you could edit the Registry using Regedt32. In that instance, you would edit the following:

- `HkeyLocalMachine` Registry entries
- `HkeyCurrentUser` Registry entries

Regedt32 offers a variety of options with fewer search capabilities than Regedit. In essence, Regedt32 and Regedit are very similar, just different flavors of the same utility. Microsoft couldn't decide which one to include, so they gave us both instead, and now we have to know the differences.

Keep in mind that you must reboot the computer before most system changes take effect. When you change users' individual settings, have users log off and back on. Remember the differences between a reboot and logging on and off. A reboot completely retstarts the computer, but logging off removes the user and any policies that apply to that user from the system.

To get to Regedt32, type the command in the RUN box as shown in Figure 10.10.

You also can access this utility by selecting the `Regedt32.exe` file from the WINNT folder.

Remember the warning given in the section on Regedit also applies here.

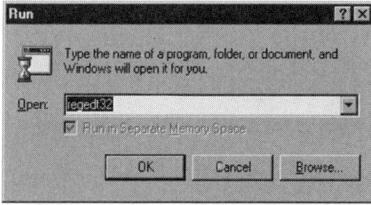

**Figure 10.10** Or use Regedt32 to inspect and edit the Registry.

- It's not a great idea to ever directly edit the Registry using Regedt32 unless you know what you're doing.
- If you must edit the Registry, make a backup of the Registry, so you can restore it in case of any problems.
- Regedt32 is not available in Windows 95.

So why would you ever use Regedt32? Well, if you know what you're looking for and how to get there, use Regedt32. If you're not sure what you're looking for and need the searching powers to find it, use Regedit.

## Services Applet in Control Panel

The Services applet gives you great control in configuring and troubleshooting the various services that exist on a Windows NT Workstation.

As shown in Figure 10.11, you access Services by selecting the following:

```
My Computer | Control Panel | Services (double-click)
```

Notice that the available services lists the services loaded on the computer. Not all the services are actually running, however.

When troubleshooting a problem in Windows NT, check Services first. In most problems that occur, more often than not a service stopped, or it has not been loaded into the system.

Suppose that DHCP is configured on the server, but the workstation you're working at isn't accessing the DHCP server properly. By checking Services, you can verify the following:

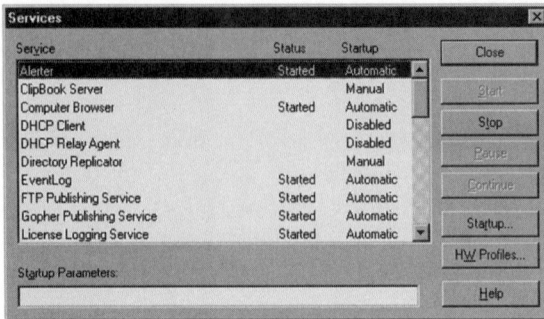

**Figure 10.11** Use the Services applet in Control Panel to start and stop services.

- DHCP Client has been added.
- Is DHCP Client running?

The previous screen is a good example of this. Notice that DHCP client is disabled. By checking services, you can immediately determine whether the service is running, disabled, or stopped. In this case, DHCP Client has been loaded onto the computer, but it has been disabled. Two possible reasons for this are as follow:

- It is not yet configured to be part of a DHCP server configuration.
- The service is no longer needed.

One certain conclusion is that the service isn't working.
You also can manipulate services in the following ways:

- Start—Start a service. Start a service only if you are sure that it will have no adverse affect upon the network.
- Stop—Stop a service. Conversely, stopping a service can be just as detrimental to a system that is dependent on it.
- Pause—Pause a service. For example, troubleshoot print problems. If the Print Spooler is jammed, you can stop the Print Spooler in the service box and restart it.
- Continue—Used for continuing a service that you have paused.

Notice the HW Profiles button. This feature is handy when you are running multiple hardware profiles on a computer. For example, one of your computers could be a laptop that uses its own hardware profile when it's docked at the office. When you are on the road, however, it uses an entirely different hardware profile. (Remember that you can configure various hardware profiles in the System Properties section of the Control Panel.)

Because differing hardware profiles use different services, you can use this HW Profiles feature to configure different services for each profile.

To accomplish this, you will do the following:

1. Select the service that you want to configure.

2. Select the HW Profiles button.

3. You see a screen that shows you how the service is configured for each profile. At this point, you can do two things:

   Enable the Profile

   Disable the Profile

4. If you're configuring the DHCP client, you may want to enable it for the DOCKED profile and disable it for the LAPTOP profile.

5. Close the dialog box by selecting OK.

In essence, the Services applet provides the most comprehensive view of everything that is running currently.

In Figure 10.12 you specify the startup options of the various services.

The three startup types are as follow:

■ Automatic—With an automatic startup, the service begins when the computer starts. It continues to run in the background until the computer is shut off or the service is stopped, disabled, or paused.

■ Manual—This setting can be altered only from the Services applet. It does not start when the computer starts. Also, it shuts off when the computer shuts off. This setting remains a manual set-

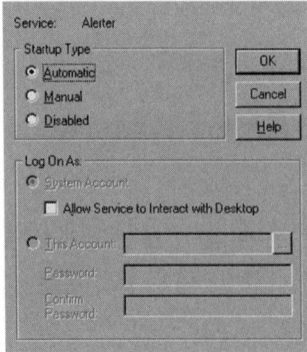

**Figure 10.12** Services may be started automatically, manually, or may be disabled.

ting unless changed to automatic or disabled. Starting it during a computer session doesn't change its default characteristics.

- Disabled—Before a disabled service can be started, it must first be changed to automatic or manual.

You need to remember these for the MCSE tests.

In any review of the many features of Windows NT, don't forget Help, as shown in Figure 10.13. You can find a plethora of information and directions to other sources. Help also is featured in the next section on the Windows Explorer enhancements.

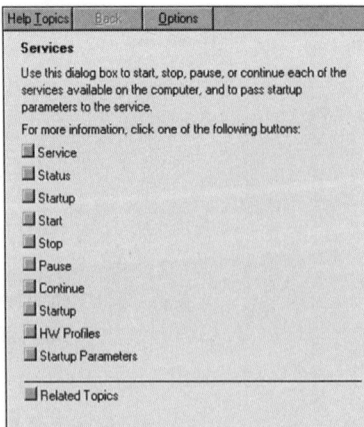

**Figure 10.13** The Services Help screen offers many options.

# Windows Explorer Enhanced with Administrative Tools

Windows NT offers enhancements to the Workstation's Explorer tools:

- Backup—This enhancement is explained earlier in the chapter. The backup enhancements apply to both the Server and Workstation.

- Disk Administrator—This GUI administrative tool performs the functions of FDISK.

- Event Viewer—This great tool lets you see details about errors, audit trails, and other events that occur while the workstation is running. It also is where you view the system, security, and application logs. Event Viewer collects data about anything and everything occurring on the system at any given moment.

- Performance Monitor—This enhancement is covered extensively in Chapter 24, "Monitoring Tools." Performance Monitor provides a real-time look at your system performance and gives you the ability to take snapshots of system performance for future review. Covered extensively in Windows NT 4.0 in the Enterprise.

- Remote Access Administrator—This utility enables you to control how users access your workstation remotely via dial-up connections.

- User Manager—A scaled-down version of User Manager for Domains with far fewer functions. User Manager was created as a tool for Windows NT Workstations. To have the capabilities of User Manager for Domains, you must download it to the Workstation.

- Windows NT Diagnostics—Enhanced version of the System configurations. Using this tool, you can get detailed information about your RAM and hard disk space. The Services applet, discussed earlier in the chapter, is a feature of this utility.

- Help—Although not officially mentioned as an Administrative Tool, Help can't be overlooked for all the terrific action-packed information it renders.

Access Windows NT Help using Start | Help or by pressing the F1 key.

# For Review

- The exam looks at how the server installs, configures, administers, and supports Windows NT Workstation computers.

- Windows NT backup supports tape drives only.

- The right to back up does not automatically give someone the right to restore data from a backup.

- Any user with read permissions on a file can perform backups on that file.

- The right to backup and restore is restricted, by default, to three groups:

  Administrators

  Backup Operator

  Server Operators

- No other group or user can restore unless the administrator gives them that right.

- By default, only Administrators and Backup Operators are available on Windows NT Workstation; the Server Operators group is not available by default on Windows NT Workstation.

- Restore data periodically to ensure the integrity of backups.

- The types of backups are as follow:

  Copy

  Daily Copy

  Differential

  Normal

  Incremental

- More backup time; more backed up; restore time reduced.

- Less backup time; less backed up; restore time increased.

- The Windows NT Workstation provides a unique group called Power User, which is not found on the server. For purposes of the

MCSE exam, the Power User group has rights to administer Workstation utilities like an administrator. A Power User cannot administer the network or Workstation as fully as the administrator account.

■ The $ is used to designate a hidden share, which designates a hidden folder.

■ Full Control is the default permission assigned to the Everyone group.

■ NT Workstation limits the maximum allowed shares to 10 users simultaneously.

■ When editing the system policy files from the workstation, the actual files remain on the domain controllers. The difference is that you are working from the workstation, logged on as the administrator with full administrative rights.

■ Remember that the alias for ntconfig.pol is netlogon.

■ Changes made to policy go into effect only after logoff/logon.

■ For the MCSE exam, you should know the five subtrees of the Registry:

```
Local_Machine

HKey_Users

HKey_Current_User

HKey_Classes_Root

Hkey_Current_Config
```

■ Regedt32 and Regedit are different flavors of the same utility. Regedit has better search capabilities and is available in Windows 95. Regedt32 has more menu options. It's not a great idea to edit the Registry unless you know what you're doing.

■ The three Startup Types in the Services applet are automatic, manual, and disabled.

■ User Manager is a scaled-down version of User Manager for Domains with far less power, created as a tool for working with Workstations only. To have the capabilities of User Manager for Domains, you must install it on the Workstation.

# From Here

Chapter 3, "Hardware Hunger," covers hardware issues. Chapter 11, "Users" and Chapter 12, "Profiles," come next.

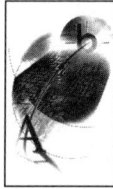

**CHAPTER 11**

# Users

This chapter discusses the User Manager application in Windows NT 4.0 Workstation. User Manager is found under Administrative Tools in the Programs group on the Start menu. Network administrators are required to control human interactions with the network. The administrator has many concerns:

Security

Access

Convenience

Turnover

Obsolescence

Etc.

User Manager consolidates many powerful functions that network administrators need every day, making it a popular and useful tool.

## User Manager

With User Manager an administrator can:

- Create user accounts
- Modify or rename user accounts
- Disable user accounts
- Delete user accounts
- Check user account information
    - Account Name
    - User Password
    - Group Memberships
    - User Profile
    - User Dial-in Access
- Create local group accounts
- Add user accounts to groups
- Set security policies
- Grant rights to user accounts and group accounts

User Manager, shown in Figure 11.1, provides a powerful tool for managing user accounts and user access to network resources.

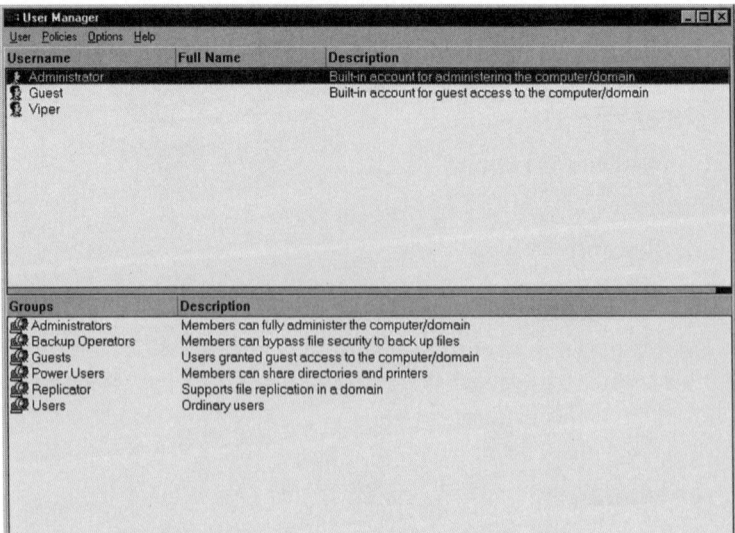

**Figure 11.1**  User Manager displays both users and groups.

When Windows NT Workstation is installed, two built-in user accounts are automatically created.

- Administrator
- Guest

The Administrator account allows the administrator(s) to perform many management functions, including managing user accounts and group accounts. The Administrator account is automatically added to the Administrators local group account. (Local group accounts are discussed later in this chapter.)

Users without an account on the network may use the Guest account. For security, when Windows NT is installed, the Guest account is disabled. The Guest account, like other user accounts, can have rights and permissions. The disabled Guest user account is automatically added to the Guests local group account, allowing the Guest user the right to log on to the workstation locally, if the account has been enabled.

A user account contains the user name, password, groups, rights and permissions information defining a user to Windows NT.

## CREATING NEW USER ACCOUNTS

For a user to log on to the network, the user must log in as a guest or have an individual user account. The New User dialog box in User Manager (Figure 11.2) allows administrators to create new user accounts from a Windows NT Workstation computer.

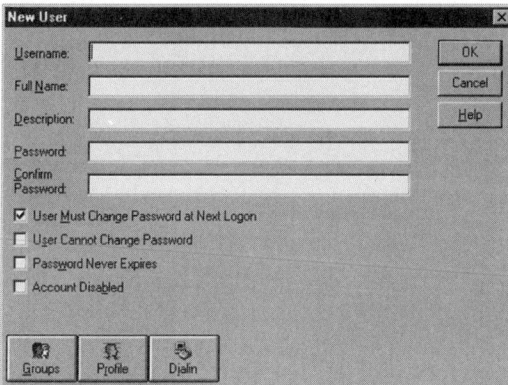

**Figure 11.2** New Users are added in this dialog box in User Manager.

### New User Information
When establishing a new user account, the following information can be entered:

Username

Full name

Description

Password

Confirm Password

### New User Options
As applicable, the following options also may be checked:

User Must Change Password at Next Logon

User Cannot Change Password

Password Never Expires

Account Disabled

If User Must Change Password at Next Logon is selected, the user will be required to change the next password at their first logon.

Selecting User Cannot Change Password prevents a user from changing the password.

Selecting Password Never Expires is a useful setting for accounts where it is not desirable to have a changing password. Accounts that represent installed services or guest accounts without security access rights are often set to password never expires.

When Account Disabled is selected, the account cannot be used.

For more information on Passwords, see the *Account Policy* section, later in this chapter.

### New User Tabs
There are three tabs available from the New User dialog box:

Groups

Profile

Dialin

### Groups
From the Groups tab, an administrator can access the Group Memberships screen shown in Figure 11.3. Administrators use Group

Memberships to add specific users to one or more available groups or to remove a user from one or more groups.

Information on creating a new local group follows. More information on local groups and global groups can be found in Chapter 15, "Groups."

### Profile

By selecting the Profile tab, an administrator can use the User Environment Profile dialog box shown in Figure 11.4 to set User Profiles and Home Directory.

The User Profile Path provides a path to a folder where information about the user's desktop environment is stored. Retaining this information allows a user's specific environment settings to be loaded during logon.

The Logon Script Name within the User Profiles section points to an executable file that runs whenever that user logs on to the network.

A home directory is a personal directory for a single user. A home directory is a private directory containing the user's files and programs that the user controls.

Information on setting up default, mandatory, and roaming profiles can be found in Chapter 12, "Profiles."

### Dialin

The Dialin Information screen, shown in Figure 11–5, accessed from the Dialin tab, allows individual user accounts to be given permission or denied permission to dial in to the workstation. If dialin permission is given, the workstation may be required to call the user back as an additional security, expense, or convenience measure.

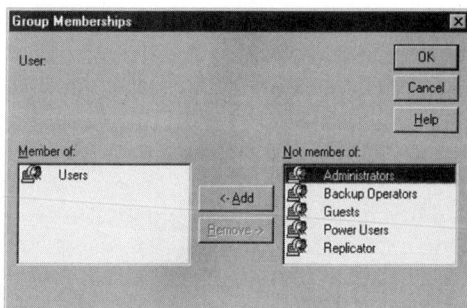

**Figure 11.3**    Add a user account to a Group account from the Group Memberships dialog box.

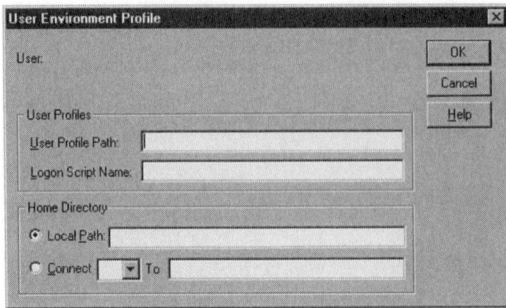

**Figure 11.4** A User Environment Profile in User Manager.

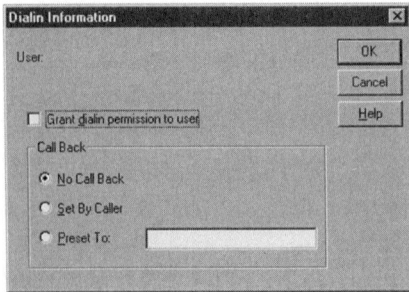

**Figure 11.5**
Set remote access permission for each user account at the Dialin Information screen.

## CREATING NEW LOCAL GROUP ACCOUNTS

From the User Menu in User Manager, New Local Groups can be created. The New Local Group dialog box is shown in Figure 11.6.

Each local group may contain user accounts, called Members. Because a local group can be granted rights and permissions, creating special purpose groups is a convenient way to aggregate similar user accounts to allow each member of the groups the same rights and permissions.

In other words, rather than assigning rights and permissions to each and every user account, created on a one-by-one basis, add that user account to a predefined group that already has appropriate rights and permissions. This technique is especially handy when the time arrives to change a permission. By changing the group's permissions, you effectively change the permissions of each member of the group.

### New Local Group Accounts

To create a new local group, provide:

- a Group Name
- add users (optional)
- add global group accounts (optional)

A local group provides access to resources only in the domain in which the local group was created.

## ACCOUNT (PASSWORD) POLICY

Controlling use of passwords is an important part of a network's overall security plan. The Account Policy dialog box, as shown in Figure 11.7, is available through the Policies menu in User Manager by selecting Account. Account Policy controls how passwords are used by user accounts on the network.

Account Policy allows an administrator to set password restrictions regarding:

Maximum Password Age

Minimum Password Age

Minimum Password Length

Password Uniqueness

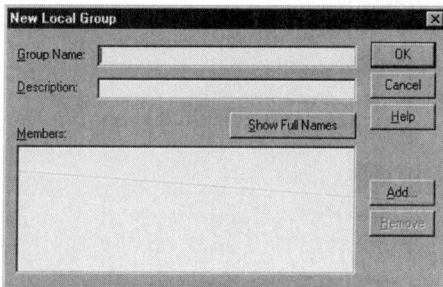

**Figure 11.6** The New Local Group dialog box in User Manager.

The account policy can be set so an account is locked out after a specified number of unsuccessful logon attempts. A locked account cannot log on to the network.

If Users Must Log On In Order To Change Password is selected, a user who does not change their password before the password expires will require assistance from the administrator to regain access to the network.

## USER RIGHTS

The User Rights dialog box, as shown in Figure 11.8, can be set through the Policies menu in User Manager after selecting User Rights. When the administrator grants a right to a user account or a group account, that account is allowed to perform certain activities on the workstation.

Table 11.1 shows user rights that can be granted using the User Rights Policy dialog box and the default built-in groups granted the right. Built-In Groups and Special Built-In Groups are discussed further in Chapter 15, "Groups."

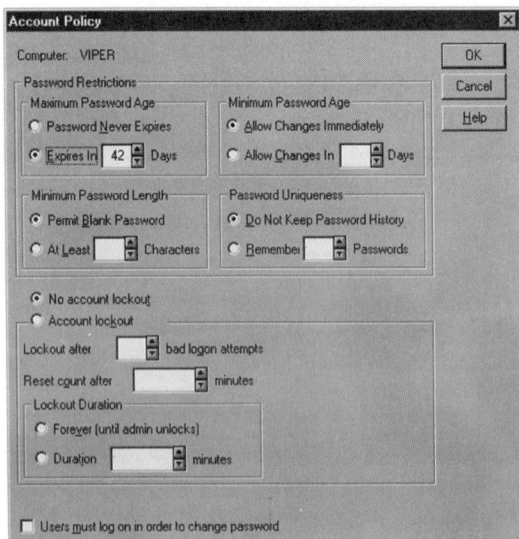

**Figure 11.7**   Account Policy provides for various password restrictions and settings.

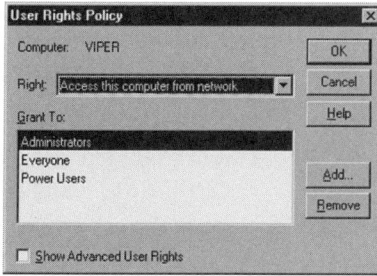

**Figure 11.8**   User Rights can be granted to user accounts and group accounts with the User Rights Policy dialog box.

**Table 11.1**  The default settings for User Rights granted to built-in groups.

| User Right | Local Group |
| --- | --- |
| Access this computer from network | Administrators, Everyone, Power Users |
| Back up files and directories | Administrators, Backup Operators |
| Change the system time | Administrators, Power Users |
| Force shutdown from a remote system | Administrators, Power Users |
| Load and unload device drivers | Administrators |
| Log on locally | Administrators, Backup Operators, Everyone, Guests, Power Users, Users |
| Manage auditing and security log | Administrators |
| Restore files and directories | Administrators, Backup Operators |
| Shut down the system | Administrators, Backup Operators, Everyone, Power Users, Users |
| Take ownership of files or other objects | Administrators |

By selecting Show Advanced User Rights, additional user rights are listed in the Right: drop-down menu. Rights available by selecting Show Advanced User Rights include:

Act as part of the operating system

Bypass traverse checking

Create a page file

Create a token object

Create permanent shared objects

Debug programs

Generate security audits

Increase quotas

Increase scheduling priority

Lock pages in memory

Log on as a batch job

Log on as a service

Modify firmware environment variables

Profile single process

Profile system performance

Replace a process-level token

## AUDIT POLICY

By selecting Audit from the Policies menu, administrators can select events for auditing and logging on the Audit Policy screen as shown in Figure 11.9. Auditing provides a way to collect information regarding system security and how the network is actually being used.

Events can be audited based on success and/or failure of the attempt and include:

- Logon and Logoff
- File and Object Access
- Use of User Rights
- User and Group Management
- Security Policy Changes

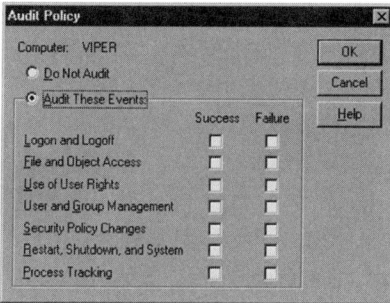

**Figure 11.9** The success and failure of events can be audited by the Audit Policy in User Manager.

- Restart, Shutdown, and System
- Process Tracking

Audit policy results are logged to the security log. The security log is only available to members of the Administrator local group. Access to the Security Log is only available through the Event Viewer located in Administrative Tools under the Programs Group from the Start menu. A Security Log is shown in Figure 11.10.

An audit entry provides information about the type of event logged, the user account involved, and the date and time of the event. Figure 11.11 shows a log entry of a failed attempt to access a secure object.

## AUDITING FILE AND OBJECT ACCESS

Auditing File and Object Access is a two-step process. The first step is to select File and Object Access from the Audit Policy screen. By turning this feature on, the global file and object access auditing policy is enabled on that workstation. The second step chooses the file or object to be audited and the type of auditing to be logged.

## FILES AND FOLDERS

To be audited, files and folders must be located on an NTFS partition. If the files and folders are located on a FAT partition, security logging cannot be enabled.

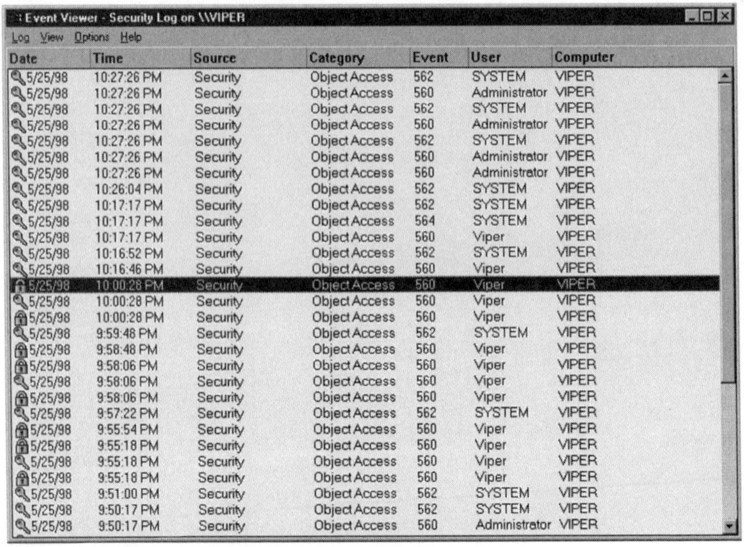

**Figure 11.10**   Access the Security Log through the Event Viewer.

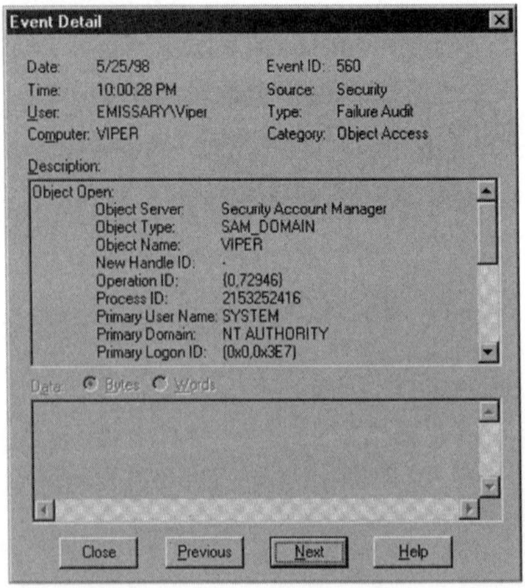

**Figure 11.11**   The Event Detail screen provides information about audited events.

After turning on an auditing policy as mentioned earlier, individual files and folders to be audited must be selected by an administrator using Windows NT Explorer. In Windows NT Explorer go to the Properties screen of the file or folder to be audited. Click the Security tab, and select Auditing. A Directory Auditing dialog box, shown in Figure 11.12, appears. From this dialog box, user and group accounts can be added and/or removed, and the success and/or failure of the following events can be selected for auditing:

Read

Write

Execute

Delete

Change Permissions

Take Ownership

Because only new files and folders will be audited once this feature is activated, you must select Replace Auditing on Subdirectories and Replace Auditing on Existing Files from the dialog box if existing files and folders are to be audited.

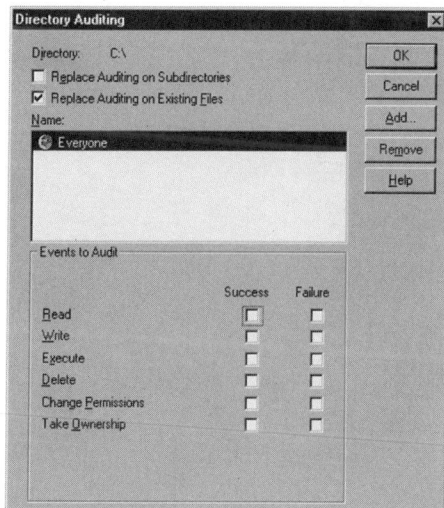

**Figure 11.12**   Administrators can use Windows NT Explorer to audit files and folders.

## OBJECTS (PRINTERS)

Printers, like files and folders, can be specified for auditing.

After first activating the Audit Policy by selecting File and Object Access from the Audit Policy screen in User Manager, select the printer to be audited. Click the Security tab, and select Auditing. Using a Printer Auditing dialog box as shown in Figure 11.13, user and group accounts can be added or removed. The success or failure of the following events can be logged for those accounts.

```
Print

Full Control

Delete

Change Permissions

Take Ownership
```

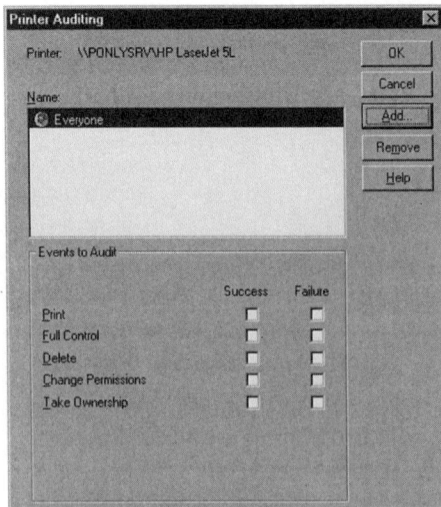

**Figure 11.13**   Use the Printer Auditing dialog box in Windows NT Explorer to audit printing.

**NOTE**

Even if auditing is selected from a file or object's Properties menu, if File and Object Access has not been selected in User Manager's Audit Policy, no activity will be logged. Auditing Files and Objects requires two separate steps.

1. Turn on the Audit Policy
2. Select the file or object to be audited

## FOR REVIEW

- Use User Manager to administer user accounts and access to the network
- Groups are a convenient way of grouping user accounts
- For security, set password restrictions in Account Policy
- Account Policies can be set so that accounts are locked out after a specified number of unsuccessful logon attempts
- Auditing events provides information on who used or attempted to use audited network resources
- The security log in Event Viewer allows an administrator to view audited events

## FROM HERE

Chapter 15, "Groups," covers local and global account groups and built-in and special built-in groups.

Default, mandatory, and roaming profiles are discussed in Chapter 12, "Profiles."

# Profiles

User profiles provide network administrators a means of controlling the environment that users experience. User profiles can be configured to allow users themselves to change the profile settings or to require users to have a mandatory desktop configuration. User profiles also allow users sharing the same workstation to create a unique profile so that each user experiences the computer as they wish to.

Windows NT Workstation requires a user profile for each user account. User profiles can be used to configure and manage desktops. A user profile, which is loaded during logon, contains a specific user's environment and preference settings. These settings include:

- Desktop arrangement and icons
- Installed applications
- Screen colors
- Screen savers
- Network connections
- Printer connections
- Mouse settings
- Shortcuts
- Window size and position

The four types of user profiles are explained next.

- Default
- Local
- Roaming
- Mandatory

## Default User Profile

The default user profile is created during the installation of Windows NT Workstation. A default user profile is the default configuration a user receives the first time they log on to a Windows NT Workstation.

When a user first logs on to a Windows NT Workstation, a fresh user profile folder is automatically created. The default profile is copied to the new user's profile folder as a starting point for each new user.

The default user profile and subsequent individual user profile folders are located in C:\Winnt\Profiles. Each profile folder contains a file named Ntuser.dat.

If the default profile is not mandatory, the user can customize the profile and the modified profile will be saved as the user's profile and stored under the Profiles folder in a specific folder identified by the username.

## Local User Profile

A local user profile is available to the user only when logged on to the workstation on which the local profile was created. Local profiles are user and computer specific. If a user does not have a server-based profile, or if the profile server is down, the local user profile will be used when the user logs on to Windows NT Workstation.

## Roaming User Profile

A roaming user profile can be set up so a user sees the same desktop even when logging onto different computers. Roaming profiles are stored on a network share. A roaming profile is set up by specifying a user profile path in User Manager. See the sidebar for more information about roaming user profiles.

A user who has been assigned a roaming user profile will receive a copy of their locally cached profile (if the user has logged on the workstation before) or the default user profile if they log on to a Windows NT Workstation when the profile server is down.

## Mandatory User Profile

A mandatory user profile is preconfigured by an administrator and cannot be changed by the user.

A mandatory profile is set up by specifying a User Profile path in User Manager and by changing the filename Ntuser.dat to Ntuser.man. (See the sidebar for more information.) When Windows NT reads the Ntuser.man file, Windows NT marks the user profile as read only. Even if the user modifies the desktop while logged on, the changes will not be saved. When the user logs on at a later time, they will receive the mandatory profile.

A user, who has been assigned a mandatory user profile, will receive a copy of the default user profile if they log on to a Windows NT Workstation when the profile server is down.

If the profile directory has also been renamed with a .MAN extension, the user will not be allowed to log on if the profile server is down.

### CREATING ROAMING OR MANDATORY USER PROFILES

A roaming user profile can be created through User Manager or the System option in Control Panel. Both methods have the same effect.

To assign a roaming or mandatory profile to a user, in User Manager | User | Properties | Profile | User Environment Profile | User Profile path, type the path name and user profile folder name as shown in Figure 12.1.

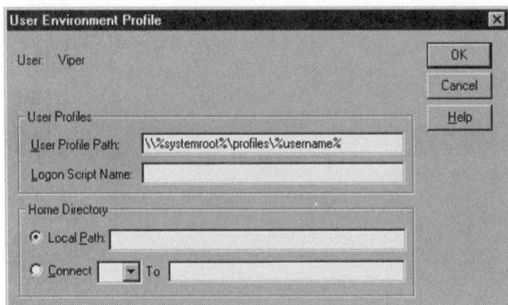

**Figure 12.1** Assign a User Profile Path in User Manager to set up a roaming or mandatory user profile.

To make a user profile mandatory, the `Ntuser.dat` file on a Windows NT Workstation must be renamed to `Ntuser.man`. A roaming user profile can also be created on a Windows NT Workstation by using the Control Panel | System | User Profiles as shown in Figure 12.2. A user's local workstation profile can be copied to a shared folder on a server by using the Copy To button available from the User Profiles tab. Once copied, configure the path and profile name of the roaming profile in User Manager.

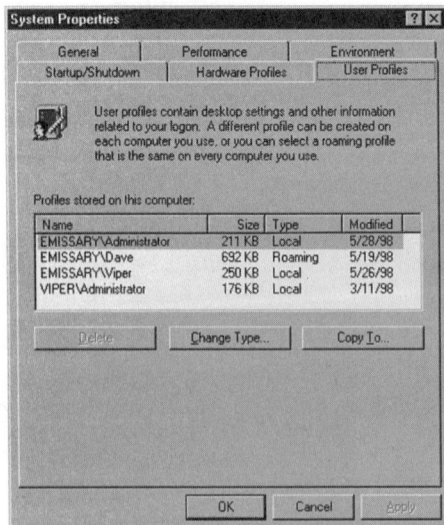

**Figure 12.2** Use the Copy To button on the User Profiles tab to copy a user's local workstation profile to a shared folder on a profile server.

## UNIVERSAL NAMING CONVENTION (UNC)

UNC names are used when entering the User Profile Path. To use a system environment variable, enclose it in percent signs.

For example, the %systemroot% environment variable is the name of the root directory where the Windows NT Workstation files are located, usually C:/Winnt. Wherever the system is located, the %systemroot% is the right name for it.

If the %username% variable is used in a profile, the system will automatically substitute the appropriate user account name so that when a user logs on the first time, the system copies the default profile and saves it under the user's account name. This automatic substitution, available in Windows NT, is helpful when dealing with many user accounts.

## PROFILES AND POLICIES

When access to system and network resources is in question, the system evaluates profiles and policies (discussed in Chapter 16, "Policies"). There is a hierarchy of profiles and policies that determines what takes precedence. For the Windows NT Workstation exam (and Windows NT Server, and Windows NT Server in the Enterprise), you should memorize the following list that shows the order of precedence:

- Individual System Policy
- Group System Policy
- Mandatory User Profile
- Personal User Profile
- Default User Profile

Policies always override profiles. An individual system policy has greater priority than a group system policy. A mandatory user profile has priority over a personal user profile. All the others have priority over the default user profile.

## FOR REVIEW

A new user profile folder is automatically created the first time a user logs on to Windows NT Workstation.

Create a roaming user profile using User Manager or the System option in Control Panel.

Make a user profile mandatory by renaming the `Ntuser.dat` file to `Ntuser.man`.

## FROM HERE

Policies are discussed in detail in Chapter 16.

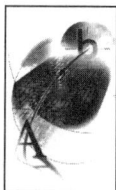

# CHAPTER 13

# Share and NTFS Permissions

Permissions cannot be assigned to individual files on a FAT partition. So when security is a concern, NTFS should be used to format the partition. With NTFS, files and folders can have permissions that control user and group access to resources (files and folders) whether or not the resource has been shared.

Permissions can be very tricky. Users can be assigned permissions as individual users and as members of multiple groups, each of which may allow different levels of access. Because of this, it can be difficult not just to restrict access but also to ensure that users are able to access the files they actually need.

As with all things in Windows NT, planning is crucial to ensure that resources are secure and accessed properly. So make sure that you give permissions to users and groups who need it. This is one reason that Microsoft stresses using groups to allow access, rather than individual user accounts. In other words, assign the user to global groups; the global groups to local groups; and only assign the permissions to the local groups. By assigning permissions to local groups, an administrator can keep better track of who has permissions to network resources. Chapter 15, "Groups," provides more information on global and local groups.

## Sharing Folders on the Network

Share permissions can be set on both FAT or NTFS partitions. In either case, to make a file accessible over the network, the folder in which the file is located must be shared.

By default, the Windows NT Workstation built-in groups that can share a folder are:

- Administrators
- Power Users

To share a resource located on either a FAT or NTFS partition, right click the resource (or share) in Windows NT Explorer. Select Sharing from the menu, and click on the Shared As: option. When setting up the share, you can assign a share name, include a comment to clarify or amplify use of the share, and set a maximum number of simultaneous users as shown in Figure 13.1.

After clicking the Permissions button on the Sharing dialog box, the Access Through Share Permissions dialog box becomes available. As shown in Figure 13.2, the Type of Access for specified users and groups can be set to:

- No Access
- Read

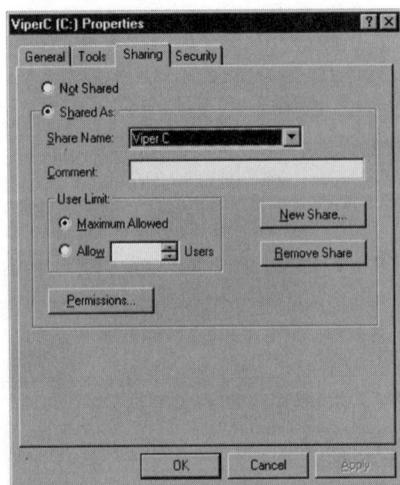

**Figure 13.1**   The Sharing dialog box in Windows NT Workstation.

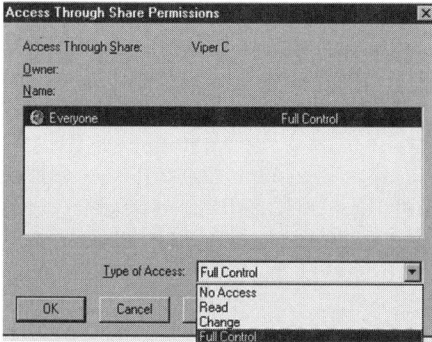

**Figure 13.2**   The Access Through Share Permission dialog box to set Permissions for shares on a Windows NT Workstation.

■ Change

■ Full Control

Table 13.1 shows several common tasks, along with the access levels allowed to perform each task.

**Table 13.1** Different tasks require different levels of share access.

| Task | Full Control * | Change | Read | No Access |
|------|------|------|------|------|
| Access Denied | | | | X |
| View Folder and Filenames | X | X | X | |
| View Subfolders | X | X | X | |
| View File Data | X | X | X | |
| Run Program Files | X | X | X | |
| Create Files and Subfolders | X | X | | |
| Change File Data | X | X | | |
| Delete Files and Subfolders | X | X | | |
| (NTFS only) Change Permissions | X | | | |
| (NTFS only) Take Ownership | X | | | |

* FULL CONTROL is the default permission assigned to the EVERYONE group and the EVERYONE group is assigned to every folder shared by default.

Users can be assigned permissions as an individual user and as a member of multiple groups; each group of which may have different levels of access assigned. To determine a user's level of access through Share Permissions, add the different levels of rights the user has been assigned. For share access, the individual rights and the rights of all the groups a user is a member of accumulate, except for No Access. In other words, the least restrictive permission is given to the user of all the user's individual and group rights, unless NO ACCESS is one of the permissions. In this case, NO ACCESS overrides all other permissions, and the user is DENIED access.

For example, a user attempts to access a shared folder. The shared folder permissions have been set to allow the individual user READ access. The user belongs to Group 1, whose shared folder permissions have been set to FULL CONTROL. When the permissions are combined, the user receives the least restrictive of the two permissions, that is, FULL CONTROL access to the shared folder.

In a second example, a user attempts to access a shared folder. The shared folder permissions have been set to allow the individual user CHANGE access. The user belongs to Group 2 whose shared folder permissions have been set to NO ACCESS. NO ACCESS overrides the CHANGE permission and the user will be denied access.

If the shared folder is located on an NTFS partition, file and folder permissions can be used to provide a finer level of security. NTFS permissions are discussed later in this chapter.

## FAT Partitions

First, it is important to understand that sharing a folder is the only way to secure it on a FAT partition. To make this concept even simpler, if you try to access a folder over a network and it is not shared, you cannot get in. Period. Keep in mind that sharing only applies to network access. Also remember that files can only be protected at the directory level when located on a FAT partition. Permissions cannot be set on individual files located on a FAT partition.

In other words, files on a FAT partition can be protected from access:

- Only at the folder level
- Only over the network
- Only if the folder is shared

If a user logs on to a Windows NT Workstation, and the user has the "Log on Locally" user right, the shares and share permissions for over the network access do not apply to FAT partitions.

Figure 13.3 shows how to resolve a user's access level to a folder on a FAT partition.

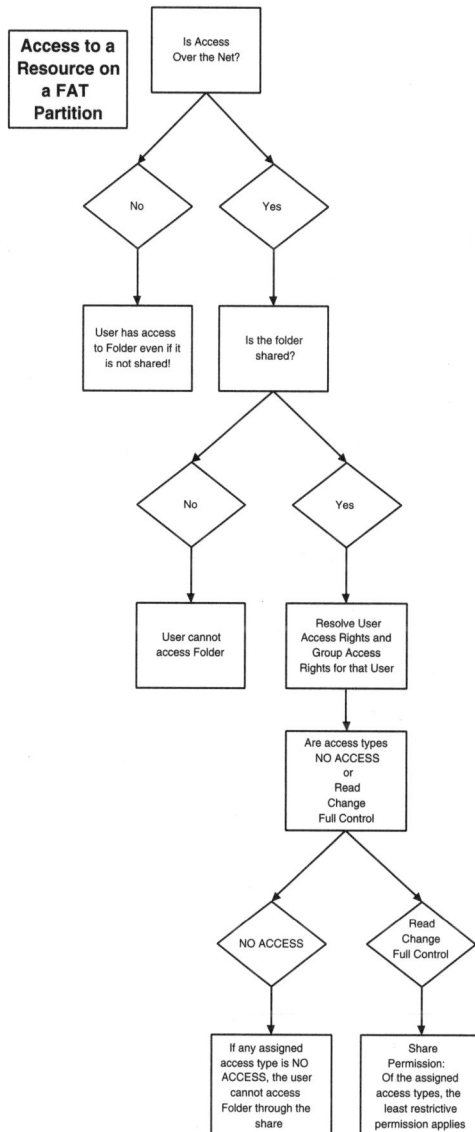

**Figure 13.3**   Resolve a user's access to a folder on a FAT Partition.

## NTFS Permissions

NTFS creates deeper levels of security than a share by securing files as well as folders. NTFS permissions, unlike a share on a FAT partition, do apply locally as well as remotely (over the network).

NTFS is more complicated than FAT shares and allows permissions to be combined. In an effort to alleviate some of the complications, Windows NT created Standard Permissions that can be used on folders and files. A Standard Permission is a combination of specific types of access.

Table 13.2 gives the details of access types for NTFS permissions. As you can see, they are much more extensive than the share permissions for a FAT partition. As you review the table, note that permissions compound, that is, they build on each other.

**Table 13.2** The six types of access for NTFS files or folders.

| | |
|---|---|
| Read | Displays folders and files data, names, attributes and permissions |
| Write | Displays folders and files data, names, attributes and permissions; Change folders and files data, names, attributes; Add files and folders |
| Execute | Displays folders and files data, names, attributes and permissions; Change folders and files data, names, attributes; Add files and folders; Run executable files |
| Delete | Delete a file or folder |
| Change Permission | Change the permissions of a file or folder |
| Take Ownership | Take Ownership of a file or folder |

As you encounter NTFS permissions, note the abbreviation for each of the permissions. The abbreviation for each permission is listed.

| | |
|---|---|
| Read | R |
| Write | W |

| Execute | X |
|---|---|
| Delete | D |
| Change Permission | P |
| Take Ownership | O |

It is also important to understand how Standard Permissions are created. Listed are the NTFS Standard Permissions. The 'code letters' beside each Standard Permission represent how regular NTFS permissions are combined. These also represent how you will see these various permission represented on the MCSE exams.

| No Access | ( ) |
|---|---|
| List | (RX) |
| Read | (RX) |
| Add | (WX) |
| Add & Read | (RWX) |
| Change | (RWXD) |
| Full Control * | (RWXDPO) |

* Full Control will be shown as (All) on Windows NT menus.

To assign NTFS permissions, right click on the resource to be shared. Then proceed to Properties | Security | Permissions to bring up the Directory Permissions dialog box as shown in Figure 13.4.

Two options that can be set from the Directory Permissions dialog box are:

Replace Permissions on Subdirectories

Replace Permissions on Existing Files

When setting NTFS permissions, by default, the permissions apply to the directory and its files. If the permissions are also to be applied to the subdirectories, check the Replace Permissions on Subdirectories box.

As stated above, by default, permissions apply to the files in the directory as well as the folder. The Replace Permissions on Existing Files should be cleared if the new permissions are to be applied to the directory only.

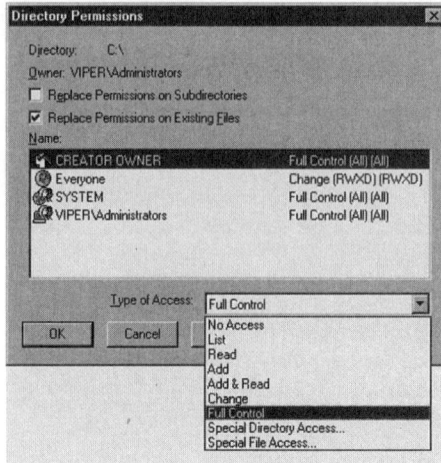

**Figure 13.4** The type of access for users and groups can be assigned with the Directory Permissions dialog box.

NTFS permissions are applied in the same manner as share permissions. Users can be assigned permissions as an individual user and as a member of multiple groups, each of which may have different levels of access assigned. To determine a user's access level through NTFS Permissions, add the different levels of rights the user has been assigned individually and through group membership. The rights accumulate, except for No Access. In other words, the least restrictive permission is given to the user, unless NO ACCESS is one of the permissions. In this case, NO ACCESS overrides all other permissions and the user is DENIED access.

Figure 13.5 shows how to resolve a user's access level to a folder on a NTFS partition.

## Share Permissions versus NTFS Permissions

Whenever NTFS file and folder permissions are combined with a share permission, the most restrictive permission is granted. This is an effective method of securing network resources. A user's level of access to a shared folder will either be the same or more restrictive than the level of access the user would have if logged on to the resource locally.

Figure 13–6 shows how to resolve a user's level of access to a shared NTFS resource.

```
          Resolve User
         Access Rights and
          Group Access
         Rights for that User
```

**Resolve User's Level of Access**
**to a Local Resource Located on a**
**NTFS Partition**

```
            Are access types
              NO ACCESS
                  or
              List  (RX)
              Read  (RX)
              Add   (WX)
          Add & Read  (RWX)
          Change  (RWXD)
          Full Control (All)
```

```
                                        List
                                        Read
      NO ACCESS                         Add
                                     Add & Read
                                       Change
                                     Full Control
```

```
   If any assigned
   access type is NO
   ACCESS, the user           NTFS Permission:
   cannot access the          Of the assigned
      resource                access types, the
                              least restrictive
                             permission applies
```

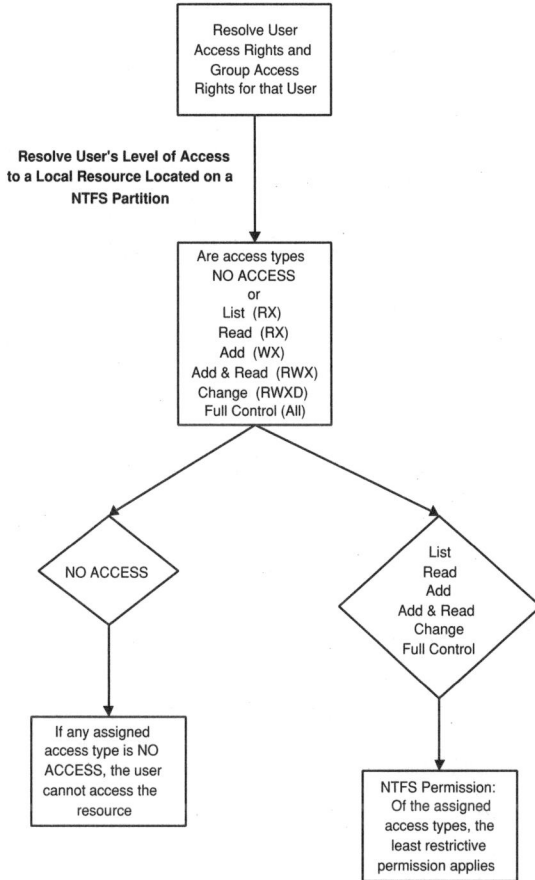

**Figure 13.5**   Resolve a user's access to a resource on a NTFS Partition.

## Resolving a User's Access to a Resource

When the Windows NT Workstation exam presents a question regarding a user's access level, follow this procedure.

1. Read the question carefully.
2. Break the question down into small parts as indicated.

   Is the resource located on a FAT partition or a NTFS partition?

   If the resource is located on a FAT partition, proceed to Part A.

   If the resource is located on an NTFS partition, proceed to Part B

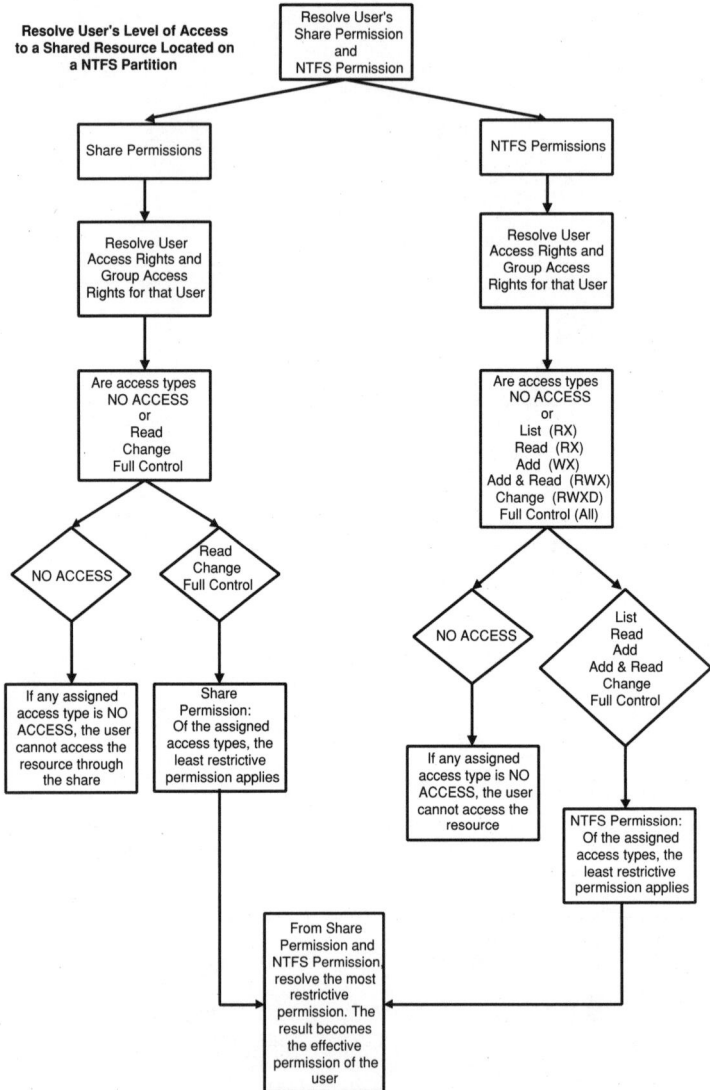

**Figure 13.6**  Resolve a user's access to a shared resource on a NTFS Partition.

Part A: Resource located on a FAT partition.

Is access to the resource local or remote?

    If access is local, the user has access to the resource.

    If access is remote, resolve the share permissions.

- User Access Rights
- Group Access Rights for the User

Share permissions are cumulative. The user is given the least restrictive permission. Unless one of the permissions is NO ACCESS. NO ACCESS prevents the user from accessing the shared resource. See Figure 13.3.

Part B: Resource located on a NTFS partition

Is access to the resource local or remote?

If access is local, resolve the NTFS permissions.

- User Access Rights
- Group Access Rights for the User

NTFS permissions are cumulative. The user is given the best permission. Unless one of the permissions is NO ACCESS. NO ACCESS prevents the user from accessing the NTFS resource. See Figure 13.5.

If access is remote (over the network), do the following three steps:

Step 1: Resolve the NTFS permissions

- User Access Rights
- Group Access Rights for the User

NTFS permissions are cumulative. The user is given the least restrictive permission. Unless one of the permissions is NO ACCESS. NO ACCESS prevents the user from accessing the NTFS resource.

Step 2: Resolve the Share permissions

- User Access Rights
- Group Access Rights for the User

Share permissions are cumulative. The user is given the least restrictive permission. Unless one of the permissions is NO ACCESS. NO ACCESS prevents the user from accessing the Share resource.

Step 3: Combine the NTFS permission and the Share permission to resolve the most restrictive permission. When a user accesses a shared resource on a NTFS partition, the most restrictive permission applies. See Figure 13.6.

## Taking Ownership

Every file and folder on a NTFS partition has an owner. The owner is the user who created the file or folder. The owner controls access by changing the permissions set on the file or folder.

Note: Members of the Administrators group can always take ownership of any file or directory. For example, if an employee leaves the organization, the administrator can take ownership of the ex-employee's files. An administrator can even take ownership when the permission is set to No Access.

Ownership can be transferred in two ways.

1. The owner can grant the Take Ownership permission to other users or groups.

2. An administrator can also take ownership of any file on the workstation. An administrator cannot directly transfer ownership, but after taking ownership, an administrator can grant Take Ownership permission on a file to other users or groups.

## Moving and Copying Files and Folders on a NTFS Partition

On an NTFS Partition, a file moved to a different folder on the same partition continues to have the permissions and attributes it had before the file was moved. When moving a file on the same partition, NTFS just updates the directory pointers—a new file is not created. The only way to move a file and keep the NTFS permissions intact is to move the file to the same partition.

If a file is moved to a different partition, the file inherits the permissions and attributes from the folder where it now resides. A new file has been created and receives the target folder permissions and attributes.

If the file is copied, even on the same partition, the file inherits the permissions and attributes from the folder where it now resides. A new file has been created and receives the target folder permissions and attributes.

When files are moved or copied from NTFS to FAT, the file permissions are lost because the FAT file system does not support file permissions.

**FOR REVIEW**

- Members of the Administrators and Power Users groups can share a folder on a Windows NT Workstation.

- NTFS file and folder permissions accumulate so the user receives the least restrictive permission.

- No Access permission overrides all other permissions

- When NTFS file and folder permissions are combined with share permissions the most restrictive permission is granted.

- An administrator can take ownership of any file.

- A file retains its permissions and attributes when it is moved to a new folder on the same NTFS partition.

- A file inherits the permissions and attributes of the target folder when it is moved from one NTFS partition to a different NTFS partition.

- A file inherits the permissions and attributes of the target folder when it is copied even on the same NTFS partition.

- File permissions are lost when files are moved or copied from a NTFS partition to a FAT partition.

**FROM HERE**

Chapter 15, "Groups," provides more information on global and local groups.

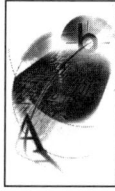

# CHAPTER 14

# Printers and Print Devices

The Windows NT printing environment is a robust component of Windows NT 4.0, and configuring printing is not difficult. This chapter discusses a variety of printing methods and numerous printing configurations supported by Windows NT. Printers can be configured to be local or remote, as well as across other operating systems.

The topics in this chapter include:

- Hardware Compatibility List
- Printers versus print devices
- Windows print architecture
- Printers (printer drivers)
- Sharing printers
- Remote printers versus local printers
- Attaching the print device
- Printer properties
- Print management
- Non-Windows printing
- Troubleshooting common print problems

## Hardware Compatibility List

Before you begin to install a printer, review Chapter 6, "Installation Overview," to re-acquaint yourself with the HCL, or Hardware Compatibility List. It is essential that you research printer hardware like any other hardware you plan to install in Windows NT. Because Windows NT 4.0 is not plug and play, attaching anything to a Windows NT 4.0 computer that is not on the HCL, you do at your own risk.

The bottom line is that you should check the HCL before purchasing print devices for use with Windows NT.

## Printers versus Print Devices

Here is some Microsoft terminology. For the examination, you must understand the following two terms as Microsoft means them to be understood. The two most basic components of any Microsoft Windows NT printing environment are:

- Printers—In a Microsoft world, the printer is the driver: the software that interfaces with the operating systems and runs the print device(s) attached to a computer or network. While it is popular to refer to the hardware device as the printer, for purposes of the MCSE exam, it is imperative you relearn the Microsoft use of this word.

Think of the printer as the software "middle-person," negotiating the communication and printing requirements of the application with the physical capabilities of the printer hardware. In Windows NT the print device hardware and application never communicate directly with each other, but use the printer (driver) as an intermediary.

Printer drivers that work fine for Windows 3.x or 95 will not work for Windows NT 4.0. Don't be tempted to waste time trying those old drivers—the Windows NT architecture is different and Windows 3.51 or Windows 95 drivers can't do the job.

Also, if the printer will be shared with clients running Windows 3.51 and Windows 95, a separate driver for each operating system will need to be installed on the print server.

- Print Devices—A print device is the actual physical print device, such as a Hewlett Packard DeskJet or an Epson Bubble Jet. The print device creates the printed output pages and is the place where you add paper, change the ribbon or ink cartridge, and so forth.

The term printer is so familiar and popular that you should not assume this distinction is easy to remember. Caution is definitely the watchword for dealing with "printers" on the exam, because familiarity may give you false confidence.

Remember the hardware is a print device, while the printer is the printer driver, or interface software.

## Windows Print Architecture

A modest portion of the Windows NT 4.0 print architecture is relevant to the MCSE exams. The balance of the architecture is also worth knowing. It will facilitate your understanding of how the components of printing interface with each other.

In fact, it is this interfacing, or modularity, that distinguishes the Windows NT Print Architecture. Each component has a specific function, yet no component is so isolated that it ignores the rest of the system.

Take some time to review the following components.

- Print Monitor—Sends the print job to the print device.

- GDI, or Graphics Device Interface—helps translate the graphic portion of a print job into something the printer and print device can understand, and therefore, print.

- Printer—The actual software that translates the print job request to the printer device. More detail on this component is provided in the next section.

- Router—Sends the print requests to the spooler.

- Spooler—A spooler, or Print Provider, can intercept print jobs for local or remote print devices. If local, it holds the job until the print device is free to print it. If it is acting like a remote spooler, the spooler intercepts the print request and then sends it on to the appropriate local spooler, where the job is printed. The default folder for the spooler is %systemroot%\system32\spool\printers.

- Print Processor—This is the last stop for the print job, where it is processed before going to the Print Monitor.

## Printers or Printer Drivers

Now we will focus on one aspect of the previous section: printers. Understanding the concept of the printer as software is often the biggest hurdle for test-takers. In order for you to overcome this obstacle, you will need to forget the slang you've learned in the real world. Pretend that everything you already know about printers is now wrong.

There are two other concepts about printers that you must also remember.

- A printer (software) can interface with multiple printing devices (hardware)
- A print device (hardware) can interface with multiple printers (software)

Let's review each of these two statements in more detail.

### A PRINTER CAN INTERFACE WITH MULTIPLE PRINT DEVICES

Many organizations do enough printing to need multiple print devices (hardware) to handle the printing volume. In this case, there may be only one printer, or driver, that determines which print device will receive a particular print job. The process of managing multiple print devices is known as pooling. When multiple print devices are combined, they form a printer pool.

The primary requirement of a printer pool is that all printers in the printer pool must be able to use the same printer driver. This means that all the print devices must be very similar. Identical print devices, or print devices all emulating the same type of print device must be pooled together.

For instance, you can have a Hewlett-Packard printer pool or an Epson printer pool, thereby creating a printer pool according to printer manufacturers of similar or identical print devices. Another method of organizing printers is also by type, that is, all laser printers, all inkjets, and so on. This method, however, can create compatibility problems. It is generally not recommended to combine different manufacturers in a printer pool regardless of the printer type.

Enable printer pools by doing the following:

1. Start | Settings | Printers

2. Select a printer to configure

3. Select Printer Properties

4. Select Ports

5. Check Enable Printer Pooling

6. Select each port you want to be part of the pool

An example of the dialog box used to configure a printer pool is shown in Figure 14.1.

In the example in Figure 14.2, client computers send their print requests to the printer. The printer then polls the network print devices to see which one is free to accept a print job. If all are free, the print job will go to the default system print device. If none are free, the print job is sent to the print queue. The queue holds the print job until it is printed or cancelled.

Note: If you work with NetWare Networks or OS/2, keep in mind that other manufacturers refer to a printer as a print queue, as

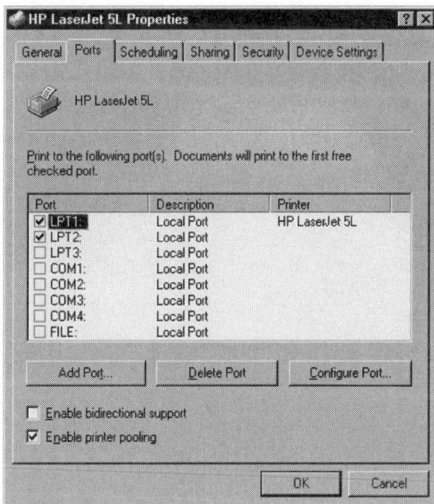

**Figure 14.1**  Enable printer pooling from the Ports tab in Printer Properties.

shown in Table 14.1. Windows NT users submit print jobs to a printer, and OS/2 and NetWare users submit print jobs to a print queue.

**Table 14.1** Novell terminology calls printers queues.

| Microsoft Terminology | Novell NetWare Terminology |
| --- | --- |
| Printer | Print Queue |
| Printers | Print Queues |

The printer can reside almost anywhere on the network. On a larger network, where printing demands are large, it is common to have a dedicated print server. On a smaller network, even a Windows 95 peer-to-peer network, a printer can reside on the client computer where you attach the print device. In addition, some print devices do not require a client computer connection, instead, they attach directly to the network with their own network interface card.

**A PRINT DEVICE CAN INTERFACE WITH MULTIPLE PRINTERS**
Sophisticated printers (the printing software interface) can support multiple printing languages. In that case, although interfacing with a single print device, there will be multiple printer icons in the Printers applet. When multiple printers are created corresponding to the same print device, and the print device is connected to a computer rather than directly to the network, then the printers are installed from the computer local to the print device.

In the example, Figure 14.3 shows a single print device configured for multiple printers. Note there are two requirements to enable one print device for multiple printers.

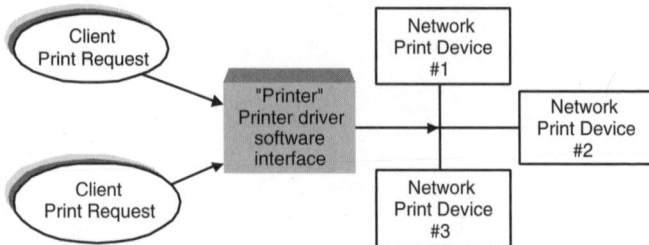

**Figure 14.2**  Printers (software) interface between the client print request and the network print devices.

- One print server contains all involved printers
- One port configured for a single print device

For the time being, the previous explanation is enough; however, you should review a Printer Properties page for a further explanation of ports.

Before a client computer can interface with the printer, the printer driver software must be loaded on the client computer. For instance, a client computer with only Language A, as shown in Figure 14.3, cannot print to the Language B interface because that client computer does not have the Language B software loaded.

In this instance, the client computer sends the print request to the appropriate alternate printer by selecting the appropriate printer from those available. Each available printer is represented as an icon in the Printers applet of Control Panel, shown Figure 14.4.

It is also possible to configure all print jobs to a specific printer by default. Just select the printer icon as shown in Figure 14.4, right-click on it, and select Set As Default.

The MCSE exam contains many references to printers, print devices, and printer pools. Therefore, it is crucial to have a clear understanding of these foundation principles before the exam.

## Sharing

Applications interface with the printer not the print device. Therefore, it is inconsequential where the print device is located and what the print device is attached to. This is ideal for purposes of administering a network because it allows sharing of print devices.

It is the responsibility of the network operating system to send print jobs to the right place. The advantage to this is that a network can facilitate and serve many different clients running many

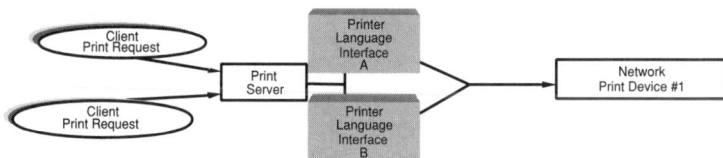

**Figure 14.3**  Print Servers may contain more than one printer.

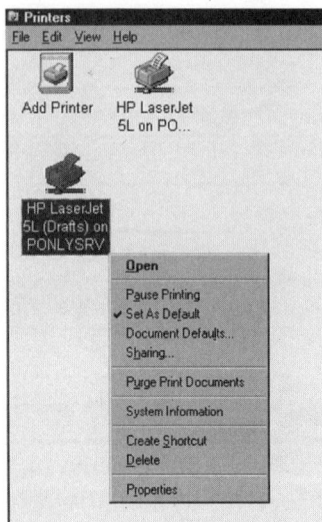

**Figure 14.4** To send all print jobs to a specific printer, set the printer as default.

different operating systems. Best of all, different clients and operating systems can all can share a single printer and print device.

For the specifics of how to share a printer on a network, see the section on printer properties later in this chapter.

For the MCSE exam, you need to understand the overview of the select print permissions shown in Table 14.2. If a user has one of the permissions across the top of the table, the consequent powers are indicated in the table with the word "Yes."

**Table 14.2** These are User or Group print permissions from most restrictive to least restrictive.

| User or Group Print Permissions | No Access | Print | Manage Documents | Full Control |
|---|---|---|---|---|
| Print All Documents | | Yes | Yes | Yes |
| Pause All Documents | | | Yes | Yes |
| Pause Own Documents | | Yes | Yes | Yes |
| Delete All Documents | | | Yes | Yes |
| Delete Own Documents | | Yes | Yes | Yes |

| User or Group Print Permissions | No Access | Print | Manage Documents | Full Control |
|---|---|---|---|---|
| Restart All Documents | | | Yes | Yes |
| Restart Own Documents | Yes | Yes | Yes | Yes |
| Resume All Documents | | | Yes | Yes |
| Resume Own Documents | Yes | Yes | Yes | Yes |
| Change Permissions | | | | Yes |
| Delete a Printer | | | | Yes |
| Share a Printer | | | | Yes |

Other assignments can also be given to printer permissions; however, these are the ones you will need to know for the exams.

Review Table 14.2. It is particularly important to note the difference between the print permission and the manage documents permission. By default, the print permission is assigned to all users through the Everyone group.

The Manage Documents permission is assigned, by default, to the Creator Owner.

Full Control is assigned to the Administrators group and the Power Users group, by default, giving them the ability to administer printing on any Windows NT computer.

No Access permission, if assigned of course, overrides all other print permissions.

Administrators can change the permissions for these groups, other groups, and individual users by going to the Printer Permissions screen shown in Figure 14.5. To get there, go to:

```
Start|Settings|Printers|File|Printer
Properties|Security|Permissions|Add
```

## Remote Printers versus Local Printers

In any discussion of printing on a Windows NT network, you must distinguish between the remote and the local printer. For instance, if the printer resides on a computer, the printer becomes local to that computer. Therefore, to any other computer on the network, that printer becomes a remote printer because it is not attached to the local computer.

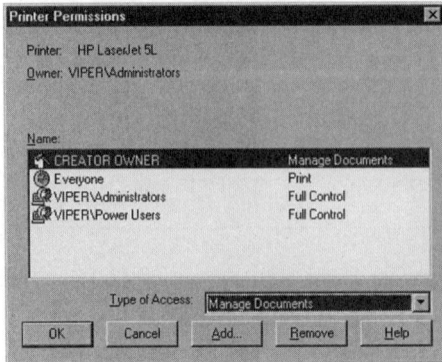

**Figure 14.5** Administer Printer Permissions from this dialog box.

To put it another way, a remote printer does not reside on the computer at which you are sitting. Because of this, when you have a print job, you send the request to the remote printer, where it is spooled and sent to a print device. So you see, your perspective of what is remote and what is local determines everything. As seen in Figure 14.6, the perspective of the print device is noted relative to which computer the print device is connected.

Please note in the example shown in Figure 14.6, the printer resides on a print server, which will spool the print jobs, and the printer must be shared to enable network clients to use it.

## Attaching the Print Device

By now, having distinguished between a printer and a print device, you realize you cannot simply attach a print device to a computer and expect it automatically to print from Windows NT. However, the process of creating a local printer is not difficult. Microsoft has supplied an Add Printer Wizard, shown in Figure 14.7, to facilitate the process. You can find the wizard two ways.

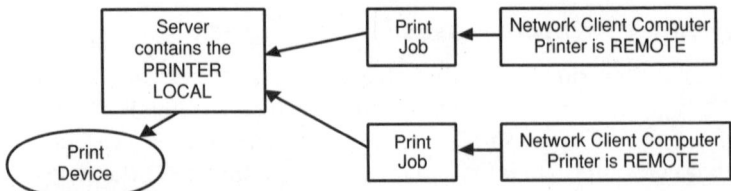

**Figure 14.6** Remote printers are not connected to the computer where you are sitting.

```
Start | Settings | Printers |Add Printer
```
or
```
My Computer | Control Panel | Printers | Add Printer
```

In configuring the print device, you may need the CD-ROM or floppy disk that came with the print device. During setup of the printer using the wizard, you will be asked these questions.

1. Local (My Computer) or remote printer (network printer server)
2. Manufacturer name or generic
3. Printer device type or model
4. Printer port, usually LPT1 or 2
5. Printer name
6. Whether the printer will be the default printer
7. Print a test page?

If you specify Remote Printer (in step 1), you'll be asked for additional information, including:

- Shared or not shared
- If shared, the share name
- Operating system(s) of computers accessing the printer

When connecting to a remote printer, you'll see the dialog box shown in Figure 14.8. Using this screen, you can browse the network to locate and add a printer. This is not only useful to the client computer adding a remote printer but also to the administrator of

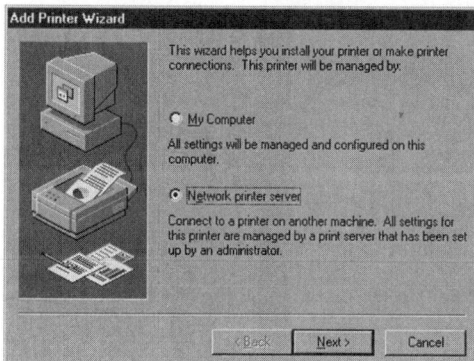

**Figure 14.7**    Add a printer by using Windows NT Add Printer Wizard.

a large network. The ability to browse a network to see the UNC
path of printers eases administration.

If you did not specify the printer as a network printer when setting it up, you can modify this property later by going to:

```
My Computer | Control Panel | Printers | select the printer |
right-click|Sharing
```

From here, you'll enter the share name and password. You can
also reach the sharing option through the Printer Properties Page of
the printer, discussed next.

## Printer Properties

You can configure the properties for the print device during or after the installation.

To reach the printer's Printer Properties page, shown in Figure
14.9, use the following route:

```
My Computer | Control Panel | Printers | select the printer |
right click | Printer Properties
```

The Printer Properties page has most of the settings you made
during the setup procedure. Here is a short list of some of those
properties you'll need to know for the MCSE exam:

### GENERAL TAB

#### Separator Page
This option allows you to configure a blank page to be printed between print jobs. There are three types of separator files. They are

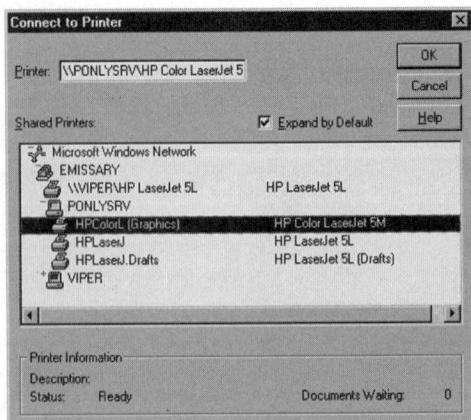

**Figure 14.8** Use the Connect to Printer screen to add a remote printer.

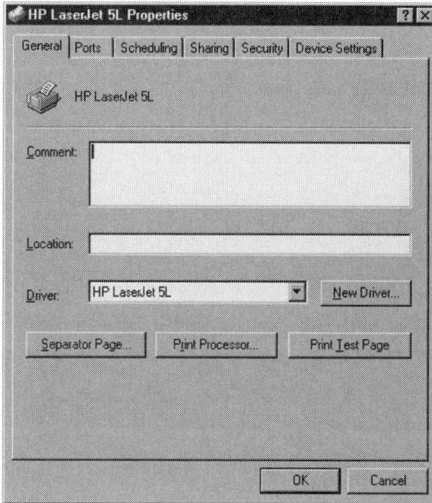

**Figure 14.9**   The Printer Properties page offers many tabs and options.

Sysprint.sep—Separates each print job with a blank page.

Pcl.sep—Separates each print job with a blank page and puts the printer in PCL mode for HP print devices.

Pscript.sep—Doesn't print a blank page between print jobs but does switch to PostScript for HP print devices.

### SCHEDULING TAB

Think of this as a way to restrict the print device much as you can control the logon hours of users. Scheduling allows you to control when the print device is in use. It also controls the queue of print jobs to the print device, giving priority to users or groups as specified. There will be several questions on the MCSE test about scheduling print jobs on network print devices. Forewarned is forearmed.

One terrific feature of scheduling, which you should know for the exam, is that you can create multiple icons for the same printer, assigning different properties for each icon. For instance, you can create an icon for Vice-Presidents, sharing it only to the Vice-Presidents group. By doing this, you can assign a higher priority to that printer. This will cause the Vice-Presidents' print jobs to print ahead of other groups, making the

VPs happy, so that the next time there is a salary review for the network administration staff . . . everyone can be happy.

Alternatively, you can create a printer icon for Large Print Jobs, configuring it to print only after business hours. By doing this, the large print jobs will not print during the day, freeing up the print device for other uses.

Remember, each icon you create for the same print device is a logical printer. To understand this better, review Figure 14.10 and the options offered.

- Available—You can exercise great control over the availability of the print device by making it available.

  - Always—Making a printer available all the time can cause traffic jams at the print spooler. Only use this option if you have low print volume on your network.

  - From specify time to specify time—As mentioned previously, you could create a Large Jobs printer icon, specifying print jobs sent through it to spool during the day and print after normal business hours.

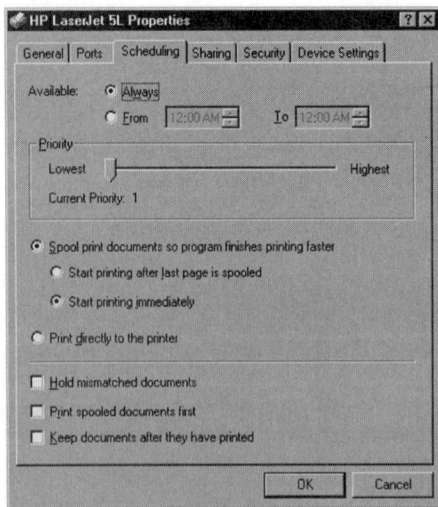

**Figure 14.10**  Schedule printer times and set printer priority from this dialog box.

- Priority—Each logical printer you configure can have a different priority. The default priority is 1, which is the lowest. The highest priority is 99. A print job with a priority of 99 will be printed before a print job with a priority of 1.

- Spool Settings—You'll want to consider this option carefully. You're options include:

  Spool print documents so program finishes printing faster— The following two choices are important to consider. Before deciding on one or the other, assess your network printing volume.

  - Start printing after last page is spooled— If you choose this option, print jobs will start printing only after the last page of the job is spooled. This is a good option to choose for large print jobs, which does not tie up the printer while the spooling is taking place.

  - Start printing immediately—With this option, print jobs will start printing after the first page is spooled. Choose this option if the printer is used primarily for smaller print jobs.

  Notice that last statement, "if the printer is designated for smaller print jobs." Planning, (there is that word again), a print strategy for your network is important. If you find large print jobs are tying up your printers, consider having two printer devices. Designate one printer for large print jobs and one for smaller and quicker print jobs.

  - Print directly to the printer—Although the print job goes through the spooler, it does not spool at all, instead it goes directly to the print device.

- There are three other options available in the Scheduling section that you should be aware of for the exam.

  Hold mismatched documents—When the print job and printer settings are not compatible.

  Print spooled documents first—Documents already spooled and waiting in the queue are given priority.

  Keep documents after they have printed—Saves a copy of all print jobs to a file on the disk.

**SHARING TAB**

You may configure and modify sharing in the Printer Properties page of the Printer. You can also restrict the printer from network access by selecting the Not Shared option.

Once printer drivers are loaded on the server, you can automatically use them from a client computer needing access to a print device. This is a feature supported by Windows 95, Windows NT Workstation, and Windows NT Server only.

The MCSE exams may ask about downloading printer drivers. Specifically, questions will focus on how to distribute printer drivers to client computers. You must understand the Windows NT concept of sharing a printer, and also how sharing enables automatic downloading of drivers to client computers.

Remember client computers can download updates of printer drivers in the same way. If, for instance, you update a printer driver on the server, the client computers who have previously downloaded the older version will automatically receive the updated version the next time they access that printer driver on the server.

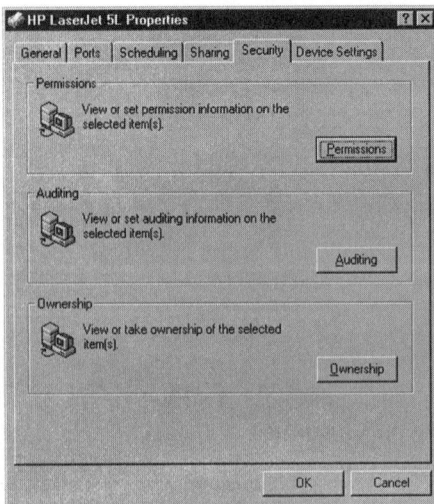

**Figure 14.11**  Access security options from the Security tab of the Printer's Property Page.

## SECURITY TAB

If configured correctly, one of the most powerful features of the Printer's Property Page is the Security section. You must know the three configurations shown in Figure 14.11.

- Permissions—From this screen you can determine which users have print and manage documents print permissions. Review the next section, Print Management, which covers this topic in more detail. To configure user rights in this area, go to:

1. Start | Settings | Printers
2. Select a printer from the screen
3. Then select File | Printer Properties | Security | Permissions
4. You can use this selection not only to give rights but also to restrict user access.

- Auditing—The auditing option will display the screen shown in Figure 14.12:

Auditing a printer allows you to track printer use and users and/or groups using a printer.

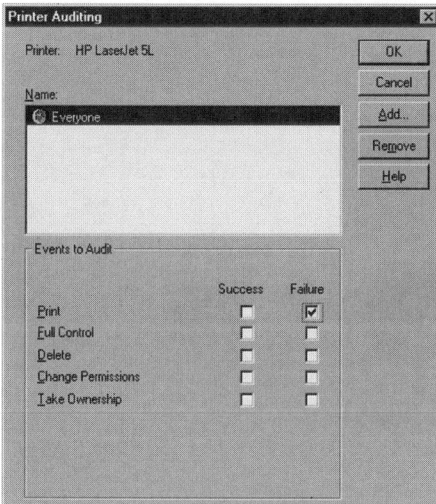

**Figure 14.12**   Setup printer auditing from this dialog box.

Remember auditing a printer is a two-step process. First select the event(s) to audit from Printer Auditing, then enable the File and Object Access option in User Manager's audit policy. See Chapter 11, "Users," for more information.

- Ownership—Literally, ownership is what this indicates. You can take ownership of the printer. Remember taking ownership requires you have the appropriate user rights. The Administrator group has the Take Ownership by default.

Review the concept of Take Ownership. Samples of the new adaptive tests for the MCSE (which you can download from the Microsoft web site) refer to this subject. It makes sense that if a sample question is about this subject one could assume Microsoft deems it a fitting subject for a future MCSE test question. Here are some other key points about ownership:

- The ownership of a printer is assigned to whomever installs it. In most cases, this is the administrator group, but not always. It could also be anyone assigned Full Control.

- Assigning ownership rights is a bit tricky. Remember the owner of something cannot give ownership to someone else. To do this, someone with Full Control rights must re-assign ownership.

- In short, don't re-assign ownership if you can avoid it. Nevertheless, for the test, you should know what ownership is, who can do it to whom, and who can't do it.

## DEVICE SETTINGS TAB

The Devices Settings page acts as a catch-all page for all the miscellaneous printer configurations. Among them, you can configure the orientation of the paper as follows:

- Landscape or Portrait
- Paper Size and Type
- Fonts
- Paper Trays Used for Printing

## Print Management

You can control each logical printer individually. Therefore, it is important to review and understand all the options available to you in the drop-down boxes as shown in Figures 14.13 and 14.14.

The first item you should note about these screens is that there is one print job in the print queue. (Although not shown in Figures 14.13 and 14.14, the print job status is noted in the lower left corner of the print window.) Also, note the document is paused.

One of the best features of printing with Windows NT is that you can stop, or pause document printing.

So if your print device jams, remember you can pause a printer using the Document drop-down menu, clear the jammed print device, and then choose resume or restart printing. These options are:

- Resume—Use this option to restart printing documents after pausing. For instance, if you paused the printer after printing page 11 of a document, Resume would start printing at page 12.

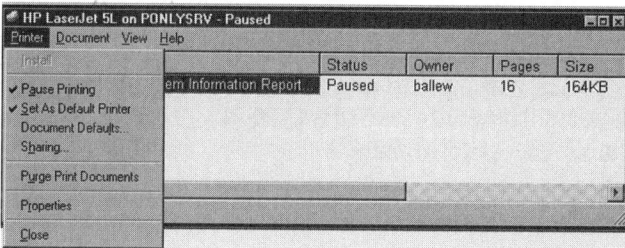

**Figure 14.13** This Printer drop-down box shows that the print job has been paused.

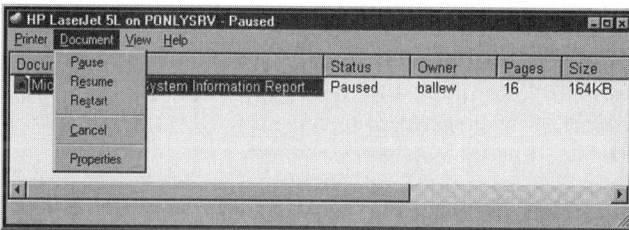

**Figure 14.14** The Document drop down box offers additional options for the selected document.

- Restart—Regardless of where the document was paused, you can use this option to start printing a document from page 1 of the document.

You can also pause printing when there are no documents in the print queue. This enables you to hold documents in the print queue until you are ready to print them.

There are numerous reasons to hold documents. For instance, suppose the default paper in the print device is 8 $1/_2$ × 11. But you are printing legal size documents on 8 $1/_2$ × 14 paper. By pausing the printer, you can change the paper and resume printing.

Documents can be paused

- individually,
- as a whole (all documents),
- or as a group (select documents).

To pause all documents, do not highlight any documents and select Pause Printing from the Printer drop-down menu. When you want to pause several documents at once, but not all documents:

- When the documents are in consecutive order, highlight the first document to be paused, hold down the <SHIFT> key, and highlight the last document to be paused. Select Pause Printing from the Document drop-down menu.

- When the documents are scattered, or not in consecutive order, highlight the first document to be paused, hold down the <CTRL> key, and highlight each document you want to pause. Select Pause Printing from the Document drop-down menu.

Notice also that you can set the printer as the default printer with the Set As Default option on the Printer menu. You can designate a printer as the default printer so all print jobs sent from a client computer always go to that printer.

Finally, notice that you can Cancel a print job and Purge Print Documents. The difference between the two is:

- Cancel is for canceling single documents in the queue. To do this, select the document and then select Cancel. Cancel a document is only offered in the Document drop-down menu.

- Purge Print Documents removes all documents from the queue. Purge is only available in the Printer drop-down menu.

In large organizations, it is common to have users regularly sending print jobs to printers. Because it impossible for these users to know if the print devices are working or not, problems can occur when the print devices break down. Print jobs sit in the queues on print servers, backlogging the computer, and using its resources. If enough print jobs are waiting, this can slow server and network performance.

In cases like this, if multiple print devices are available, you may want to consider sending the print jobs to other print devices using a process called *redirecting*, while you arrange for repairs on the broken print devices.

To send print jobs to other printers, use the following method:

1. Go to Start | Settings | Printers

2. Select the printer that is not working

3. Select Printers | Properties

4. Select Ports | Add Port

5. Select Local Port

6. Select New Port

7. Enter the UNC path to the printer you want to use temporarily, for example, \\computername\hp9

When you want to revert to the default printer, remove the new port you just added.

## Non-Windows Printing

### APPLE PRINTING

Apple computers, specifically, but not limited to Macintoshes, require the AppleTalk protocol to interface with Windows NT print networks. To enable this interface, you must install Services for Macintosh, which comes with the services utilities on Windows NT Server.

Services for Macintosh allows two things.

- Apple Computers to access printers attached to Windows NT clients
- Windows NT Computers to access Apple printers

## NOVELL NETWARE PRINTING

Microsoft Client Services for NetWare allows an individual Windows NT Workstation with Client Services for NetWare installed to access NetWare server resources.

Client Services for NetWare (CSNW) installs a Control Panel applet that allows the user to specify print options. Print options allow a user to specify certain settings regarding how NetWare will handle a print job.

- Add Form Feed—adds a form feed after each print job has printed
- Notify When Printed—notifies the user after the print job has printed
- Print Banner—prints an announcement page prior to the actual print job

More information on NetWare can be found in Chapter 20.

## UNIX PRINTING

To connect a computer using a UNIX operating system to a Windows print environment you must first create a share to the UNIX computer and install TCP/IP Printing Services. The Lpd (Line Printer Daemon) service is then installed, allowing UNIX clients to connect using the Lpr command. The UNIX computer will need to be configured with the IP address of the print server and the printer name so that TCP/IP will know where to send the print job.

### Installing TCP/IP Printing Services

To install TCP/IP Printing Services, select:

```
Start | Settings | Control Panel | Network | Services | Add |
Microsoft TCP/IP Printing
```

Each UNIX client computer must install the appropriate printer driver software. This also applies to other non Windows NT-compatible client operating systems such as MS-DOS, OS/2, Windows 3.1, and Windows for Workgroups 3.11.

## LAN MANAGER 2.X PRINTING

LAN Manager also requires each client computer to install the printer software. As a non-Windows NT system, LAN Manager can access Windows NT network printers using the net use command.

## DLC PRINTING

You should remember that DLC is a special communication protocol used by network printers that have their own network interface cards and are directly connected to the network and for mainframe connections. Some HP print devices that have their own network interface cards, particularly those called Jet Direct print devices, require DLC. Lexmark also has print devices and other devices requiring the DLC protocol.

## Troubleshooting Common Print Problems

When troubleshooting the print process, you can be certain the failure will almost always originate in one of the three areas shown in Figure 14.15. Somewhere along the path from the request to the logical printer interface to the actual hardware of the print device, a problem exists.

Here are some recommendations for troubleshooting a printer problem on the network.

**Check the cables**—Make sure the cables connecting the hardware are firmly attached. If possible, check the integrity of the entire cable by examining the length of it. Cuts in the cable can disable the communication process.

**Drivers**—It is not uncommon for a printer, that is, the software driver, to become corrupt. In this case, re-install the driver. Re-installing will probably not disrupt the system, so go ahead and do it if you're not sure of the nature of your problem. Remember to re-boot after re-installation.

**Check the printer**—Are any lights blinking on the print device? Consider turning the machine off and back on again. Sometimes a solution as simple as power-cycling the print device will solve what seems to be a baffling problem.

**Printer Diagnostics**—Some printers have their own diagnostic programs that enable you to investigate problems.

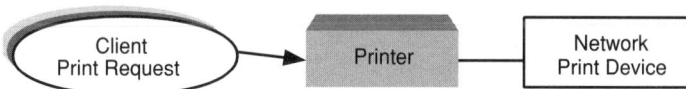

**Figure 14.15** Troubleshoot printer problems with this schematic in mind.

**System Properties**—Don't forget to check the Control Panel System Applet to see if there is an IRQ or I/O conflict with the printer.

**Are you using the correct Printer?**—Has the network changed printers or print devices recently? If so, use the Add Printer Wizard to add the printer to your computer.

The Spooler is Confused—Sometimes, due to a variety of networking factors, the spooler needs to be reset. To reset the spooler:

```
Start | Settings | Control Panel | Services | Spooler | select
Stop | then select Start
```

Stop and start the spooler service as the first course of action. If that doesn't fix the problem, try deleting the print job in progress to see if that particular print job is causing the problem. Then re-send the print job.

**Is the Printer or Print Job Paused?**—Have you recently paused the printer? If so, it will not print until you resume the printer.

**What's the priority of the printer?**—If your print job is not printing, yet other clients' print jobs are, you might consider the priority. Perhaps your printer has a low priority.

**Is the printer accessible during the day?**—If your printer has been configured for specific operating hours, you should check to make sure you're not attempting to print illegally.

**Application Problems**—Don't assume the printer or the hardware is always the problem. Try printing from a different program. If it works, the problem may be a particular software application.

**Print Device Out of Control**—Turn it off. There is no better way to test a printer problem than to simply turn the hardware off, wait, and turn it back on. Alternatively, try selecting a pause button on the print device (if there is one.)

**Re-boot**—If all else fails, sometimes rebooting is a solution. In addition to clearing the cache, rebooting sets the system back to a proper environment.

**FOR REVIEW**

- Printer drivers that work fine for Windows 3.51 or Windows 95 will not work for Windows NT 4.0.

- If the printer is to be shared with clients running Windows 3.51 and Windows 95, a separate driver for each operating system will need to be installed on the print server.

- Know the distinction between a printer and a print device:

    - The printer is the driver, or software that runs the print devices attached to a computer or network. While it is common to refer to the hardware as the printer, for purposes of the MCSE exam, it is imperative you make this distinction.

    - The print device is the physical machine, the Hewlett Packard DeskJet printer or the Epson Bubble Jet printer, for example. The print device is where you change the ribbon or ink cartridges.

- The default folder for the spooler is %systemroot%\system32\spool\printers.

- The process of managing multiple print devices is known as pooling. When multiple print devices are combined, they form a printer pool. The only requirement of a printer pool is that all the print devices must be similar.

- One terrific feature of scheduling that you should know for the exam is that you can create multiple icons for the same printer assigning different properties for each icon. Each icon you create for the same print device is a logical printer.

- Each logical printer can have a different Priority. The default priority is 1, which is the lowest. The highest priority is 99. A printer with a priority of 99 will print before a printer with a priority of 1.

- If printer drivers are updated on the print server, the clients who have previously downloaded the older version will automatically receive the updated version the next time they access that printer driver on the server.

- Auditing a printer is a two-step process. First select the event(s) to audit from Printer Auditing, then enable the File and Object Access option in User Manager's audit policy.

- If a print device jams, remember you can pause a printer using the Document drop-down menu, clear the jammed print device, and then choose resume or restart printing.

- Use the Resume option to start printing documents from the point at which it was paused. If it was paused after printing page 18 of a document, resume would start printing at page 19.

- Regardless of where the document was paused, you can use the Restart option to start printing a document from page 1 of the document.

- Apple computers, specifically, but not limited to the Macintosh, require the AppleTalk protocol to interface with Windows NT print networks.

- Client Services for NetWare (CSNW) installs a Control Panel applet that allows the user to specify print options. Print options allow a user to specify certain settings on how NetWare will handle a print job.

  - Add Form Feed adds a form feed after each print job has printed.

  - Notify When Printed notifies the user after the print job has printed.

  - Print Banner prints an announcement page prior to the actual print job.

- A UNIX computer will need to be configured with the IP address of the print server and the printer name so that TCP/IP will know where to send the print job.

- Some HP print devices that have their own network interface cards, particularly those called Jet Direct print devices, require DLC.

**FROM HERE**

Chapter 6, "Installation Overview," provides details on the HCL, or Hardware Compatibility List. Chapter 11, "Users," contains more information on Auditing and Chapter 20, "Implementing and Supporting Windows NT 4.0 Workstation in a Mixed or NetWare Environment" discusses NetWare.

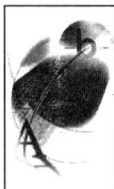

**CHAPTER 15**

# Groups

A Windows NT group is an account containing other accounts, called *members*. When a user account is a member of a group that has been assigned a right, the user can perform the activity associated with that right. Various in-common user rights establish what a group can do on the network and are further discussed in Chapter 11, "Users."

With Windows NT Workstation's User Manager, management of user accounts can be simplified by assigning a user account to a group that already has the appropriate rights, rather than assigning each individual user account the rights.

Windows NT Workstation, by default, has six built-in groups, and three special built-in groups, described below. Each built-in group has automatically been assigned a standard, reasoned set of user rights. For management and control, administrators can add user accounts to a built-in group; thereby granting a user the group's rights, or even change the standard rights for the built-in groups, if necessary.

Local groups, a particular kind of Windows NT group, can be created on a Windows NT Workstation and are discussed later in this chapter.

# Windows NT Workstation Built-In Groups

The six Windows NT Workstation built-in groups are:

- Administrators
- Backup Operators
- Guests
- Power Users
- Replicator
- Users

The Windows NT Workstation built-in groups are also shown in the bottom panel of User Manager, Figure 15.1.

## ADMINISTRATORS

The Administrators local group on a Windows NT Workstation has complete control over the workstation and is assigned a broad set of built-in rights. These rights include:

- Access this computer from network
- Back up and restore files and directories
- Change the system time
- Create a pagefile
- Debug programs
- Force shutdown from a remote system
- Increase quotas
- Increase scheduling priority

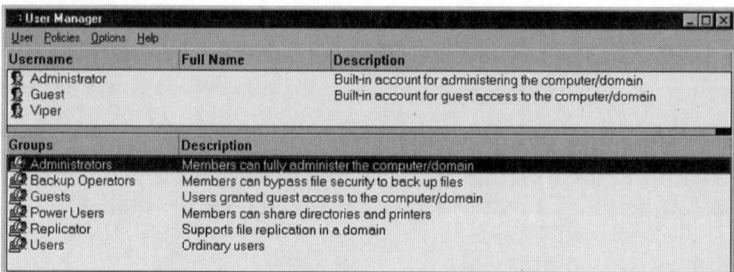

**Figure 15.1**   Windows NT Workstation has six built-in groups.

- Load and unload device drivers
- Log on locally
- Manage and view the security log
- Modify firmware environment values
- Profile single process
- Profile system performance
- Shut down the system
- Take ownership of files or other objects

## BACKUP OPERATORS

Members of the Backup Operators local group have the right to backup and restore files on the workstation. While any user can backup and restore files where the user has appropriate permissions, the Backup Operators local group can back up and restore files regardless of permissions.

## GUESTS

The Guests local group grants limited rights and allows infrequent or one-time-only users to log on to Windows NT Workstation interactively.

## POWER USERS

The Power Users local group has the ability to perform some administrative functions. These include:

- Access this computer from network
- Change the system time
- Increase scheduling priority
- Log on locally
- Profile single process
- Create, modify, delete user accounts and groups
- Add and remove users from the Guests, Power Users, and Users groups
- Share folders on the network
- Local or remote system shut down
- Manage printers

Note: The Power Users group is not available on Windows NT Server unless the operating system as been installed as a Member Server.

## REPLICATOR

The Replicator local group supports the directory replicator service. The directory replicator service automatically copies files between Windows NT computers. Actual user accounts should not be added to the Replicator group. A special user account must be created and added to the Replicator group. The directory replicator service logs on to the workstation using this special account.

## USERS

By default, each Windows NT Workstation user is a member of the Users built-in local group on that computer.

---

### TWO RIGHTS: LOG ON LOCALLY AND SHUT DOWN THE SYSTEM

By default, the Log on Locally right and the Shut Down the System right are given to the following Windows NT Workstation built in groups:

- Administrators
- Backup Operators
- Power Users
- Users

The built in Guest group also has the right to log on locally; however, by default, the Guest group does not have the right to shut down the system.

---

## Windows NT Workstation Special Built-In Groups

These three special built-in groups are not listed in User Manager because the group membership cannot be changed. The special built-in groups do appear in lists an administrator will encounter while managing the workstation.

The Windows NT Workstation special built-in groups are:

- Everyone
- Interactive
- Network

### EVERYONE

Any user logged on the workstation will be a member of the Everyone group. The Everyone group includes local (Interactive) and remote (Network) users.

### INTERACTIVE

Any user accessing the computer locally is a member of the Interactive group.

### NETWORK

Any user accessing the computer over the network is a member of the Network group.

## Windows NT Workstation Local Groups

Local groups are the only type of group that can be created on an ordinary Windows NT Workstation. Local groups are used to grant permission to access resources on the computer where the local group is created. Local groups are specific to the computer on which that local group was created. After administrative tools have been added to a workstation, administrators can use a Windows NT Workstation to do most tasks they could accomplish on the domain controllers.

### GLOBAL GROUPS

If a Windows NT Workstation belongs to a Windows NT domain, a global group from the domain can be added to a local group on the Windows NT Workstation. Global groups cannot be created with the ordinary User Manager applet on a Windows NT Workstation.

Global groups are used to organize users based on a common denominator such as a need to access a resource, location, or type of work performed.

Global groups cannot contain anything except users—no global or local groups may be included in a global group.

---

Local groups can include users and global groups (see sidebar). Local groups cannot include other local groups.

Creating a new local group account using User Manager on a Windows NT Workstation is described in Chapter 11.

A local group gives an individual user or the members of an included global group permission to do something with the resources on the network. These permissions can include accessing a printer or folder, or permission to administer various functions on the network.

## For Review

- The Administrators local group on a Windows NT Workstation has complete control over the workstation and is assigned a broad set of built-in rights.

- The Power Users group has the ability to perform some administrative functions.

- Local groups are the only type of group that can be created on an ordinary Windows NT Workstation.

## From Here

Chapter 11, "Users," discusses user rights. Chapter 12, "Profiles," and Chapter 13, "Share and NTFS Permissions," discuss user choices, preferences, and access rights.

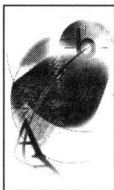

# CHAPTER 16

# Policies

Policies are useful in every organization, but especially so in the largest ones. Implementing policies allows administrators to control computer work areas and to maintain consistency where desired. A policy can apply to the whole domain or to as few as one or two users, groups, or computers. System policies are created with System Policy Editor.

User profiles are another tool used to control the work environment and are discussed in Chapter 12, "Profiles."

## System Policy Editor

As discussed in Chapter 10, "Configuring and Using Software Services," the System Policy Editor is not automatically part of Windows NT Workstation. System Policy Editor is one of the Network Administration tools that you can install from the NT Server Setup disk. Placing the System Policy Editor on the Windows NT Workstation allows the Administrator to work from a computer other than a domain controller. This is often preferable for security and convenience.

A few points to remember about the System Policy Editor:

- The policy file is saved to the Netlogon share on the PDC as `Ntconfig.Pol`
- The `Ntconfig.Pol` file is saved in `\winnt\system32\repl\import\scripts\` (This folder is shared as Netlogon)
- The \Netlogon folder should be replicated to all BDCs in the domain

Keeping policy files in this folder enables the Netlogon service to find them during logon.

- Changes made to a policy go into effect only after logoff/logon. Users must log off and back on to the system before any new policies go into effect.

## Policies and Profiles

When assessing policies and profiles, there is a hierarchy that determines which takes precedence. You should memorize the following list, which shows the order of precedence.

1. Individual System Policy
2. Group System Policy
3. Mandatory User Profile
4. Personal User Profile
5. Default User Profile

Policies override profiles. An individual system policy has greater priority over a group system policy. Within profiles, *mandatory* has priority over *personal*. Everything has priority over the default user profile.

During logon, several dynamics are at work in the background: checking the various policies and a profile and deciding which one has priority over the other. The diagram in Figure 16.1 gives a visual aid for understanding how this takes place.

In viewing this diagram, focus on the merging that takes place. Merging occurs between the profiles, the policies, and also the computer settings. To recap:

After the user is authenticated by the SAM, the user profile is applied.

Next, the `Ntconfig.pol` file is consulted to see if a user policy exists. If one exists then it is applied.

If an individual user policy does not exist, then group policies for any groups the user is a member of are applied in their order of priority.

Next, the individual computer policy is applied. If no policy exists, the default computer policy is applied.

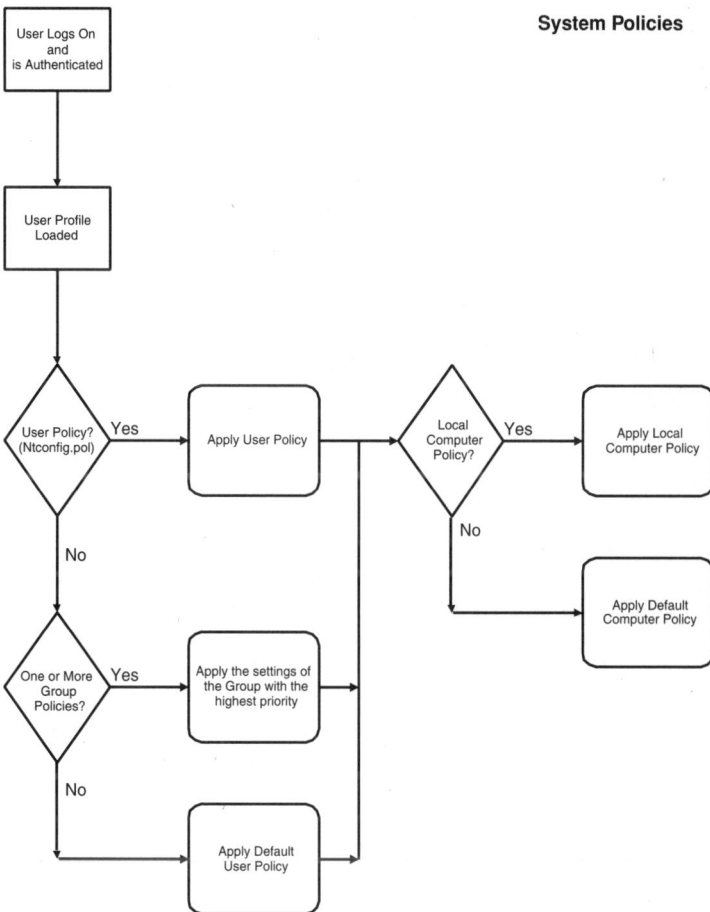

**Figure 16.1**    Flow of merging system policies during logon.

## FOR REVIEW

■ The policy file is saved to the Netlogon share on the PDC as Ntconfig.Pol

■ Changes made to policy go into effect only after logoff/logon. Users must log off and back on to the system before any new policies go into effect.

■ The order of precedence for policies and profiles is

1. Individual System Policy
2. Group System Policy
3. Mandatory User Profile
4. Personal User Profile
5. Default User Profile

■ Policies override profiles.

■ An individual system policy has greater priority over a group system policy.

■ Within profiles, mandatory has priority over personal.

■ Everything has priority over the default user profile.

## From Here

Chapter 10, "Configuring and Using Software Services," provides further discussion on the System Policy Editor. Chapter 12, "Profiles," discusses how user profiles can also be used to control the work environment.

**CHAPTER 17**

# Available Protocols

## What Is a Protocol?

Aprotocol is like a language or a special vocabulary with a group of rules that computers use to communicate with other computers on a network. If you attempt to speak exclusively in Japanese (or Russian) to ordinary folks in the United States you may not be able to communicate. Similarly, a computer attempting to use just one protocol, such as TCP/IP, with another computer that does not "know" TCP/IP, probably won't be able to communicate.

A *protocol suite* is a collection of protocols used together. It's reasonable to assume that protocols in the same suite should be compatible and possibly even cooperate with each other. One example of a protocol suite is (IPX) and (SPX), which were developed by Novell. To avoid the need to pay royalties to Novell, Microsoft created the Microsoft NWLink protocol. NWLink is completely compatible with and slightly faster than Novell's IPX/SPX suite. Microsoft is so proud of the NWLink IPX/SPX compatible protocol that Microsoft once used NWLink as the default protocol for Windows NT networks.

**TIP**
The Microsoft exam questions always refer to NWLink as NWLink IPX/SPX compatible protocol. NWLink is Microsoft's baby, and NWLink is completely able to do all the work that IPX/SPX used to do on NetWare networks. NWLink is one of the methods Microsoft uses to ease the transition for companies switching from Novell networking to Microsoft networking.

Another example of a protocol suite is TCP/IP, which includes Internet Protocol (IP) and Transmission Control Protocol (TCP) as well as many other related services. While one name would have probably been enough, the name TCP/IP rolls off the tongue so well that the compound name has stuck. The name TCP/IP also gives equal acknowledgement to the indispensable contributions of two protocol development groups who, together, created TCP and IP.

When two people do not speak in turn, and simply shout at each other simultaneously, little communication takes place. Computers, of course, have the same difficulty. So one thing that protocols must do is to define when, and under what circumstances, each computer may communicate, and when each computer may be expected by other computers to communicate. Protocols set the rules for exactly these kinds of communication interactions among computers.

Computers use several varieties of protocols. At the lowest level of the OSI reference model you'll find protocols that define how the hardware speaks to other hardware.

When you install Windows NT Workstation software on a computer connected to a network, you must choose one or more protocols to use for network communication. Until Windows NT knows what protocol (rules) to obey, no communication with other computers on the network can occur. Unlike humans, computer network protocols can easily be added or removed at any time after installation using the Windows NT Control Panel Network applet.

Your choice of protocols, and protocol binding order, is very important. Sometimes, the other computers you intend to communicate with will determine the protocol required. At other times, the choice may be left up to the network administrator. In every case, the choice must based on several factors, including protocol speed, efficiency, and availability of that protocol on other systems.

**TIP**
Sometimes special security or administrative privileges are required to
have the right to install or modify existing protocols.

One factor that makes the protocol choice easier is Windows
NT's ability to *bind*, or attach, multiple protocols to a single network interface card (NIC). When multiple protocols are in use on a
network, the computer initiating communication attempts to use
its first priority protocol. If the intended recipient computer can
understand that first protocol, it will be used. If not, each succes-
sively bound protocol is tried until a common protocol is found.

The order of protocol binding can greatly affect the performance
of a network computer. During an attempt to establish communications with another computer each protocol is tried in binding order from top to bottom. The protocol most often used, or most
important protocol, generally should be moved to the top of the
binding order list.

Although multiple protocols can be bound to the same network
card, this should only be done as necessary. Each additional protocol can slow down network performance because, as mentioned
above, each successive protocol is tried in each attempt to establish
communication. Even at the bottom of the list, additional protocols use up valuable memory and overhead.

**Figure 17.1**  Control Panel | Network applet's Bindings tab, where you can
change the binding order.

## Routable Protocols

Protocols can be broken down into two categories: those that can be routed and those that cannot. If a computer is on an isolated, free-standing network, then a non-routable protocol may be an appropriate choice. However, if the network is connected to a second network, a routable protocol must be used for communication to take place across the routed connection between networks. Routable protocols carry addressing information to indicate which network the data is coming from and going to.

Most protocols used by Windows NT are routable. Two important exceptions are Local Area Transport (LAT) protocol and NetBIOS Extended User Interface (NetBEUI) protocol, which are not routable. While LAT and NetBEUI can be used on a small network, once the network is expanded to include a router, the protocol must be switched to a routable protocol. The LAT protocol is typically used in a DEC/VAX environment.

LAT is a Digital Equipment Corporation proprietary network communication protocol. The LAT protocol is based on a relatively small known number of hosts on a local network sending small network packets at regular intervals. LAT will not work on a wide area network, as TCP/IP does.

**TIP**
The two most popular protocols for use with Microsoft networks are NetBEUI for non-routable networks and TCP/IP for routable networks.

## Frame Types

All data is transmitted in frames. A frame consists of header and data. The header typically includes such information as the source address and the destination address. The header can be organized in many ways depending on protocol and frame type.

Most protocols used by Windows NT use only one type of frame. On the other hand, NWLink uses several types. The frame type does not need to be set for other protocols; however, frame type may well need to be set in the case of NWLink. This peculiarity of the NWLink protocol is highly likely to help you answer one or more test questions.

## Transport Protocols

Transport protocols are used by Windows NT Workstation to communicate with other computers on a network. Each of these protocols can be installed via the Network applet in the Control Panel.

### MS Loopback Adapter

As discussed under Windows NT Workstation installation, one of the network card options is not even a network card—it's Microsoft's way to allow Workstation installation to proceed without a network adapter in the computer. The MS Loopback adapter is a software program that emulates a network card, so that the operating system can pretend it has an NIC and can therefore install communication protocols needed for the computer to participate in a network after a network adapter card is eventually installed.

### NETBIOS EXTENDED USER INTERFACE (NETBEUI)

NetBIOS Extended User Interface (NetBEUI) is the easiest protocol to install and use on Windows NT. It is commonly seen in small office environments of ten or fewer computers, particularly where there is not a computer-savvy staff available to handle a more complicated protocol.

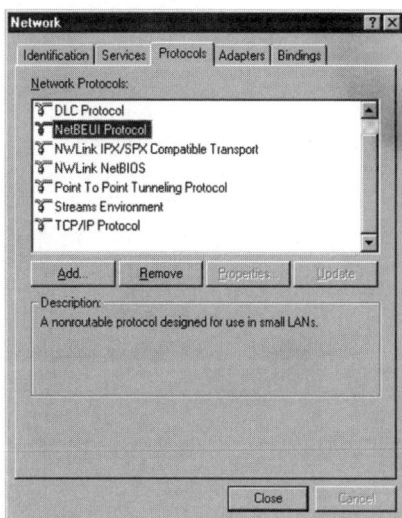

**Figure 17.2**   The Control Panel | Network applet's Protocols tab, showing the NetBEUI protocol.

NetBEUI has two great advantages: speed and ease of installation. There are no options to choose when installing NetBEUI. NetBEUI is one of the fastest protocols Windows NT Workstation can use.

The major disadvantage of NetBEUI is that it cannot be routed. Because NetBEUI cannot be routed, it is limited in its usefulness to networks of around twenty computers or fewer.

**TIP**
Use of a bridge, router, or other connection to the Internet requires the binding of an additional protocol or a replacement of NetBEUI with a protocol that is routable.

## IPX/SPX AND NWLINK IPX/SPX COMPATIBLE TRANSPORT PROTOCOL

NWLink is Microsoft's answer to Novell's IPX/SPX protocol suite. Novell uses Internetwork Packet eXchange/Sequenced Packet eXchange (IPX/SPX) in its flagship product NetWare. Microsoft's NWLink is compatible with the original IPX/SPX suite and can communicate with computers using IPX. (In fact, independent tests have shown that NWLink is faster than the original IPX/SPX). Also, when installing Client Services for NetWare (CSNW) or Gateway Services for NetWare (GSNW) on a Windows NT computer, the NWLink protocol is automatically installed if it's not already on the computer.

**TIP**
Installing NWLink IPX/SPX Compatible Transport Protocol on a Windows NT Workstation does not, by itself, allow the Windows NT Workstation to use file and print services on a Novell NetWare server. In addition to NWLink, to use native Novell file and print services, either Microsoft's Client Services for NetWare must be installed on the Workstation or the Workstation must access the NetWare server through a Windows NT server that has Gateway Services for NetWare installed.

The IPX/SPX protocol suite uses the IPX protocol at the OSI Reference Model network layer to handle connectionless transmissions. Broadcast messages are a typical example.

Sitting above IPX at the OSI Reference Model transport layer is the SPX protocol. SPX is used for connection-based transmissions. SPX handles error checking, confirmation of transmission receipt, and retransmission of flawed data.

### Service Advertising Protocol

Another member protocol of the IPX/SPX protocol suite is the Service Advertising Protocol (SAP). SAP is used by servers to announce the availability of resources. A Novell server broadcasts a SAP packet announcing the available resources every 60 seconds. SAP informs Novell client computers of what network resources are available to them. SAP resides at the session layer of the OSI Reference Model.

Because SAP broadcasts can cause network congestion, especially over larger networks, Microsoft's NWLink does not make SAP broadcasts.

### Microsoft File and Print Services for NetWare

Novell is the most popular LAN networking environment in the world. Microsoft wants to be the most popular. From that point of view, a step in the right direction is the introduction of the first Microsoft Windows NT Server into any Novell network. The more Windows NT servers the better of course, but the first one is the most significant step. In order to put its foot in the door, so to speak, Microsoft needed a smooth way to get that first server into Novell networks. Microsoft File and Print Services for NetWare (FPNW) provides an ideal vehicle to accomplish this purpose.

File and Print Services for NetWare is a Windows NT server-based utility that allows the Microsoft server to look and function like a NetWare file and print server in a Novell network. This free adjunct service is available for installation on any Windows NT server, so any Windows NT server can join and interoperate with a Novell network by sharing the Windows NT server's directories and printers.

Of course, any Microsoft NT client or Windows 95 client computers on the network will also be able to access and use Windows NT server at the same time that the server appears to Novell clients to be a Novell server. So there is no loss in service to any client by adding this service to a Novell network. In fact, it adds services by allowing Microsoft clients to access NetWare printers.

### Installing NWLink

When NWLink is installed on a Windows NT Workstation, two new entries to the network protocols list will be available: NWLink IPX/SPX Compatible Transport and NWLink NetBIOS.

Two choices required during NWLink installation are the frame type and the NetWare network number.

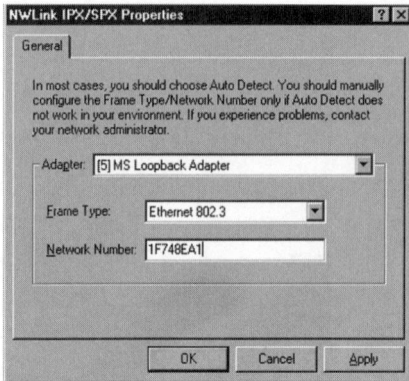

**Figure 17.3** Installing the NWLink protocol entails entering the network number and possibly setting a frame type.

### NetWare Network Number
The network number is an eight-digit hexadecimal number set by the network administrator and is associated with the network cable and all the computers on it. The number is bound to the specific network adapter on the server attached to the cable, not the Net-Ware server itself. So every NetWare server and workstation attached to the same cable must have the same network number in order to communicate.

### NetWare Frame Types
The IPX protocol allows the use of several types of frame. The frame type describes the type of headers added to data prior to transmission. Windows NT supports four frame types for IPX with Ethernet:

- 802.2
- 802.3
- Ethernet II
- Ethernet SNAP (SubNetwork Access Protocol).

Windows NT supports two frame types in a token-ring environment. An administrator can choose between token-ring and token-ring SNAP.

Initially, the frame type should be set to Auto Detect. This will automatically set the frame type and network number, the second property setting, based on traffic detected on the network when the workstation is started. If no traffic, or a mix of traffic, is detected, the frame type and network number must be manually set. The frame type must also match between all computers that wish to communicate.

> **TIP—MISMATCHED FRAME TYPES—802.3 VERSUS 802.2**
> A major cause of problems on an IPX network is mismatched frame types. Novell NetWare versions prior to 3.12 used Ethernet 802.3 as default. NetWare 3.12 and later versions use Ethernet 802.2 as default. One of the simplest ways to avoid frame type mismatches is to ensure that all NetWare servers are manually set to the same frame type. If an entire network already uses a frame type other than the default (802.2 for Windows NT), the frame type on a client computer new to the network must be set to match the network.

NWLink, in addition to its ease of connecting to NetWare servers, is faster than TCP/IP and easier to configure.

NetBEUI is fast and has no configuration, compared to NWLink. NWLink has no standardized numbering scheme like TCP/IP. While this is fine in smaller networks, connecting NWLink to a WAN environment is a major challenge.

NWLink is automatically installed, if it's not already present, whenever any of the Microsoft adjunct services for Novell NetWare is installed. Chapter 20 covers this in more detail.

## TCP/IP

The Transmission Control Protocol/Internet Protocol (TCP/IP) suite is used on the world's largest network of networks, the Internet. TCP/IP was first used on the Internet in 1983. TCP/IP is designed to work over almost all known communication media:

- Ethernet
- Token-Ring
- Telephone
- Cellular
- Microwave
- Satellite
- Short Wave Radio

The minimum required to install TCP/IP is:

- A unique IP address
- A subnet mask

**TIP**

For the examination, you should also consider a setting for default gateway to be at least an important setting, if not an essential setting. Some networks do require the default gateway to be set for Internet access to succeed—other networks do not. If a network operates as a routed environment, the default gateway is an essential setting. If the network is not routed the default gateway is not an essential setting.

**TIP**

If the exam question requires two answers, remember the IP Address and Subnet Mask must be known for the computer to participate on the network. If three answers are needed, assume you're dealing with a routed environment and add the default gateway to the list of required settings.

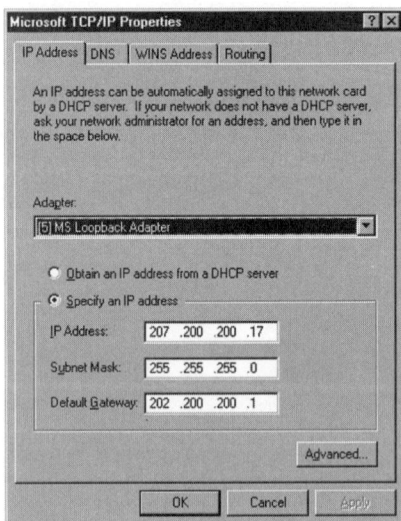

**Figure 17.4**   TCP/IP Properties IP Address tab in Windows NT.

**TIP**

The IP address is a unique address assigned to the computer. The Subnet mask breaks the IP address into a network portion and a host or node portion. If a message needs to go to a network other than the originating network, it is routed to the destination network through the default gateway.

The DNS tab allows an administrator to configure the Domain Name Service (DNS) settings for the protocol. DNS translates from Internet "wordy" names to IP numerical addresses.

**TIP**

Do not confuse Internet domains with Windows NT domains. Internet domains, such as microsoft.com, consist of a group of computers with the same subnet mask and network address portion of their IP address. On the other hand, a Windows NT domain defines a group of computers connected to a Windows NT server acting as a domain controller and controlling security for that Windows NT domain.

Windows Internet Name Services, or WINS, is a Microsoft protocol that helps track and resolve computer names on a network.

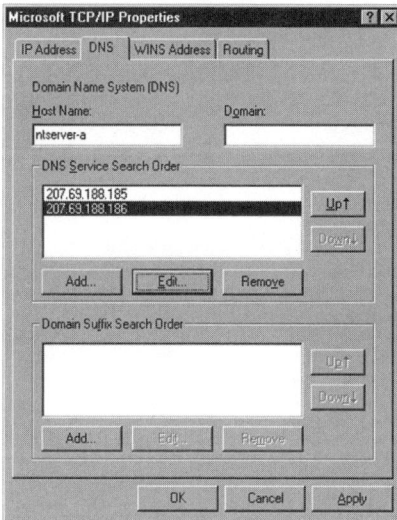

**Figure 17.5**   TCP/IP Properties DNS tab in Windows NT.

Additionally, WINS can work with DNS in resolving Internet names to computer addresses.

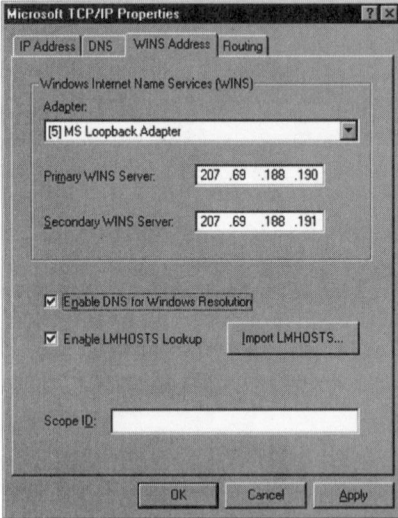

**Figure 17.6** TCP/IP WINS Address Tab in Windows NT.

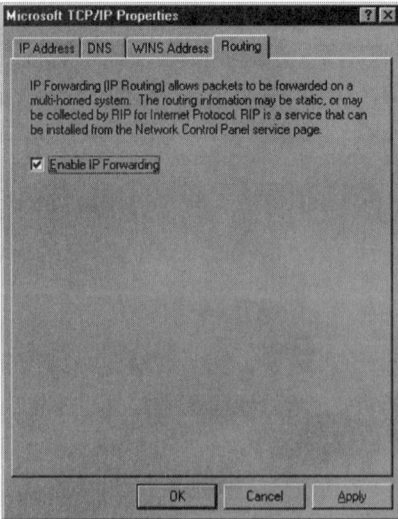

**Figure 17.7** TCP/IP Properties Routing Tab for IP Forwarding in Windows NT.

The greatest advantage of TCP/IP is its continued growth as a worldwide de facto standard. For compatibility with the Internet, many businesses are choosing TCP/IP. Additionally, the TCP/IP addressing scheme allows each computer connected to the Internet to be uniquely identified.

If a network does not need Internet access, TCP/IP may not be the protocol of choice. TCP/IP requires more configuration than other protocols Windows NT Workstation uses, either on each client computer or on a separate Dynamic Host Configuration Protocol (DHCP) server. Also, NWLink and NetBEUI both run quicker than TCP/IP.

### Simple Network Management Protocol (SNMP)

Simple Network Management Protocol (SNMP) is another Internet-based protocol that Microsoft has embraced. SNMP runs over TCP/IP and must be installed on any computer that you want to remotely monitor with Windows NT Performance Monitor. See the chapter on Monitoring for further details.

## AppleTalk Protocol

AppleTalk was developed by Apple Computer as the protocol suite for use with its Macintosh and other products. It was originally designed for use in small networks and has been expanded by Apple to handle networks as large as sixteen million nodes. Because it is included on each Macintosh computer shipped, without requiring a separate network card purchase, it has become the overwhelming leader of Apple networking. AppleTalk provides stability and reliable delivery through the AppleTalk transaction protocol (ATP) located at the OSI Reference Model Transport Layer. ATP employs socket-to-socket transmissions, requiring both a transaction request and a transaction response.

The default zone must be set when using AppleTalk. AppleTalk networks are divided into zones. Zones are logical divisions of network resources and each zone has a name.

AppleTalk is a required protocol if Macintosh computers are to be included on a network. Client Services for Macintosh must be installed to allow Macintosh computers to share files and printers with Windows NT computers. AppleTalk is also required for Windows NT computers to print to any Apple print device.

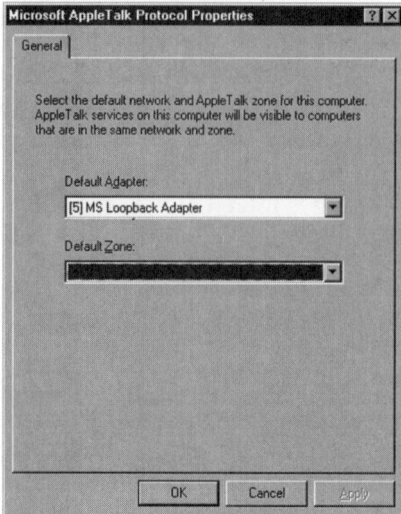

**Figure 17.8** AppleTalk Configuration in Windows NT.

However, AppleTalk is slow. At 230.4 Kbps, AppleTalk is rarely used as a primary protocol in larger networks.

## Data Link Control (DLC) Protocol

Data Link Control (DLC) protocol allows Windows NT to communicate with some older IBM mainframes and is used for direct network printing on some Hewlett Packard (HP) and Lexmark print devices with their own network interface cards. Newer HP print devices use TCP/IP to communicate.

There are no parameters to be set when installing DLC.

DLC is not routable, making it the third non-routable protocol available on a Windows NT network. (Reminder: The other two non-routable protocols are NetBEUI and LAT. Please remember these three protocols in a special, warm part of your heart.)

The only advantage of using the DLC protocol is allowing a computer to communicate with an already installed IBM mainframe or an HP or Lexmark print device connected directly to the network with its own network adapter.

## STREAMS

The STREAMS Environment protocol enables transport drivers developed in the STREAMS environment to port to Windows NT. This protocol is not used unless you are connecting a Windows NT network to a UNIX computer running STREAMS.

## Dial-up Protocols

### Serial Line Internet Protocol (SLIP) and Point-to-Point Protocol (PPP)

When a user is remotely dialing in to the network, a dial-up protocol is used. Serial Line Internet Protocol (SLIP) and Point-to-Point Protocol (PPP) are both dial-up protocols. SLIP is the older and more primitive of the two protocols. PPP offers additional error checking, security, and other features.

SLIP does not provide an automatic IP address number for TCP/IP applications to use in interacting on the Internet. The newer PPP protocol can provide an automatic IP address upon connection to the Internet, which allows TCP/IP applications (such as Web browsers or WHOIS service) to interact with other Internet connected computers.

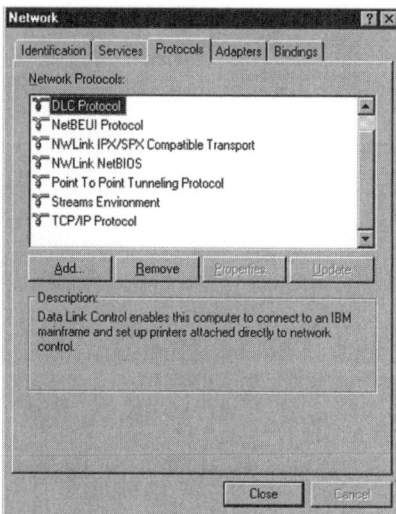

**Figure 17.9**  The Control Panel Network applet's Protocols tab, showing the DLC protocol.

### Point-to-Point Tunneling Protocol (PPTP)

Windows NT also offers the Point-to-Point Tunneling Protocol (PPTP). PPTP is a method that allows the encrypted passage of a transport protocol, such as TCP/IP or NetBEUI, over the Internet. This is accomplished by encrypting the original packet, then treating it as the data in a larger TCP/IP packet.

## Other Protocols

### X.25

X.25 is an older, standard packet-switched network communications protocol used for WANs. Some organizations use the X.25 protocol over an elaborate worldwide network and packet forwarding nodes called Data Communications Equipment nodes (DCEs). After the X.25 protocol has been installed, a Windows NT Workstation can use the X.25 protocol either by creating a dial-up networking connection to an X.25 Packet Assembler/Dissembler (PAD) service or by adding an X.25 hardware network card and connecting a cable directly from an X.25 network.

### Routing Information Protocol (RIP)

Routing Information Protocol (RIP) is a network layer protocol used to route network traffic. Each routing device keeps a routing table and broadcasts the table at regular intervals. Other routing devices listen for other routing table broadcasts and update their own tables. RIP uses these tables to choose a path when routing data from source to destination.

RIP protocol updating is performed using a vector distance algorithm to choose optimum routes. RIP is used with both NetWare and in the TCP/IP protocol suite.

### Server Message Block (SMB) Protocol

The Server Message Block (SMB) Protocol operates at the OSI Reference Model Application Layer. SMB is characterized by a block of data that contains client-server requests or responses. The SMB protocol is used in all areas of Microsoft network communication and was developed originally by Microsoft, Intel, and IBM.

### The Network File System (NFS) Protocol

The Network File System (NFS) protocol was developed by SUN Microsystems and is used primarily in UNIX computers. UNIX computers commonly share files using NFS on TCP/IP networks. Using NFS may become necessary on a Windows NT network if a UNIX workstation has shared files that must be accessed by Windows NT computers or if UNIX workstations must have access to shared files on a Windows NT computer.

## FOR REVIEW

- For two computers to communicate, they must share at least one protocol.

- Windows NT can bind multiple protocols to a single network adapter.

- Binding order affects the order that bound protocols are tried in an attempt to find a common protocol between two computers before communication can occur.

- NWLink is routable and faster than TCP/IP.

- The network number and frame type must match between two computers before communications using NWLink can occur.

- NWLink is needed for communications with a NetWare server.

- TCP/IP is the primary protocol suite used on the Internet.

- While slower and more complex to configure, TCP/IP offers a wealth of optional settings.

- DHCP can be used to centralize and ease configuration of workstations.

- DNS and WINS are used to allow the use of human-friendly text addresses rather than IP addresses.

## From Here

Chapter 18, "Binding Order," reviews binding order issues, and both Chapter 19, "Mixing and Matching Resource Access," and Chapter 20, "Implementing and Supporting Windows NT 4.0 Workstation in a Mixed or NetWare Environment," discuss topics also covered here. Chapter 21, "Dial-up Networking," also goes into more detail on SLIP and PPP, etc.

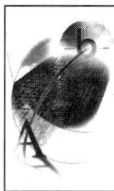

# Binding Order

There is at least one question on the Windows NT exam that tests your understanding of binding order. This chapter prepares you by reviewing what you'll need to know about protocol binding order for the exam, and a little bit more.

First, network communication protocols are installed and adjusted using the Control Panel Network applet, as shown in Figure 18.1.

From the same applet, on the Bindings tab, the protocol binding order may be adjusted as shown in Figure 18.2. You may move them up or down.

Because it is the initiating computer that selects the communication protocol in a client-server pair, it is important that Windows NT Workstation computers in client-server networks have their binding order set in the most beneficial fashion. Otherwise, users could wait needlessly every time they make an over-the-net resource request.

Why would users wait unnecessarily if the binding order is less than optimal? Because each time the computer attempts to set up a communication session with another computer, each available protocol is tried in the binding order from top to bottom. This means that each protocol higher in the binding order must be tried, fail, and be abandoned before the correct, lower protocol is finally tried.

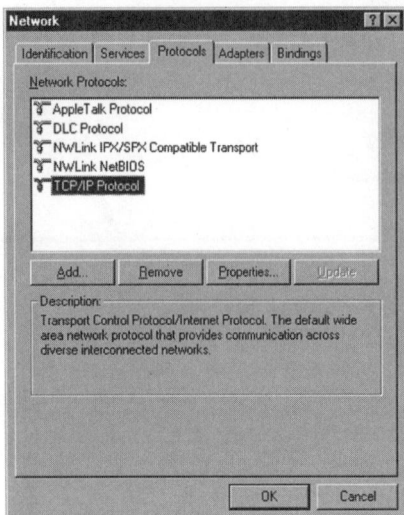

**Figure 18.1**   Use the Network applet in Control Panel to install protocols.

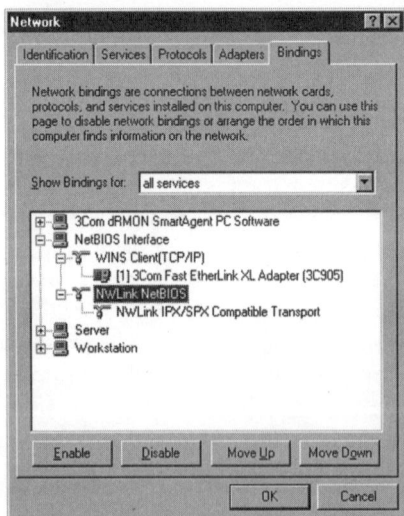

**Figure 18.2**   Use the Network applet in Control Panel to review and adjust binding order.

Generally, the more a protocol is used on a network, the higher in the binding order sequence it should appear. Protocols that are little used on the network should generally appear at or near the end of the protocol binding order, and the protocol that is most used should appear first in the protocol binding order.

## A SCENARIO WITH BINDING ORDER

Let's say you have a single computer with four SCSI hard drives of 2 gigabytes each. Each hard drive is formatted with a 2-gigabyte FAT partition. There are some very large files on the computer, and these files must be shared and available on the network.

The computer has 32 MB of RAM. The Pagefile is on the boot partition.

Each workstation on the network uses multiple communication protocols. The computer is responding slower than it should.

## REQUIRED RESULTS

Improve the speed/performance of the computer.

## OPTIONAL RESULTS

Faster paging
Faster network access

## PROPOSED SOLUTION

A) Configure the four hard drives so that one is for the boot/system partition, and the other three drives are a large stripe set. Put the large shared files on the stripe set.
B) Move the page file off the boot partition.
C) Move the most-used protocol to the bottom of the binding order list.

## ANALYSIS

Solution A satisfies the required result by creating the fastest possible hard drive response time with a stripe set.

Solution B speeds up paging.

Solution C does not work. Moving the most used protocol to the bottom of the binding order ensures that network access from this computer will be slower, not faster.

## FOR REVIEW

- Move the primary protocol to the top of the binding order for each Workstation.

- Move more important protocols up in the binding order.

- Never move the most-used protocol to the bottom of the binding order.

## From Here

Chapter 19, "Mixing and Matching Resource Access," and Chapter 20, "Implementing and Supporting Windows NT 4.0 Workstation in a Mixed or NetWare Environment," discuss protocol issues. Chapter 17 covers the protocols tested on the Windows NT exam.

# Mixing and Matching Resource Access

Transmission Control Protocol/Internet Protocol (TCP/IP) is a suite of networking protocols. A TCP/IP network allows data exchanges to occur between Windows NT computers, other Microsoft computers, and computers using other operating systems such as UNIX.

When running the TCP/IP protocol suite on a Windows NT Workstation, there a few topics to be familiar with:

TCP/IP requirements

Name Resolution Services

Peer Web Services

## TCP/IP Requirements

When configuring a Windows NT Workstation with TCP/IP on a routed network, the following items are required:

- IP address—a unique number that identifies the workstation on the TCP/IP network. The address is represented by four numbers separated by dots. This address identifies the workstation and the network where the workstation is located.

- Subnet Masks—provides the information necessary to identify, from an IP address, the network ID and the host computer ID.

- Default gateway—a router that forwards non-local messages.

If the Windows NT Workstation is on a non-routed network, only the IP address and the subnet mask will be required for configuration.

## DYNAMIC HOST CONFIGURATION PROTOCOL (DHCP)

Microsoft DHCP dynamically assigns IP addresses to computers on the network. It is a Windows NT Server-based service. With DHCP, an administrator does not have to manually configure IP addresses for each computer.

## Name Resolution Services

Name resolution services provide a way for computer names to be matched to IP addresses and IP addresses to be matched with computer names.

### NETBIOS

NetBIOS is the naming convention used by Windows NT. NetBIOS performs a computer name to IP address translation.

### Windows Internet Name Service (WINS)

For those networks with a WINS server, the Windows Internet Name Service resolves NetBIOS computer names to IP addresses.

The WINS server cannot directly perform name resolution for a non-Microsoft operating system, such as UNIX.

An LMHOSTS file maps IP addresses to NetBIOS computer names and will be consulted if there is no WINS server available.

### DOMAIN NAME SYSTEM (DNS)

DNS is the naming convention used by TCP/IP. DNS resolves host names to IP addresses.

A HOSTS file provides a static configuration for use when DNS is unavailable.

## Peer Web Services

Windows NT Workstation 4.0 includes Peer Web Services, which can be used to publish a test bed of web pages. Peer Web Services can also be used for Web application development.

Figure 19.1 shows the options available when installing Peer Web Services. A few of these options are:

- World Wide Web Service
- Gopher Service
- FTP Service

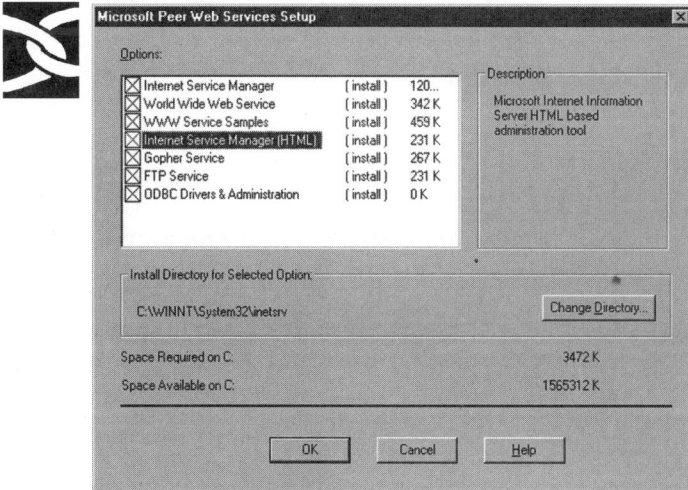

**Figure 19.1**  Customize Peer Web Services during Setup.

**FOR REVIEW**

- When configuring a Windows NT Workstation with TCP/IP on a routed network, the following items are required:

  IP address

  Subnet Masks

  Default gateway

- If the Windows NT Workstation is on a non-routed network, only the IP address and the subnet mask will be required for configuration.

- DHCP dynamically assigns IP addresses to computers on the network.

- WINS resolves NetBIOS computer names to IP addresses.

- DNS resolves host names to IP addresses.

- If static name resolution files are used:

  - LMHOSTS for WINS
  - HOSTS for DNS
- FTP Service can be installed as a component of Peer Web Services.

## From Here

Chapter 20, "Implementing and Supporting Windows NT 4.0 Workstation in a Mixed or NetWare Environment," talks about Novell NetWare, and Chapter 21, "Dial-up Networking," covers RAS and DUN.

# Implementing and Supporting Windows NT 4.0 Workstation in a Mixed or NetWare Environment

## Windows NT and NetWare

Novell NetWare is the leading competitor to Windows NT as a local area networking solution. Microsoft has made an intense effort to ensure compatibility with existing installations of NetWare and to design simple methods to migrate from NetWare to Windows NT.

Microsoft includes several features in Windows NT Workstation to improve compatibility with NetWare. These include the Microsoft NWLink IPX/SPX compatible transport protocol and Microsoft Client Services for NetWare. Windows NT Workstation computers can also make use of NetWare services through Microsoft Gateway Services for NetWare, which is included with Windows NT Server.

## NetWare Directory Services (NDS) or Bindery?

Before release of NetWare 4.0, NetWare used a bindery to store security and resource information. The bindery was located on each NetWare server. A user needing access to resources on NetWare would specify the NetWare server on which the resource resided and a user account and password valid for that resource.

Novell changed this with the release of NetWare 4.0. NetWare 4.0 uses NetWare Directory Services (NDS) to handle security similarly to Windows NT Domains by having security and resource information for all computers in a group (a group is a tree in NetWare terms) stored in one location. A user needing access to resources with NDS specifies the tree and the context (context is a location within the tree) instead of a specific server and a valid user account and password for the tree and context.

NetWare 4.x servers can run in bindery emulation mode. Bindery emulation mode was required for NetWare servers to be accessible to previous versions of Windows NT. Many older programs designed around older versions of NetWare require bindery emulation mode. Bindery emulation mode is the default for NetWare 4.x servers.

By changing the Bindery Context setting on the NetWare server to " ", bindery emulation may be disabled. Changing the Bindery Context setting is done from the console prompt. Leaving bindery emulation mode enabled sets a fixed context within the NDS tree. This setting allows applications designed for the older bindery mode to function properly. However, this also disallows browsing the NDS tree. By default, Windows NT computers will connect to NetWare servers in bindery emulation mode if possible. However, if no programs requiring bindery emulation are in use, disabling emulation mode allows Windows NT computers to navigate the NDS tree structure freely.

### NWLINK PROTOCOL

NWLink is Microsoft's improvement on Novell's very successful IPX/SPX protocol suite. Novell uses IPX/SPX in its flagship product, NetWare. NWLink is a Transport Driver Interface (TDI) compliant transport protocol, and NWLink is 100% compatible with IPX. Microsoft went to great lengths to ensure complete compatibility. (In fact, independent tests have shown that NWLink is faster than the original IPX/SPX). When you install Microsoft Client Services for NetWare or Microsoft Gateway Services for NetWare, the NWLink protocol is automatically installed—if NWLink is not already installed on the client or server computer.

### TIP

Installation of NWLink IPX/SPX Compatible Transport alone on a Windows NT Workstation does not allow use of file and print services on a Novell NetWare server. Either Microsoft Client Services for NetWare must also be installed on the Windows NT Workstation, or it must access the NetWare server via an NT server with Microsoft Gateway Services for NetWare installed.

NWLink is not limited to Microsoft networks that need to connect to NetWare servers. In fact, NWLink can be used on networks with no Novell resources on them at all. NWLink has several advantages over either NetBEUI or TCP/IP. NWLink is routable, unlike NetBEUI, allowing NWLink to be used in larger networks where NetBEUI would be impractical. The current release of NWLink is also somewhat faster than TCP/IP for Windows NT computers, and administration of NWLink is significantly easier than TCP/IP.

Many network administrators use NWLink as a primary transport protocol, binding TCP/IP as a second protocol only on computers that access the Internet. This security measure may help limit the exposure a firm's computers have to intrusion risks from the Internet onto the internal network.

When NWLink is installed, Windows NT Workstation adds two entries to the network protocols list, as shown in Figure 20.1; one for NWLink IPX/SPX Compatible Transport, the other for NWLink NetBIOS. The NWLink NetBIOS entry is for the OSI reference model Session layer NetBIOS that runs on top of the NWLink transport. NWLink automatically runs NetBIOS on top of IPX/SPX at the OSI session and presentation layers.

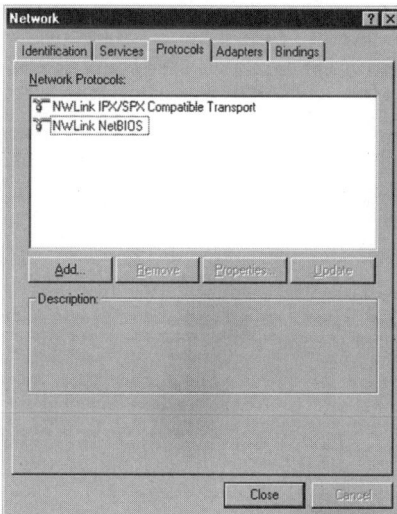

**Figure 20.1** Windows NT Network Control Panel.

In the Windows NT Control Panel Network applet, some protocols have configurable properties and others do not. NWLink IPX/SPX Compatible Transport has configurable properties. Two choices an administrator must make during installation are the frame type and the Novell network number, as shown in Figure 20.2.

The IPX protocol uses several frame types. The frame type specifies the kind of headers added to data prior to transmission. Windows NT supports four frame types for IPX with Ethernet.

- IEEE 802.2
- IEEE 802.3
- Ethernet II
- Ethernet SNAP (SubNetwork Access Protocol)

In a Token Ring environment, an administrator can choose between Token Ring and Token Ring SNAP.

Novell NetWare versions before 3.12 used Ethernet 802.3 as default. NetWare 3.12 and later versions use Ethernet 802.2 as default.

Some network interface cards may be able to handle only a limited number of frame types. This is particularly true with older network cards.

The network number is an eight-digit hexadecimal number set by the network administrator. The network number is associated with the network cable and all the computers connected to the network. The network number is bound to one specific network

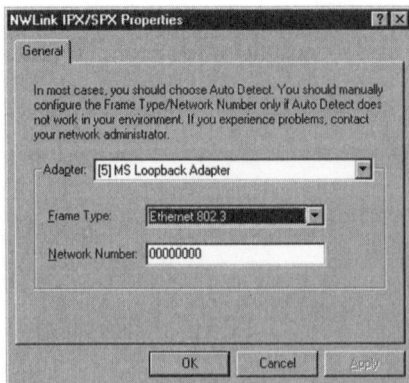

**Figure 20.2** Supply the frame type and network number on the NWLink IPX/SPX Properties tab.

adapter that is attached to the network cable, not the NetWare server. So in order to communicate, every NetWare server and every Windows NT Workstation attached to the network must have the same network number associated with each network adapter card attached to the cable for them.

Initially, the frame type should usually be set to Auto Detect. This allows Windows NT to automatically set the frame type and the network number based on the traffic detected on the network when the workstation is started. If no traffic or a mix of traffic is detected, the frame type and network number must be set manually. The frame type must match on all computers that wish to communicate.

**TIP**

Networks including NetWare services frequently have problems with default frame types. Different NetWare versions have different default frame types. To prevent or minimize problems, ensure that all NetWare servers are set to the same frame type, or ensure that all NetWare servers have multiple frame types bound to each network adapter card.

The administrator can also manually configure Windows NT Workstation to use multiple frame types if a mix of frame types is being used on the network.

If the frame type is manually set, the network number can be left to its default of zero. This allows Windows NT to detect the network number automatically. If the default network number of zero is not used, then the administrator must ensure that the network number matches the network number for the network adapter card on the server the workstation needs to access.

**FOR REVIEW**

- Microsoft's NWLink protocol is compatible with Novell NetWare's IPX/SPX protocol suite.

- The frame type used must be consistent on all computers on the network.

- Not all frame types are available on all network adapters.

- NetWare 3.11 and earlier use Ethernet 802.3 frames as default.

- NetWare 3.12 and later use Ethernet 802.2 frames as default.

- The network numbers assigned to network adapter cards of communicating computers must match.

## RIP and SAP

NWLink uses RIP and SAP in the same way that IPX does—recall that NWLink is 100% compatible with the IPX/SPX protocol suite.

Routing Information Protocol (RIP) is the default protocol for routing information to be exchanged between routers on an IPX protocol network. Each router on the network broadcasts the contents of its routing table every 60 seconds. Routers update their routing tables based on the information received in broadcasts from neighboring routers. Routers use their routing tables to ascertain the best route to forward data.

Service Advertising Protocol (SAP) is used by servers to let clients know of their presence. Servers automatically announce their available services (such as attached print devices) by broadcast every 60 seconds.

Both RIP and SAP can contribute to broadcast storms. An administrator should be wary of the NWLink protocol if the network is vulnerable to broadcast storms.

## Client Services for NetWare

Windows NT Workstation computers can access file and print resources of Novell NetWare networks as easily as any other client operating system. Two methods of access are available.

- Windows NT Server running Microsoft Gateway Services for NetWare
- Client Services for NetWare installed on the Windows NT Workstation

Microsoft Client Services for NetWare allows an individual Windows NT Workstation with Client Services for NetWare installed to access NetWare server resources without any additional software installed on the Windows NT Server or the Workstation.

NetWare file and print services are accessed in the same manner as resources on Microsoft Windows-based systems. This is accomplished through Client Services for NetWare acting as a Transport Driver Interface (TDI)-complaint NetWare compatible redirector that interfaces with NWLink at the Transport layer. NWLink then interfaces with NDIS complaint network adapter drivers completing the journey down the OSI model to the physical layer.

Client Services for NetWare requires NWLink as a transport protocol and installs NWLink if it is not already present before Client Services for NetWare is installed. The Workstation service on the client computer must also be active for Client Services for NetWare to operate, just as the Workstation service is required for any network service request to be sent from a client computer to a server.

In order to access resources controlled by user level security on the NetWare server, at each logon to Windows NT, the Windows NT Workstation user provides a user account and password that is valid on the NetWare server. Client Services for NetWare can be installed during installation of Windows NT Workstation from the Services screen.

After Windows NT Workstation installation, Client Services for NetWare can always be installed by:

1. Opening the Control Panel Network Applet

2. Choosing the Services tab

3. Selecting Add

4. Choosing Client Services for NetWare from the list

5. Shutting Down and Restarting Windows NT

On restart, a user may be able to use NetWare services immediately. The default settings of no preferred server and Auto Frame Detection attach the user to the first available pre-NetWare 4.*x* server or to a NetWare 4.*x* server using bindery emulation mode. If the user has an account on the NetWare server that matches the user's Windows NT user account in name and password, the user

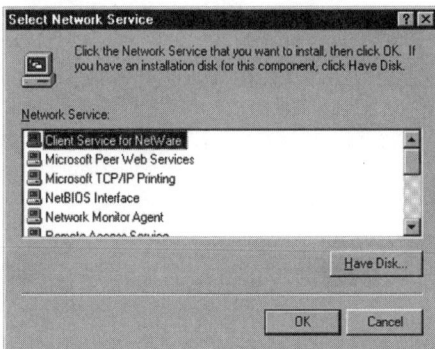

**Figure 20.3**  Network Control Panel Applet, Add Services pop-up.

will have access to the NetWare server without providing further information. Otherwise, the user is presented with an additional logon dialog box after the Windows NT login screen.

The user must then specify either the server or the tree and context of the resource they wish to access. If the user is logging into a
NetWare 3.*x* server (or a NetWare 4.*x* server running in bindery emulation mode) they should choose the Preferred server radio button
and specify the server that contains their user account. If the user is
attempting to log on to NetWare 4.*x*, they should specify a tree and
context.

Client Services for NetWare installs a control panel applet, which
allows the user to specify:

- Preferred Server or Default Tree and Context
- Print Options
- Optional running of the NetWare login script

Specifying a preferred Server or Default Tree will cause Windows
NT to attempt to connect the user to the specified server or tree
first. If a user does not specify one, Windows NT will attempt to
connect the user to the nearest server or tree.

**Figure 20.4** Control Panel with the Client Services for NetWare (CSNW)
applet in the top row.

Print options allow the user to specify several settings on how NetWare will treat a printout. "Add Form Feed" will add a form feed after each page printed. This is needed on some printers to cause the page to be ejected. "Notify when printed" will notify the user after the job has been printed. "Print Banner" will print an announcement page prior to the actual job.

The user can also optionally run the NetWare login script associated with the user account specified for logging into the NetWare server.

## FOR REVIEW

- Client Services for NetWare allows a Windows NT Workstation to access file and print resources on a NetWare server.

- NWLink and the Workstation service must be installed for Client Services for NetWare to function.

- A valid NetWare user account and password must be provided before use of NetWare resources.

- Printing to a NetWare printer is identical as printing to a Windows printer.

- No software needs to be installed at the NetWare or Windows servers.

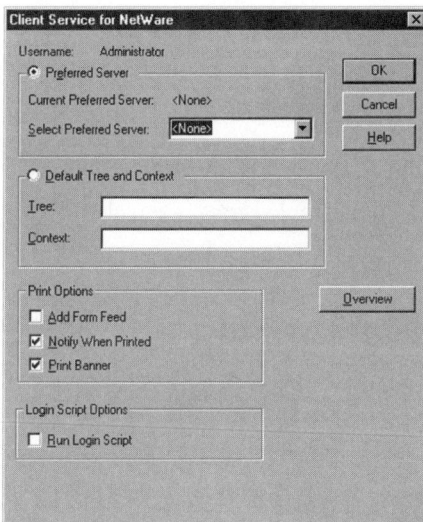

**Figure 20.5**  Client Services for NetWare applet.

## Gateway Services for NetWare

Gateway Services for NetWare is an easy method for Windows NT networks to allow Windows NT Workstation clients access to NetWare resources. After Gateway Services for NetWare is installed and configured on a Windows NT Server, NetWare resources appear to Microsoft clients as ordinary shares on the Windows NT Server computer.

After Gateway Services for NetWare is installed on a server, a Windows NT Workstation user on the network simply needs to browse the Network Neighborhood to that Windows NT Server to see and access the shared NetWare resource(s). After Gateway Services for NetWare is installed, printing to a NetWare printer is the same as printing to a Windows network printer.

Gateway Services for NetWare requirement that each shared resource must be set up in a formal share by the Windows NT Server administrator can be a limitation. On a large network, this may become burdensome. Also, if the Windows NT Server with Gateway Services for NetWare is out of service for any reason, all Windows users will be unable to access NetWare resources unless they also have Client Services for NetWare installed and configured on their local workstations.

### Gateway Services for NetWare versus Client Services for NetWare

The primary advantage of Gateway Services for NetWare over the use of Client Services for NetWare in a network is the centralization of control and ease of administration. Gateway Services for NetWare requires installation on only a single server. Each client computer that wishes access to NetWare resources needs only to have network access to the Windows NT Server with Gateway Services

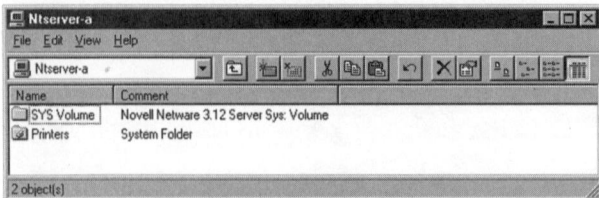

**Figure 20.6** Network neighborhood with an available Gateway Services for NetWare share.

for NetWare. This does not require NWLink to be installed on the client computers because they can access the Windows NT Server for all their NetWare resource needs.

The Windows NT Server that Gateway Services for NetWare is installed on does have an additional load. If only a small number of Microsoft clients need access to NetWare resources, having Client Services for NetWare on a few specific client computers rather than Gateway Services for NetWare may be warranted.

Another consideration is access security. Gateway Services for NetWare uses Windows NT share security to determine access to NetWare resources. Client Services for NetWare relies on NetWare security to limit access to NetWare resources.

## FOR REVIEW

- NWLink must be installed on any computer that has Client Services for NetWare or Gateway Services for NetWare installed.

- If Client Services for NetWare is used, it must be installed on all Windows NT Workstations requiring access to NetWare resources.

- Client Services for NetWare requires the login to a NetWare server, but otherwise file and print resource access is treated the same as if the resources where on the Microsoft network.

- If Gateway Services for NetWare is used, it must be installed only on the Windows NT Server that will act as the gateway to the NetWare server where needed resources reside.

- Accessing file and print resources through Gateway Services for NetWare is the same as accessing resources through a network share.

- Gateway Services for NetWare does not require any software to be installed on client workstations.

## From Here

Chapter 21, discusses dial-up networking and remote access services, Chapter 17 covered network protocols and Chapter 18 discusses protocol binding order.

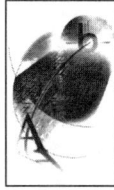

# Dial-Up Networking

The Windows NT Remote Access Server (RAS) allows users to dial into a remote network using modems and telephone lines. The RAS acts as a gateway giving the remote workstation user access to network resources as though directly wired to the network. The client side of RAS is called Dial-Up Networking (DUN). This chapter covers the installation and configuration of both RAS and DUN.

## REMOTE ACCESS SERVER AND DIAL-UP NETWORKING

RAS allows organizations to use the public telephone system, including digital services such as ISDN, X.25, and the Internet to extend networks.

Remote clients use DUN to connect to the network as though they were directly cabled to it. RAS and DUN support Windows NT security features, several protocols and WAN connections.

## Modem

Windows NT often detects installed modems. Modems may also be manually installed using the Modem applet in Control Panel. RAS uses standard modem connections over the telephone lines to establish communication between

RAS and the client. In addition, DUN can also be used to connect to an Internet Service Provider (ISP).

ISDN (Integrated Services Digital Network) is a special kind of telephone service using regular telephone wires. ISDN is much faster than the regular telephone system. In order to use an ISDN connection, special digital equipment must be used rather than ordinary analog equipment.

## X.25

X.25 uses a packet-switching protocol for transmitting data. DUN clients can access the X.25 network using an X.25 packet assembler/disassembler (PAD) and the telephone number of the PAD service. RAS provides access in one of two ways:

If the operating system is Windows NT or Windows 95, then a PAD is automatically installed. If the network is Windows NT only, then an X.25 smart card may be used instead.

## Point-to-Point Tunneling Protocol

The Point-to-Point Tunneling Protocol (PPTP) allows the use of the Internet to securely access a remote network. PPTP allows the use of IP, IPX, or NetBEUI over a TCP/IP network. It does this by encapsulating the data. PPTP also provides for data encryption.

The exam will expect you to recall these three protocols available with PPTP.

- TCP/IP
- NetBEUI
- IPX

The biggest advantages of using PPTP are improved security, lower costs, and administrative time involved in providing for remote access. Because the Internet is used, modems are required only for some remote workstations. In addition, dedicated leased lines are not needed for a secure connection. Less hardware means less time spent managing access.

### WAN CONNECTION PROTOCOLS

RAS supports two types of protocols, LAN and WAN protocols. LAN-based protocols are TCP/IP, IPX/SPX, and NetBEUI. WAN, or remote access, protocols are PPP, SLIP and Microsoft RAS protocol.

### Serial Line Internet Protocol (SLIP)

SLIP was first developed in 1984 to provide TCP/IP access over slow serial connections. SLIP is unable to use DHCP or WINS, and it only supports TCP/IP—preventing the use of other protocols. SLIP transmits authentication information such as username and password in clear text. Windows NT RAS server cannot act as a SLIP server, only as a SLIP client.

### Point-to-Point Protocol (PPP)

PPP is a considerable improvement over SLIP. It allows the use of DHCP and WINS and supports several protocols. In Windows NT 4.0, PPP supports TCP/IP, IPX, and NetBEUI. The big advantage PPP has over SLIP that the Microsoft exams focus on, is that PPP is typically configured for the PPP server (often an Internet Service Provider) to supply a temporary IP address to the dial-in client computer. SLIP cannot pass an IP address assignment from the PPP server to a remote dial-in client computer.

When RAS is installed, it binds to the protocols already installed on the server. If needed, additional protocols can be added. Each protocol is individually configured.

### Microsoft RAS Protocol

Older versions of RAS only supported connections from clients using NetBEUI as the protocol. Currently, the Microsoft RAS protocol provides a gateway to access network resources running any of the three supported protocols.

#### Gateways

RAS acts as a NetBIOS network gateway. It provides access to network resources using NetBIOS. RAS also has the ability to act as an IP or IPX router to link networks—both LANs and WANs.

#### RAS INSTALLATION

RAS can be installed on Windows NT 4.0 Server or Windows NT 4.0 Workstation. There is also a version that will run on Windows 95. The minimum hardware requirements to install Windows NT RAS are:

A network adapter card

One or more modems

Appropriate ISDN equipment if using an ISDN line

An X.25 smart card or other X.25 equipment if using an X.25 network

RAS can also be configured to directly connect two computers using a null modem cable attached to a serial port.

RAS can be installed after installation of the operating system from the Network Applet | Services tab. Before installing the RAS service, collect the following information:

The type of communication port

The modem model and any required modem settings

Whether the RAS server will support Dial-In Only, Dial-Out Only or both Dial-In and Dial-Out

The protocols to be installed

Figure 21.1 shows the Remote Access Setup dialog box. This box is presented during installation if you select to install RAS at that time. If changes need to be made later, access this box by highlighting the RAS Service on the Services tab of the Network Properties dialog box and click on the Properties button.

The first step in configuring a RAS server is to set up the hardware the RAS server will use including the port and type of modem. The Configure button at the bottom of the dialog box is used to specify whether the port will be used for dial in and/or dial out purposes. The Configure Port Usage dialog box is shown in Figure 21.2.

If multiple modems are installed on the RAS server, each one must be configured separately using the Configure Port Usage dialog box.

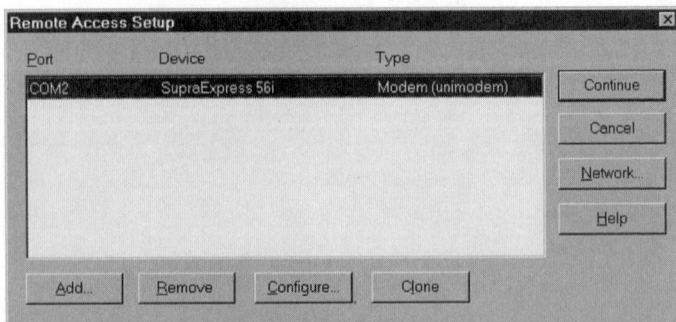

**Figure 21.1** Use the Remote Access Setup dialog box to configure RAS.

## Protocol Configuration

Clicking on the Network button displays the Network Configuration dialog box that allows for configuring each installed protocol. Configuring the dial-in protocols determines the amount of network access a user will have when calling in using that protocol.

### TCP/IP

When configuring TCP/IP, two parameters are configured: Network Access and IP address, as shown in Figure 21.3. Access may be limited to the RAS server only or granted to the entire network.

There are two ways to assign an IP address to a RAS client. If a DHCP server is running on your network, RAS can be configured to

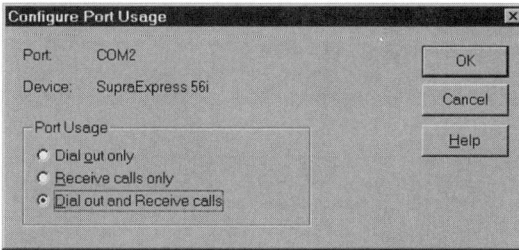

**Figure 21.2** Use this dialog box to decide if communication will be one-way or two-way.

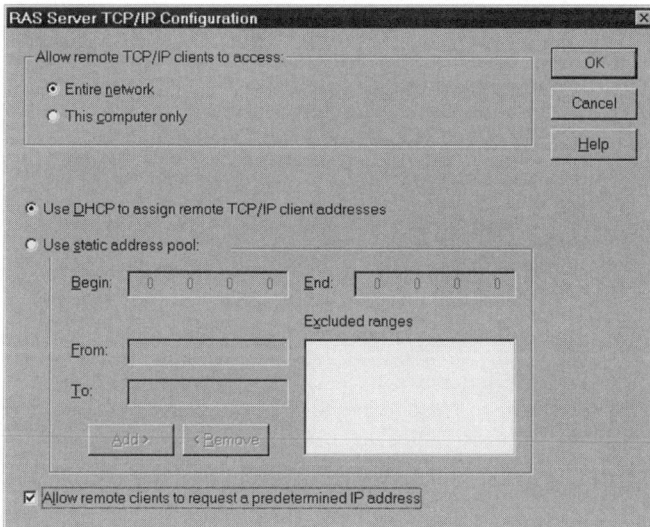

**Figure 21.3** Should remote clients have access to one computer or the whole network?

obtain the IP addresses from the DHCP server and assign them to the client.

The second way to assign client IP addresses is by creating a pool of addresses on the RAS server. The RAS server then assigns an IP address to each client upon connection. Remote clients may request a reassigned IP address if the "Allow remote clients to request a predetermined IP address" check box is checked.

### IPX/SPX

Remote IPX/SPX clients may likewise be allowed to access only the RAS server or the network, like when configuring TCP/IP.

Parameters for IPX/SPX are configured from a similar dialog box. A network number may be automatically assigned or a static number entered. By default, "Allocate network numbers automatically" and "Assign same network number to all IPX clients" are selected. Unless you have a specific need, leave these settings as they are.

### NetBEUI

The only configuration necessary for NetBEUI is the degree of user access like with the previous protocols TCP/IP and IPX/SPX. If the client is running NetBEUI, the RAS Server acts as a NetBEUI gateway to allow access to network resources running either TCP/IP or IPX/SPX.

### *Authentication Configuration*

In addition to configuring the protocols, this dialog box is also used to set the authentication level and to enable Multilink. There are three levels of authentication.

The "Allow any authentication including clear text" option is used to allow access to the RAS server by clients `unable to use a higher level of security. This is the least secure of all the authentication levels. Select this option to support the largest variety of dial-in client computers.

### TIP
Additional security can be added by installing an intermediary security host. This host is located between the RAS clients and the RAS server. The client must enter a password or code before gaining access to the RAS server. This is a good choice when you need to provide access to a variety of clients and want to have a higher level of security.

The "Require encrypted authentication" option permits a connection using any type of authentication. The type is requested by the client. Passwords are encrypted when using this option.

With the "Require Microsoft encrypted authentication" option, the only type of authentication that will be accepted is MS-CHAP. When selecting this level of user authentication, you may also have all data sent across the connection encrypted by checking the Require data encryption check box.

**TIP**

Most questions on authentication levels are scenarios. Select the most secure type of authentication that will provide access to all RAS clients. Be sure and pay attention to the operating system used by remote clients.

The "Multilink" option provides the ability to combine multiple connections to provide increased bandwidth. It works with two or more modems, ISDN or X.25, and must be configured on both the RAS server and the RAS Client. In fact, Multilink also works with a combination of connection types. The RAS server can be configured to use Multilink by checking the Enable Multilink checkbox on the Network Configuration dialog box.

**TIP**

If RAS is configured for call-back security, then Multilink will not work (except for some ISDN users whose ISDN B channel's both have the same phone number). With Multilink, only one call back phone number may be installed in a user's account and only that number will be called, thereby bypassing the Multilink capability.

### Dialin Access Rights

After RAS is installed and configured, users must be granted the right to connect to the RAS server. This can be done using the RAS Admin utility, User Manager (workstation), or User Manager for Domains (server).

Figure 21.4 shows the Remote Access Permissions dialog box. This box may be opened via Users | Permissions from the RAS Admin utility menu. The top part of the box lists all users. Select the desired user account and check the Grant dialin permission to user check box.

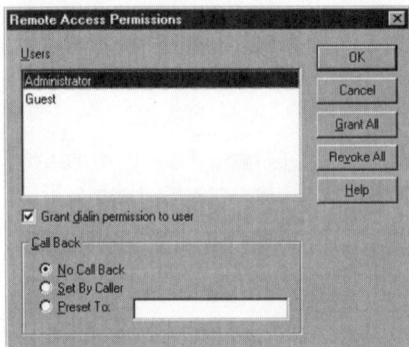

**Figure 21.4** Use the RAS Admin utility to grant dialin access.

At the bottom of the Remote Access Permissions dialog box are the options to configure Call Back. Providing for Call Back increases the security of the RAS server. Once a call is received and the user authenticated, the RAS server disconnects and then dials the user back. The three options are:

- **No Call Back.** The user continues with the session after the connection has been established and authentication completed. The user then disconnects when finished with the call.
- **Set By Caller.** After authentication, the user is prompted to enter a callback number. This is helpful for supporting travelling users. The cost of the call is then covered by the organization.
- **Preset To.** This is the most secure of the callback options. When a user connects to the RAS server, the RAS server calls back to a preconfigured number.

When using User Manager or User Manager for Domains, select the user to configure access rights and open the properties dialog box. Clicking on the Dialin button opens the dialog box used to grant rights. This box provides the same functionality as when using the RAS Admin utility. The only difference is that only that user's access status is displayed when using User Manager. The RAS Admin utility lists all users, and is a quicker way to handle multiple users' access rights.

### INSTALLING DIAL-UP NETWORKING (DUN)

Connection to a RAS server is made from the client workstation through the use of Dial-Up Networking. Once the connection is made, the DUN Client functions as though directly connected to the remote network.

Dial-Up Networking is automatically installed during installation if Remote Access Services are installed. Similar to the RAS procedure, DUN can be installed after the installation of the operating system. On the Services tab of the Network Properties dialog box, select Remote Access Services. If only DUN is to be installed, configure the modem for Dial Out connections only.

DUN has the same hardware requirements as those for installing a RAS server.

Once DUN is installed, several options may be configured. These are:

- Telephony API
- Phonebook entries
- Remote logon
- Auto-dial

### Telephony API (TAPI)

TAPI acts as a device driver for the telephone system thereby enabling the use of the telephone system as an extension to your computer. TAPI configures the dialing properties for your system. DUN is a TAPI-aware application, and TAPI configuration is done during installation of DUN. It can also be altered later by using the Telephony applet in the Control Panel.

### Locations

A location is set up to configure how TAPI dials numbers to establish a connection. A location may be related to a geographic location but may also be related to a particular site in a geographic location such as a hotel room. The information needed to configure a location includes:

Area or city code

Country code

How to access an outside line

Calling card information

Figure 21.5 shows the My Locations tab of the Dialing Properties dialog box. Use this dialog box to create, modify, or remove locations. A location may be used by any TAPI-aware application, not just DUN.

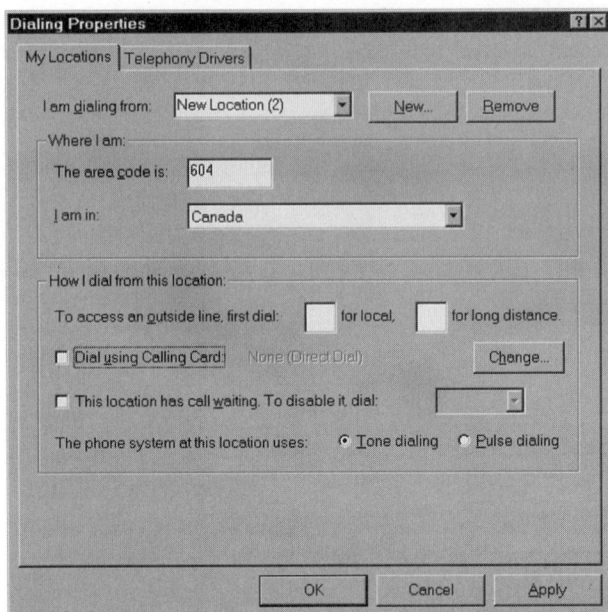

**Figure 21.5** Use the Dialing Properties dialog box to configure Location parameters.

When creating a new location, use a meaningful name. This name is selected when configuring Phonebook entries, which is covered later in this chapter. If dialing from a location outside of North America, enter the City Code in the Area Code text box. The Country Code is configured by selecting the country name from the "I am in" dropdown box.

If dialing an additional number is necessary in order to access an outside line, such as through a PBX, enter that number. Different entries for accessing a local line and a long distance line may be entered.

Two optional parameters may be configured.

- Dial using Calling Card.—This number is stored in a scrambled format and is not displayed again after entering. Multiple calling cards may be configured.

- This location has call waiting. To disable it, dial:—If Call Waiting is not disabled, the connection may be severed when a second call comes in.

Specify whether the phone system you are attached to uses tone dialing or pulse dialing.

### Phonebook Entries

Phonebook entries contain all the information necessary to establish a connection. Phonebooks may be individual or shared by multiple users.

Phonebook entries may be configured using the New Phonebook Entry wizard or can be configured manually by selecting "I know all about phonebook entries and would rather edit the properties directly." A new phone book entry is created by opening Dial-Up Networking and then clicking on the New button. Figure 21.6 shows the New Phonebook Entry dialog box.

Enter a name that is meaningful in the Entry name text box. An optional comment may also be entered. If the Use Telephony dialing properties is not checked, then the fields for Country Code and Area Code will not be displayed.

**TIP**

Multilink may be enabled by selecting Multiple Lines in the Dial using drop-down box. The number of telephone numbers to dial determines how many phonebook entries need to be created. For example, if using ISDN with two channels that have the same phone number, only one telephone number entry is required.

**Figure 21.6**   The New Phonebook Entry has five tabs and is used to record the settings necessary to establish a remote connection.

**TIP**
Although many ISDN lines are provided with two different telephone numbers, if your ISDN lines are supplied with only one telephone number, then you can use Windows NT Multilink with call-back protection.

Enter the phone number to be called and the modem to be used. Multiple phone numbers may be configured by clicking on the Alternates button. If multiple modems are available, check the Use another port if busy checkbox.

Use the Server tab to select the type of dialin server. Protocols are also included on this page and may be configured if necessary depending on the type of server being called.

The Script tab is used to indicate if a script should be run before or after dialing to establish a session. Using a script bypasses the need for manual intervention to establish the connection. Alternatively, a terminal window can be configured to pop up after a connection is established. Windows NT comes with sample scripts for CIS, SLIP, and PPP. Each script must have the extension *.scp; you'll typically find them in the C:\WINNT\system32\ras folder.

The Security tab is used to configure the type of Authentication and Encryption Policy. These choices correspond to the authentication methods discussed earlier in this chapter. They are:

- Accept any authentication including clear text
- Accept only encrypted authentication
- Accept only Microsoft-encrypted authentication

If the last option is selected, The "Require Data Encryption" and "Use Current Username And Password" options become available. Encrypting the data transferred across the connection provides for a more secure connection. If the username and password on the DUN client corresponds to the username and password on the remote network, using this option automates the logon process.

The last tab, X.25, is used to specify the network provider and its address. Optionally, user and facility information may be entered.

**Remote Logon**
Windows NT allows the use of Dial-Up Networking for logging into a domain by placing this option on the logon dialog box. If this is checked, the user is able to select which phonebook entry to use to establish a connection.

To configure the logon parameters, click on the More button in Dial-up Networking. Then select Logon Preferences to display the Logon Preferences dialog box shown in Figure 21.7.

The Dialing tab is used to configure the number of redial attempts, how long to wait between attempts, and the idle time before hanging up. The Callback Tab, shown in Figure 21.7, is where the DUN client is configured for callback.

The Appearance tab configures the user's interaction during logon. An individual phonebook or the system phonebook is selected using the Phonebook tab.

When logging on to a Windows NT domain using a roaming profile, the profile is downloaded to the client computer. This can result in a very slow logon process using DUN. One way to prevent this is to specify that the locally-cached profile is used rather than the server-based one. In order to specify use of the locally cached profile, use the System applet from the Control Panel on the User Profiles tab. See Chapter 12, "Profiles," for more information on using profiles.

## AutoDial

RAS AutoDial maps network addresses to phonebook entries in the AutoDial mapping database. The database can include IP addresses, NetBIOS names, or Internet host names.

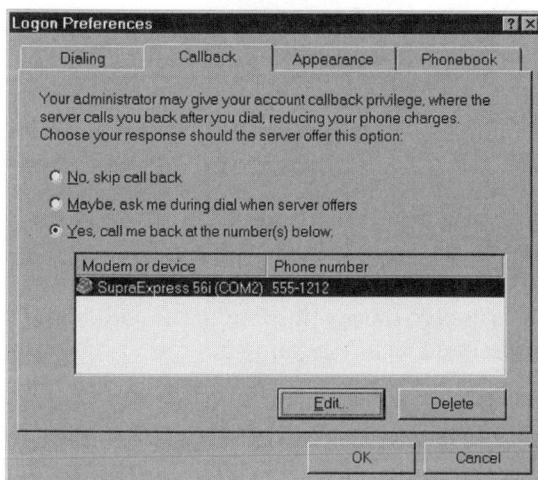

**Figure 21.7**  The Logon Preference dialog box is used to configure how a logon occurs.

AutoDial is enabled by default. To disable it, use the User Prefer-
ences dialog box. This is accessed by clicking on the More button in
Dial-up Networking. Then select User Preferences to display the
User Preferences dialog box shown in Figure 21.8.

### Troubleshooting

There are several common types of errors that may occur when using RAS. Various approaches are used to diagnose and correct the
problems. Event Viewer is frequently used to diagnose problems.
RAS events are logged in the System Log.

Problems with PPP Connections. A ppp.log file can be
created to help diagnose problems related to authentication
over PPP. To enable logging, edit the registry parameter
`\HKEY_LOCAL_MACHINE\System\CurrentControlSet\Services\Rasman\`
`PPP\Logging` and change its value to 1.

Authentication Problems. Try the lowest authentication on both
the server and the client computer. If a successful connection is
achieved, try the next higher type of authentication, etc.

Dial-Up Networking Monitor. The Dial-Up Networking Monitor
displays the status of the connection and is helpful in diagnosing
problems. Dial-Up Networking Monitor is available in the Control
Panel.

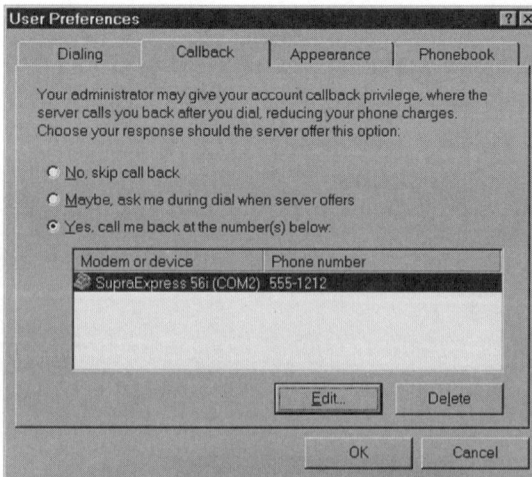

**Figure 21.8** The User Preferences dialog box is used to enable or disable
AutoDial.

By using a RAS Server, you are able to expand the size of your network by connecting remote offices and allowing network access for users who travel.

## FOR REVIEW

- RAS allows the use of the public telephone system to connect remote users to your network.

- PPTP provides a secure connection using the Internet.

- RAS supports TCP/IP, IPX/SPX, and NetBEUI protocols.

- WAN connections can be made using SLIP, PPP, or Microsoft RAS protocols.

- RAS supports three levels of authentication: Clear text, Encryption, and MS CHAP.

- The use of multilink increases bandwidth by combining two or more lines.

- Users must be granted access in order to connect to the RAS server.

- TAPI is configured by creating or modifying locations.

- Create a phonebook entry for each server to be called.

- RAS may be used to log on remotely to a Microsoft domain.

- Dial-Up Networking Monitor may be used to troubleshoot problems with RAS.

## FROM HERE

You may want to review Chapter 17, "Available Protocols," or Chapter 18, "Binding Order," for more information about communication protocols. Coming up, Chapter 24, "Monitoring Tools," Chapter 25, "Performance Tuning and Optimization," both discuss network protocol issues, as well.

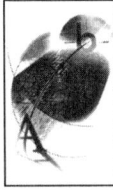

# CHAPTER 22

# Go App, Go!

As the Windows interface has developed, more options have become popular for starting and running applications. This chapter gives you a brief review of the Windows NT 4.0 interface in terms of various ways to start applications.

## Multitasking, Multithreading and Multiprocessing

### MULTITASKING

In a single-tasking environment such as DOS, one process must finish before another can begin. Windows 3.1 was Microsoft's initial foray into multitasking environments and Windows NT 4.0 is much further down the road.

Multitasking is a technique used by Windows NT that allows a single processor to be shared among multiple threads. On a single processor system, multiple programs or tasks don't actually run at the same time. It just appears to the user that all the tasks are being executed at once because the operating system is able to switch quickly between the active processes allowing what appears to be continuous progress on all of them.

Multitasking computer operating systems control and distribute CPU work more carefully so the CPU does not necessarily waste time waiting for I/O devices and/or user input. Instead, time that would otherwise be wasted is used for other tasks that don't need I/O right now.

### Pre-emptive and NonPre-emptive (Cooperative) Multitasking

Windows 3.1 used nonpre-emptive, also known as cooperative, multitasking. In nonpre-emptive multitasking, a task must voluntarily yield control of the processor before any other task can run. For many programs to run cooperatively together on Windows 3.1, each program was required to be specially written so it would frequently yield, or offer to yield, control of the CPU to other programs.

With pre-emptive multitasking, the Windows NT operating system can take back control of the processor even if the program doesn't cooperate. With preemptive multitasking, an application can also voluntarily cooperate with the operating system and release control of the CPU, as it could in Windows 3.1. Pre-emptive multitasking means the operating system, not the application, controls which programs run and for how long.

Windows NT takes away control of the processor from a task in two ways:

- **When a task's time runs out.** Each task is allocated a small amount of time to control the CPU. After this time is up, the operating system interrupts and decides which task to run next based on the priorities of the tasks that are ready to run.

- **When a higher priority task is ready to run.** The current task loses control of the CPU if a higher priority task is ready to run, even if the current task had time left in its turn.

When a program's allotted time expires, the operating system saves all the information about the current program's state so the program can later begin execution exactly where it left off. Then Windows NT loads the next program for execution. The process of saving one program's state and loading another is called context switching.

### MULTITHREADING

Windows NT is a multithreaded operating system, so more than one thread can progress in a single task or process during a given time period. This offers speed advantages because more work can be done in the same amount of time. Background printing is a good example of multithreading—in a single threaded application, the user must wait for printing to complete because the operating system (or application) cannot multithread. In a multithreaded application on Windows NT, users can continue other work and the computer will continue to respond to input even though a print job is being processed in the background.

In a multithreaded process, every thread of the process uses the same memory address space. This provides for quick communication among the threads of a process, speeding things up. Threads can also be created more quickly than processes because threads don't use a separate address space, and processes do.

## MULTIPROCESSING

Computers with more than one processor are capable of multiprocessing. With multitasking on a multiple-processor system, there can be as many threads running simultaneously as there are processors in the computer.

By distributing the system requirements across multiple processors, the computer can balance requests and perform with more stability. This provides multithreaded applications with the opportunity to maximize their output. Keep in mind that multithreaded applications running across multiprocessors do not necessarily mean more speed. Thread performance is inter-dependent; that is, applications execute threads based on the output of other threads. Therefore, threads will still wait for each other. Nevertheless, the potential for increased speed exists. Remember that single thread applications will still only execute on a single processor.

## The Kernel's Dispatcher

Thread scheduling and context switching is performed by the kernel's dispatcher. The kernel's dispatcher decides which thread runs on each processor based on the thread's current dynamic priority. When the processor is busy, thread priority determines which threads get to run at all. The kernel's dispatcher also performs context switching to save one thread's volatile state (its CPU register contents) and restore the next thread's volatile state so each thread can continue running in its next turn exactly where it left off in its last turn.

## THREADS

A process can have many threads. All threads in the same process share the same memory, and the same system resources. The process owns these assets, rather than a thread. Programmers writing multithreaded applications are responsible for ensuring that various threads of the same process do not interfere or conflict with each other.

On computers with only one CPU, only one thread actually executes at a time. On computers with multiple CPUs, more than one processor may run various threads in the same process simultaneously. As you would expect, using Windows NT with multiple processors can substantially increase application speed. Multithreading cannot reach its full potential until multiple processors are available.

Each thread has a dispatcher state that describes its status. The three most interesting thread dispatcher states are:

- Running—Only one thread runs at a time (on each processor).

- Ready—Threads in the Ready state may be scheduled for execution the next time the kernel dispatches a thread. The Ready thread with the highest priority executes next.

- Waiting—Waiting threads are on hold contingent on an event when they may become Ready.

Real-time threads always run at their original priority—their priorities are not adjusted by algorithms. Variable or dynamic priority threads are assigned a base priority when they are created based on the priority of their parent process. Setting an application's priority is discussed in Chapter 23, "Setting Application Priority."

The kernel's dispatcher dynamically adjusts each thread's priority by complex algorithms and strategies designed to improve performance and optimize responsiveness. The dispatcher also keeps a priority queue of ready tasks. When the dispatcher is prompted, it changes the state of the highest priority Ready task to Standby. Next, the context switch occurs and the Standby thread goes into Running state.

Lower-priority threads with time remaining in their turn always get pushed out by higher-priority threads even if the lower-priority thread is running on a different processor.

> A thread is the smallest unit of a process that can be scheduled by the Scheduler Service or kernel.

## EACH PROCESS HAS A BASE PRIORITY

An application or program may have many threads but they all run as part of the same process. A process is a collection of one or more threads that share the same memory, files, and system resources. Because threads share the same memory they can work together easily. Each process has a base priority that applies to all threads of that process. Threads independently do their work by executing program code. The microkernel or kernel schedules threads to run on the processor(s).

### WINDOWS NT PROTECTS THE MEMORY OF EACH PROCESS

To ensure that each process will not interfere with other processes, each Windows NT process has a private address space through which all its threads access memory. This is intended to help make the operating system more reliable, robust, and secure.

Communication between processes must be channeled through the Windows NT executive interprocess communication (IPC) manager. The IPC manager provides methods for threads of different processes to send each other messages, without allowing them to step on each other's toes.

## DOS Applications

A DOS application is implemented as a Win32-based application through a virtual DOS environment on Windows NT. The NTVDM.exe utility creates a Virtual DOS Machine (VDM) for each DOS application so each DOS application runs in its own address space. By running each DOS application in its own VDM, Windows NT is mimicking the single-tasking nature of the native DOS operating system.

Windows NT pre-emptively schedules DOS applications.

## WIN16 Applications

By default, Windows-based 16-bit applications share a single VDM. The single VDM emulates the native Windows 3.1 environment where multiple Win16 applications shared a single address space.

A VDM running a WIN16 application has an extra layer of software called the Win16onWin32 (WOW) layer. This layer is referred to as WOW. WOW mimics the nonpre-emptive multitasking environment expected by WIN16 applications.

Whereas running all WIN16 applications in the same VDM provides compatibility, it does have its disadvantages. One of these disadvantages occurs when a WIN16 application does not yield control of the processor and crashes the other WIN16 applications. On Windows NT, when this occurs, neither other VDMs nor 32-bit applications are affected.

> Within the default VDM, the WIN16 applications' threads are scheduled cooperatively. However, Windows NT treats the WIN16 default VDM like a 32-bit application in that it is scheduled pre-emptively with 32-bit applications.

If a WIN16 application does not 'play nice' with the other WIN16 applications, the misbehaving WIN16 application can be started in its own VDM. This provides the WIN16 application its own address space and it will be pre-emptively multitasked.

> To run a WIN16 application in its own VDM, do one of the following:
>
> Use the Run command from the Start menu

　　or

Start the application from a command prompt using the Start command (see Chapter 23, "Setting Application Priority," for more).

## Running Programs on Every Startup

Programs on the Windows NT StartUp menu start automatically every time you start Windows NT. To start a program each time Windows NT starts, use this path:

```
Start | Settings | Taskbar | Start Menu Programs | Add | Browse
```

Browse to the location of the program you want to start each time you start Windows NT and then double-click the program. Then choose Next and double-click the StartUp folder.

There will then be a blank to fill-in with the program name that you will later see on the StartUp menu. Choose an icon if you must, and then choose Finish. When the operating system next boots, the change you made will be evident.

By dragging a program's or batch file's icon from My Computer to the Start button, you can easily add a program to the top of the Start menu.

### DOS Key Combinations May Conflict with Keyboard Navigation
The standard Windows NT keyboard shortcuts are:

- Alt+Tab to switch between running programs.
- Alt+Esc to cycle through programs according to the order they were started.
- Ctrl+Esc to display the Start menu.
- Print Screen to copy an image of the entire screen to the Clipboard.
- Alt+Print Screen to copy an image of the active window to the Clipboard.
- Alt+Enter to switch a program between a window (if possible) and a full screen.
- Alt+Spacebar to display a program's System menu.

These key combinations can doubtless conflict with reserved key combinations of old DOS applications. If the standard Windows NT shortcuts conflict with the keyboard commands of a DOS application, you can disable one or all of them in the dialog box shown in Figure 22.1.

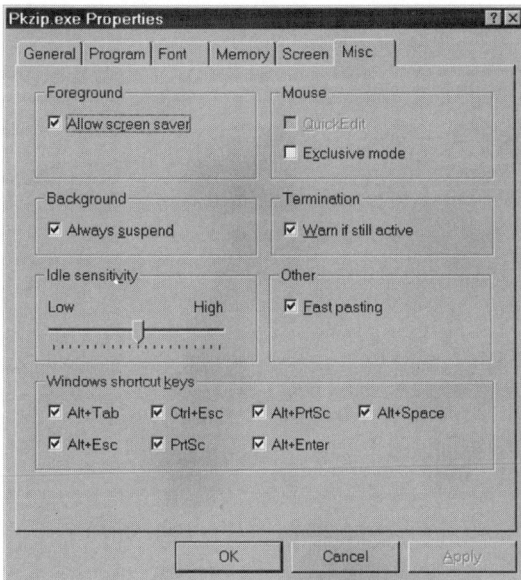

**Figure 22.1** Deselect Windows shortcut keys for an application through the Misc tab of the Properties page.

Right-click the icon for the DOS program's shortcut in My Computer or the Windows Explorer, then click Properties. In the Properties window, choose the Misc tab, and then in the lower, Windows Shortcut Keys area, deselect the shortcut keys you want to reserve for use with a program other than the Windows NT operating system.

## FOR REVIEW

- A thread is the smallest unit of a process that can be scheduled by the Scheduler Service or kernel.

- Each DOS application runs in its own address space.

- Windows NT pre-emptively schedules DOS applications.

- By default, Windows-based 16-bit applications share a single VDM.

- Within the default VDM, the WIN16 applications' threads are scheduled cooperatively.

- To run a WIN16 application in its own VDM, do one of the following:

  Use the Run command from the Start menu
  or
  Start the application from a command prompt, using the Start command

## From Here

Chapter 23, "Setting Application Priority," covers how the Start command and the Task Manager are used to control application priority.

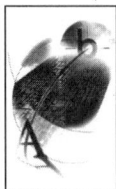

# Setting Application Priority

This chapter focuses on three methods of controlling application priority:

- The Start Command
- The Task Manager | Processes tab
- System Properties | Performance tab

Using Task Manager and the `start` command, you can monitor and change process priorities, and by using the Control Panel | System Properties | Performance tab, you can change the relative priority of foreground and background applications.

Although it takes some effort to learn to adjust application priorities, unless you know how to make these adjustments you are not using the Windows NT operating system to its fullest advantage.

You can run applications at higher or lower priorities either on a one-time basis or an every-time basis. Task Manager allows you to immediately adjust priorities for the current session—any adjustment will last until that application is closed or you change the adjustment. By using the `start` command in a batch file, you can run an application with an adjusted priority every time you use it.

To fine tune hardware and software configurations for maximum efficiency, eventually you'll need to examine and adjust priorities. The Windows NT operating system automatically does a lot to adjust thread priorities to optimize processes.

## PERFORMANCE MONITOR OBSERVES PROCESSES

It is possible to monitor the priority status of each process object with Performance Monitor. Several available processor and thread object counters also observe threads and priority status. Although running these monitors does absorb a small amount of system resources while they run, during the process of performance tuning your system it is quite appropriate to monitor and adjust application priorities as needed. See Chapter 24, "Monitoring Tools," for more information on Windows NT Performance Monitor. This subject is also covered in detail in TechNet, under the heading "Priority Bottlenecks."

## The start Command

The start command opens a separate DOS window to run a specified program or command. In a DOS window, type start /? | more to see the help file and the full syntax for start.

```
START  [/SEPARATE | /SHARED] [/LOW | /NORMAL | /HIGH |
/REALTIME] [command/program] [parameters]
```

Some of the start command switches relevant to this discussion are shown in Table 23.1.

**Table 23.1** The start command allows you to adjust an application's priority every time you run that application.

| Switch | Used For |
| --- | --- |
| /separate | Run a 16-bit Windows program in separate memory space |
| /shared | Run a 16-bit Windows program in shared memory space |

| Switch | Used For |
|--------|----------|
| /low | Run an application in the Idle priority class |
| /normal | Run an application in the Normal priority class |
| /high | Run an application in the High priority class |
| /realtime | Run an application in the Realtime priority class* |

*—Realtime priorities are only available to administrators because they can interfere with the operating system and should be used sparingly if at all.

## The Task Manager | Processes

To open Task Manager, right click in a blank portion of the taskbar, or press the Ctrl+Alt+Del keyboard combination. Figure 23.1 shows the Processes tab of the Task Manager with a process ready for priority adjustment. Notice that the Realtime priority is available—this means that an administrator is logged into the computer because only administrators are able to choose Realtime priorities.

To adjust the priority of a process, right click on the process from the Processes tab of the Task Manager. The new priority will endure until the application is closed or until you adjust it further.

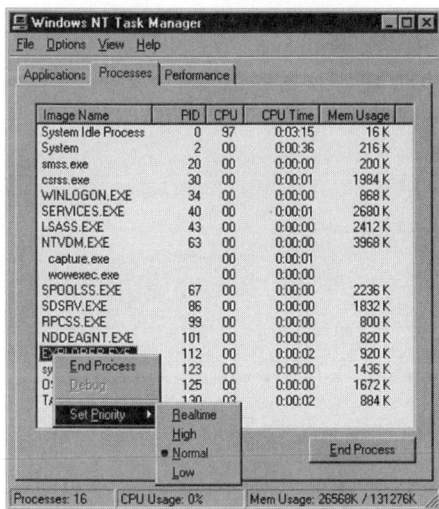

**Figure 23.1** By right clicking on a process, you can end the process or set its priority.

## Control Panel | System Properties | Performance

The Control Panel | System applet's Performance tab adjusts the relationship of foreground and background application priorities. A foreground application is the one that is selected and active on the Windows NT desktop. All other applications are background applications.

Use the Performance Tab of the System applet in the Control Panel, as shown in Figure 23.2, to set the relative weight of foreground applications in reference to background applications.

The most unusual feature of this configuration is that it uses a sliding dial. Although it may appear that you could set the slider at any point along the range, you cannot. There are no numbers showing, and only the three positions marked with notches are valid. The three notches correspond to settings in the registry.

If the Boost setting is on None, then the foreground application priority is not changed. Use this setting when background applications should not be slowed down, such as on an application server.

However, if the Boost setting is set to the middle setting, background applications retain their base priorities, but the foreground priority is increased by one level. This setting works well when an application running in the foreground needs a faster response time.

The Maximum setting increases the foreground application by two levels. Use this to run a critical application that needs to have as much processor time as possible while still allowing background applications to run. You might use this setting when recalculating a spreadsheet while a file is being spell checked in the background.

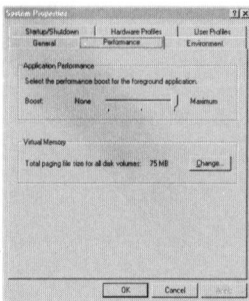

**Figure 23.2** Use the Performance Tab of the System applet in the Control Panel to set the boost factor for the foreground application.

**Table 23.2** Choose your foreground boost based on these values.

| Foreground Application<br>Performance Boost | Priority Adjustment |
|---|---|
| None | 0 |
| Intermediate | +1 |
| Maximum (Default) | +2 |

If the maximum boost of +2 does not make the foreground application responsive enough, try adjusting the priority of that application in the Task Manager. If that works, then create a batch file to always run the application at the higher priority using the start command.

## FOR REVIEW

- Use Performance Monitor to monitor the priority status of each process object.

- The start command opens a separate DOS window to run a specified program or command.

- start command switches relevant to setting application priority:

  Low

  Normal

  High

  Realtime

- Adjust the relationship of foreground and background application priorities with Performance Tab of the System applet in Control Panel.

## FROM HERE

Chapter 22, "Go App Go!" covers executing applications in ways.

# CHAPTER 24

# Monitoring Tools

Monitoring the network and creating a baseline for your network are important steps in maintaining a healthy network. A baseline establishes the performance of the network under normal operating conditions. Baseline measurements should be taken over a seven-day period or longer. As a continuation of the monitoring process, future network operations are regularly compared to the baseline measurements. These comparisons can be analyzed to reveal resource use and to:

Record typical network usage

Plan for future growth of the network

Isolate bottlenecks causing a decrease in network performance

A bottleneck is the step or resource using the most time during a larger operation and constricting the workflow of the network. Bottlenecks can occur due many conditions, including:

Inefficient use of resources

Resource speed

Inadequate resource capacity

Two tools that are useful in creating a network baseline and for monitoring a Windows NT network are:

Performance Monitor

Task Manager

Windows NT Performance Monitor and Task Manager are reviewed next.

## Performance Monitor

Windows NT built-in Performance Monitor provides a network administrator with a graphical tool to collect and log data regularly throughout each day so that trends can be determined through analysis of the data. By monitoring the network, an administrator knows whether a network needs more memory here, a faster hard drive there, or a new processor in another place.

Performance Monitor can be found on Windows NT Workstation in the Administrative Tools Programs group. Data from Performance Monitor can be viewed in real time, logged for future comparisons, and easily used in charts and reports. The log files can also be exported for further analysis in other applications such as Microsoft Excel or Microsoft Access. Alerts can be set to warn the administrator when custom threshold values have been exceeded.

Performance Monitor collects data about system resources (objects), and statistical information (counters).

A few of the objects available for monitoring are:

| | |
|---|---|
| Cache | Process |
| LogicalDisk | Processor |
| Memory | Redirector |
| Objects | System |
| Paging File | Thread |
| PhysicalDisk | |

Each object in Performance Monitor has many subcategories, called counters. A fixed set of counters for an object can be selected depending on your monitoring needs. For a specific counter definition, open the Add to Chart dialog box, select (highlight) the counter, and click on the Explain button.

Although additional resources (objects) might also be monitored, data on the following four object resources should definitely be included in a network baseline.

- Memory
- Processor
- Hard Drives
- Network

## MEMORY

To find out if the computer needs additional RAM, set Performance Monitor to log data on:

Object: Memory          Counter: Pages/sec

If a computer maintains a high rate of hard page faults, there is a memory bottleneck. Hard page faults occur when a program cannot find the data in memory (RAM) and must retrieve the data from the hard drive. If the computer has over five hard page faults a second for an extended time, additional RAM should be installed.

To obtain more information about the computer's memory use, log data on:

Object: Memory          Counter: Available Bytes

Object: Memory          Counter: Committed Bytes

Object: Memory          Counter: Pool Nonpaged Bytes

Figure 24.1 shows an example of a Performance Monitor chart with the previous four counters.

## PROCESSOR

One way to monitor a CPU is to log data from:

Object: Processor          Counter: % Processor Time

Processor: % Processor Time monitors the amount of time the CPU is in use. If the CPU operates over 75% processor time for extended periods, a faster processor or additional processors may be required.

For more information about CPU activity, the following counters can be logged:

| | |
|---|---|
| Object: Processor | Counter: % Privileged Time |
| Object: Processor | Counter: % User Time |
| Object: Processor | Counter: Interrupts/sec |
| Object: System | Counter: Processor Queue Length |
| Object: Server Work Queues | Counter: Queue Length |

Figure 24.2 shows an example of a Performance Monitor chart with counters monitoring Processor usage.

## HARD DRIVES

Performance Monitor (perfmon at the command prompt) can also log data for both PhysicalDisk and LogicalDisk objects. PhysicalDisk can monitor the hard disk drive(s) for troubleshooting and capacity planning. LogicalDisk monitors the logical partitions on the hard disk drive(s). By finding the partition that is generating the disk activity, the network administrator can track down an application that is generating excessive requests.

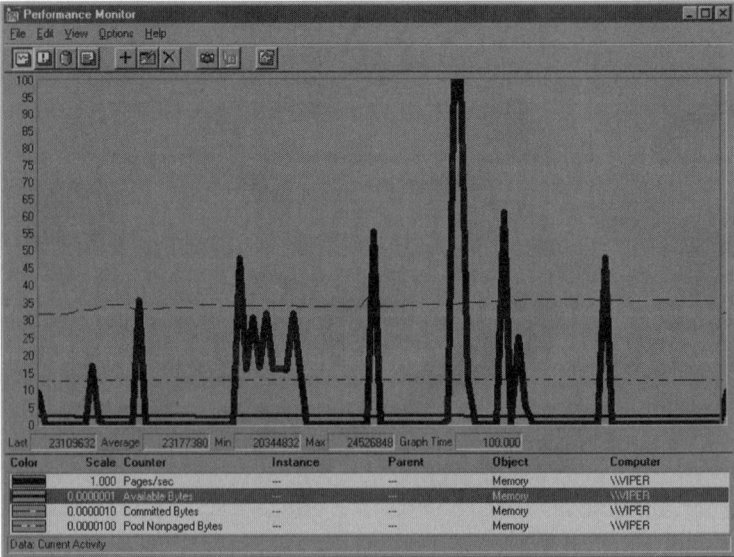

**Figure 24.1** A Performance Monitor chart logging data on Memory resources.

Because Performance Monitor disk counters can reduce performance by increasing disk access time approximately 1.5 percent on older x86 computers, disk counters are not automatically started in `perfmon`. Disk counters must be started manually by typing:

```
Diskperf -y
```

at a command prompt.

You will receive the following message.

**Disk performance counters on this system are now set to start at boot. This change will take effect after the system is restarted.**

Once the system has been restarted, the disk counters in Performance Monitor can be started.

PhysicalDisk: % Disk Time charts the amount of time a hard disk drive uses to process read and write requests. If % Disk Time remains close to 100%, a faster controller, faster hard drives, or more hard drives in a RAID environment are indicated, assuming the computer has adequate RAM.

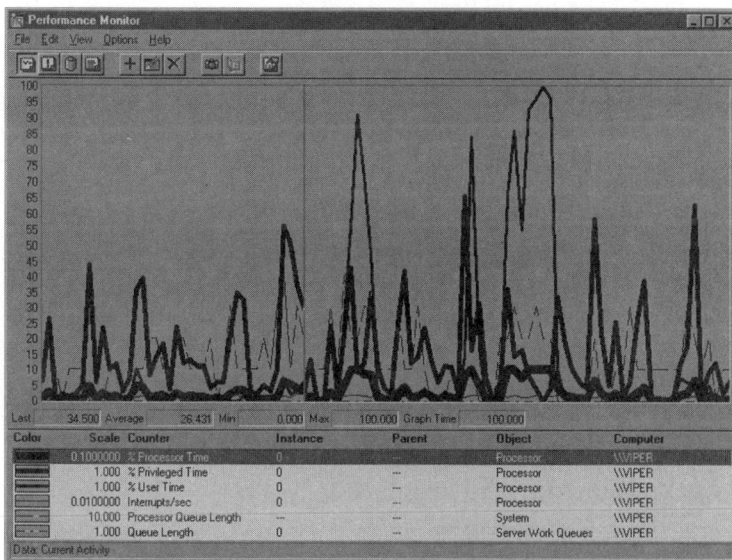

**Figure 24.2** A Performance Monitor chart logging data on Processor resources.

Object: PhysicalDisk        Counter: % Disk Time

Other objects and counters to monitor for disk usage are:

Object: PhysicalDisk        Counter: Avg. Disk Bytes/Transfer

Object: PhysicalDisk        Counter: Disk Bytes/sec

Object: LogicalDisk         Counter: % Free Space

Figure 24.3 shows an example of a chart with counters monitoring hard disk drives.

## NETWORK

To determine the number of bytes the server is sending and receiving over the network, monitor the following:

Object: Server    Counter: Bytes Total/sec

If this number is high, an additional network adapter card may be needed or the network may benefit from segmentation.

Other objects and counters to monitor in gathering data on your network are:

Object: Network Interface        Counter: Bytes Sent/sec

Object: Network Interface        Counter: Bytes Total/sec

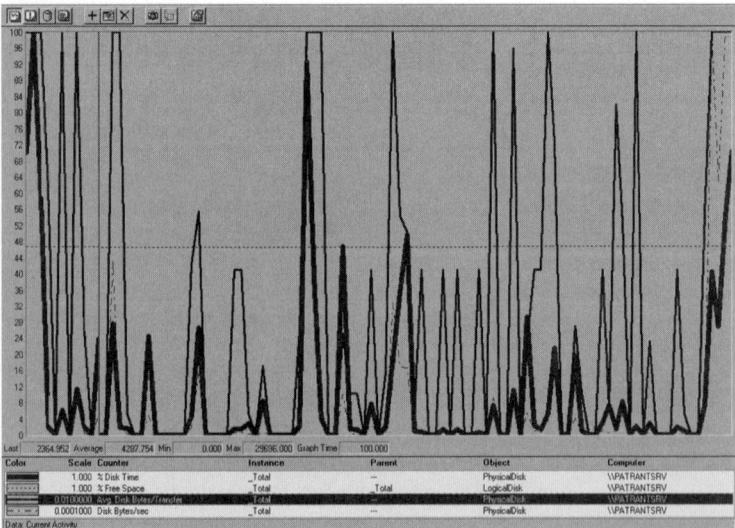

**Figure 24.3** A Performance Monitor chart logging data on Disk resources.

In order to use the Performance Monitor counters for these objects:

- Internet Control Message Protocol
- Network Interface (a NIC performance counter)
- TCP/IP
- UDP

the Simple Network Management Protocol (SNMP) service and the TCP/IP network protocol must be installed on the computer you will be monitoring. SNMP is not automatically installed when TCP/IP is installed. To install SNMP, open Control Panel, choose the Network Icon, select the Services menu, select the SNMP service, and click on Add.

## NETWORK MONITOR AGENT

**Network Monitor Agent gathers statistics for traffic on the network. By installing Network Monitor Agent, you can use the Network Segment object in Performance Monitor.**

**To install Network Monitor Agent, open Control Panel, choose the Network Icon, select the Services menu, select the Network Monitor Agent service, and click on Add. The object Network Segment will be added to Performance Monitor.**

To determine the percentage of bandwidth being used on the network, monitor the following:

| | |
|---|---|
| Object: Network Segment | Counter: % Network utilization |
| When Object: Network Segment reaches 40–50%, the network has slowed operations enough to be a bottleneck. | Counter: % Network utilization |

Other objects and counters to monitor in gathering data on your network are:

| | |
|---|---|
| Object: Network Segment | Counter: Broadcast frames received/second |
| Object: Network Segment | Counter: Multicast frames received/second |

## Task Manager

Task Manager is a Windows NT tool for monitoring applications, CPU, and memory. With Task Manager you can get a quick view of the CPU and memory use of an individual application or process. Or you can view a summary of the system's overall CPU and memory use.

There are several ways to start Task Manager, including:

- Press the Ctrl+Alt+Del key combination and select Task Manager
- Right click in the taskbar on the desktop and select Task Manager
- Press the Ctrl+Shift+Esc key combination
- Type Taskmgr at a command prompt or from the Run command

The Task Manager status bar shows the total number of processes, the CPU usage, and the memory usage for the system.

Task Manager has three tabs:

- Applications
- Processes
- Performance

### THE APPLICATIONS TAB

The Applications screen shows the status of a task and can be used for shutting down tasks or starting new tasks.

### THE PROCESSES TAB

The Processes screen provides information on individual processes running in their own address space on the system. The default columns as shown in Figure 24.4 are:

- Processes (Image Name)
- ID number (PID)
- Percentage of CPU being used (CPU)

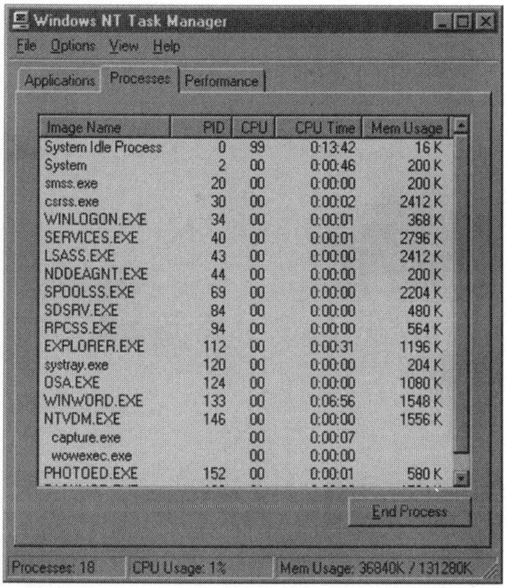

**Figure 24.4** The default columns found within the Processes Tab from the Windows NT Task Manager.

- Amount of CPU time (CPU Time)
- Memory being used (Mem Usage)

Other columns are available for viewing on the Processes screen. See Figure 24.5 for the column choices.

### THE PERFORMANCE TAB

The Performance screen as shown in Figure 24.6 provides details on a system's

Current CPU and memory utilization

Recent CPU and Memory Usage History

Statistics on file handles, threads, and processes

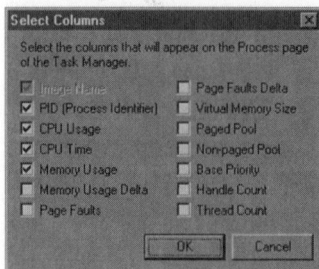

**Figure 24.5** Columns available with the Processes Tab from the Windows NT Task Manager.

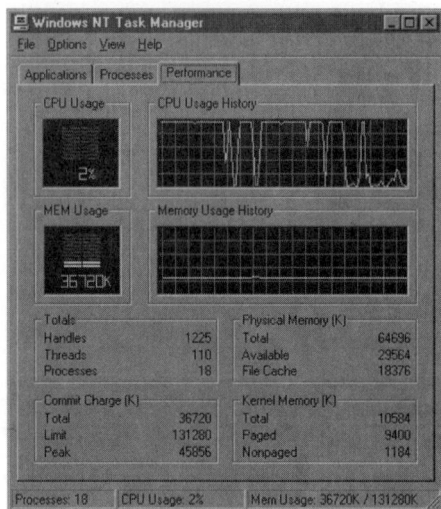

**Figure 24.6** The Performance screen from the Windows NT Task Manager.

Physical memory

Kernel memory

The information provided on the Task Manager Performance screen is similar to the information available from the Processor and Memory objects in Performance Monitor.

**FOR REVIEW**

- Use the Memory: Pages/sec counter in Performance Monitor to see if computer needs additional RAM.

- Use Processor: % Processor Time in Performance Monitor to track the percentage of time the CPU is in use.

- Monitor PhysicalDisk: % Disk Time for disk usage information.

- To monitor traffic on the network use the Server: Bytes Total/sec counter.

- The Simple Network Management Protocol (SNMP) service must be installed before the TCP/IP counters can be used in Performance Monitor.

- The Network Monitor Agent must be installed before the Network Segment object can be used in Performance Monitor.

- Performance Monitor and Task Manager can provide information on a system's CPU and memory usage.

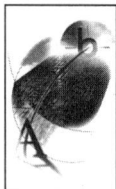

# CHAPTER 25

# Performance Tuning and Optimization

When Microsoft designed Windows NT, their goals included creating a dependable, stable, general-purpose operating system. In most cases, Windows NT has fulfilled that goal and more. Although Windows NT does load balancing and takes care of many ordinary tuning and optimization tasks without human intervention, there are a few little things that system administrators and ordinary users can do to optimize system performance.

- Pagefile Optimization
- Document Optimization
- Reboot Optimization

Remember to make changes to your system one at a time, and document them. Unnecessary changes can adversely affect system performance and cause unexpected problems.

## PAGEFILE OPTIMIZATION

By adjusting the location of the paging file, you may be able to improve performance.

**CAUTION**
If you want to use the Crashdump utility to create memory dumps when a Kernel STOP error occurs, do not move the page file from the boot/system partition.

If the Crashdump recovery feature is not required, you can boost system performance by moving the pagefile off the physical hard disk drive containing the boot/system partition.

Moving the pagefile off the physical hard drive containing the boot/system partition is meant to remove any pagefile performance decrement related to competition with the operating system for disk read/write access to the drive.

To help keep it from becoming fragmented, the pagefile can be placed on its own partition.

The Windows NT operating system creates a paging file on the physical hard drive disk where the operating system is installed. In addition to changing the physical drive where the page file is, you can also change the size of the paging file, and you can create an additional paging file on each physical disk in the computer. Having the pagefile on each hard drive (other than the drive containing the boot/system partition) allows page file reads and writes to be distributed to more than one hard drive, speeding the swapping process. Each hard disk on a computer can have all or part of the page file.

Increasing the size of the paging file can temporarily resolve a virtual memory shortage until you can install more RAM.

### *Virtual Memory*
Virtual memory is a method that allows the computer to simulate RAM on the hard disk. The official Microsoft name for this process is demand paging, which uses the Pagefile.sys file as a repository for the exchange of data. Pagefile.sys is also known as a swap file.

Physical RAM cannot always contain all the pages of memory that are open at any given time. So the swap file holds the inactive pages of memory awaiting their summons for execution by the CPU.

Swapping, however, can significantly compromise system performance. Every time a hard disk performs swapping, the hard disk must execute a write operation. This is significantly slower than RAM, which performs more quickly with less overhead.

Consequently, the larger the physical RAM the less time the system spends on swapping pages and the healthier the system performance.

For the exam, remember that more RAM or physical memory is the preferred remedy to reduce paging.

If you see Out Of Memory error messages, check the Virtual Memory settings at:

```
Start | Settings | Control Panel | System | Performance | Change
```

Configure the virtual memory from the dialog box shown in Figure 25.1.

For Windows NT Workstation, you cannot configure the Pagefile.sys to be less than 2 MB. By default, the size is set to the amount of RAM on the computer plus 12 MB. The maximum size for a page file is the amount of free space on the formatted partition. If you add to or enlarge the files a disk where the maximum free space is already used for paging, don't forget to reduce the paging file size.

This caution also applies to the minimum size. If you accept the default minimum, which is the size of the RAM plus 12 MB, and

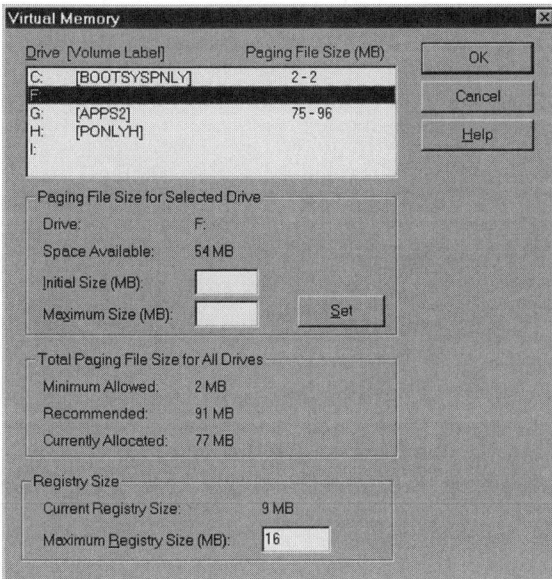

**Figure 25.1** Pagefile size and location both influence performance.

later free disk space falls below that minimum, there will be problems. For instance, if there is 48 MB of RAM on the computer, 60 MB will be the default minimum page file size. If free disk space falls to 45 MB, you must re-enter the minimum and maximum page file sizes.

If the server's paging file expands beyond its specified maximum size, the paging file fragments the disk and increases the start and response times for applications. Disk fragmentation slows down performance—page file fragmentation can seriously affect performance.

Adding RAM will give a boost to system performance by increasing caching and reducing paging.

### DOCUMENTS OPTIMIZATION

If a Windows NT Workstation user is commonly using an application whose ordinary files do not appear in the recently used Start | Documents menu, you can edit the registry to add them. This procedure allows you to add any file extension to the list shown on the recently used Documents menu.

This registry entry defines files to be considered "documents" by Windows NT:

```
HKEY_CURRENT_USER\SOFTWARE
      \Microsoft
           \Windows NT
                \CurrentVersion
                     \Windows

Documents      REG_SZ

Range: extensions
```

This registry change will not change the file associations for that computer. Filename extensions should be typed with a space between them and should not include preceding periods.

By reducing the time users must spend looking for recently used files, this method can help users gain time for productive work.

### Reboot Optimization

Another time saver is to reduce the time Windows NT waits for user selection of a dual-boot option during every re-boot. This setting is adjustable by either editing the boot.ini file, or from the Show List

For spinner on the Startup/Shutdown tab of the System applet in the Control Panel.

If users reboot daily, leaving the wait time at 30 seconds possibly wastes a half minute each day.

## FOR REVIEW

- Move the page file to hard disks other than the hard disk containing the boot/system partition.
- Add RAM to resolve paging problems.
- Any file extension can be added to the recent Documents menu.

## FROM HERE

Other areas related to topics in the chapter include Chapter 23, "Setting Application Priority," and Chapter 24, "Monitoring Tools."

# Index

## About the Authors

**Dave Kinnaman**, MCSE, from Austin, Texas, has coauthored many books and articles about computers and the Internet. Dave is particularly involved in information-access issues, including Internet filtering software, disability access, and retirement issues on the Internet.

After more than 18 years as an underpaid state employee, Dave is exploring options in the private and not-for-profit sectors.

With spouse LouAnn Ballew, Dave operates several health-related Internet discussion groups—their three-year-old open discussion of allergies has more than 800 members in 40 countries.

**LouAnn Ballew**, MCSE, is a networking consultant with 17 years in the computer industry and interests in online research methodology, doctor-patient and patient-patient communication issues caused by the current health care system and relocation to the Pacific Northwest.

# Windows NT 4.0 Workstation

Certified Professional Exam 70-73
Implementing and Supporting Microsoft Windows NT 4.0 Workstation
90 minutes, 51 questions, requires 705 of 1000

## Planning

### Storage Disks
Volume sets are not fault tolerant. NTFS volume sets *can* be expanded. Neither system nor boot files can be placed on a volume set. A volume set is read sequentially—least efficient first.
A stripe set is one logical partition. A stripe set *cannot be extended.*

#### FILE SYSTEM
Supported          CDFS, FAT, NTFS
Not Supported      FAT32, HPFS, Mac

#### INSTALLATION
/u—unattend.txt, UDF, and SYSDIFF (windiff.exe and setup.inf are incorrect)
unattend.txt is the *answer file*—All computers get default settings.
    The UDF provides specific information for individual computers.
    One unattend.txt for every hardware configuration
    The sysdiff.exe utility is used to install software applications that don't support scripted installations. Sysdiff.exe is OK; windiff.exe is not.
*SNAP*—Registry, files, and folders
*DIFF*—SNAP plus installed applications
*APPLY*—performs configurations

### Installation and Configuration
Workstation: 12M RAM, 486/25, 124M HDD, CD-ROM drive, or a floppy disk drive and an active network connection
Use Winnt32 to upgrade 3.51; use winnt for all new installs.
Use the Tape Devices applet to detect and configure a tape drive and install driver.
Windows NT 4.0 cannot be installed on a 386 computer.
To join a domain *during installation*, provide Administrator account and password.
Windows 95 cannot be upgraded to Windows NT Workstation 4.0.
The SCSI Adapters applet is used to install or remove SCSI adapter drivers.
Windows NT 3.x and Windows 95 printer drivers do not work with Windows NT 4.0.
The hardware is a *print device*; the *printer* is the *printer driver*, or interface software.
When multiple print devices are combined, they form a *printer pool.*

### Managing Resources
**MRS: M**—Move; **R**—Retain; **S**—Same (partition)
System policy changes go into effect only after user logoff/logon.
Account Policy in User Manager controls password restrictions.
Make a user profile mandatory by renaming Ntuser.dat to Ntuser.man.
NTFS rights accumulate, except for No Access. The least restrictive permission is given to the user, unless No Access.
Whenever NTFS file and folder permissions are combined with a share permission, the most restrictive permission is granted.
*Extra page after print*—Add Form feed in CSNW
*Alert print job*—Notify when printed in CSNW
*Separate jobs*—Print Banner

AppleTalk is required for Apple computers to print to NT printers and for NT to print to Apple computers. Install services for Macintosh.

The policy file is saved to the Netlogon share on the PDC as `Ntconfig.pol`.

## Connectivity

To access a NetWare server, install *Client Services for NetWare* (CSNW).

TCP/IP requires a unique IP, subnet mask, optional gateway if routed, automatically supplied by DHCP.

DLC protocol allows communication with a mainframe or a print device connected directly to the network with its own network adapter.

Peer Web services—FTP, Gopher, and WWW can be installed.

The Modems applet is used to install, modify, or remove modems.

PPP supports TCP/IP, IPX, and NetBEUI. A PPP server (Internet Service Provider) can supply a temporary IP address to the dial-in client computer. Slip cannot.

RAS acts as a NetBIOS network gateway. RAS also can act as an IP or IPX router to link LANs and WANs.

Authentication including clear text supports the widest variety of clients and allows Microsoft clients to use better encryption.

Multilink call back security allows only one call back phone number.

Password changes for Novell 3.x use *setpass*; for Novell 4.x NDS, use Alt+Ctrl+Del.

## Running Applications

Each DOS application runs as a single VDM, preemptively scheduled, with its own address space.

Windows 16-bit applications all share a single VDM by default. Within the VDM, threads are scheduled nonpreemptively. The VDM is scheduled preemptively with other VDMs and 32-bit apps.

Run 16-bit applications in a separate VDM, with the Run command or Start command. The Start command allows low, normal, high, or real-time (administrator only) priorities.

## Monitoring and Optimization

The most used protocol should appear first in the binding order.

A thread is the smallest unit of a process scheduled by the Scheduler Service or kernel.

SNMP runs over TCP/IP and must be installed on any computer that you want to remotely monitor with Windows NT Performance Monitor.

Both logical disk and physical disk counters require `Diskperf -y`.

Performance Monitor or Task Manager can be used to obtain information about Processor and Memory objects.

More RAM or physical memory is the preferred remedy to reduce paging.

Network Monitor Agent gathers statistics for traffic on the network.

## Troubleshooting

The ERD is not bootable. To use the ERD, you must have the three setup disks. Create the ERD with `rdisk /s`.

If the screen goes blank when testing the monitor type, the refresh frequency may be set incorrectly.

Nonsupported CD-ROM—Boot to Windows 95 or DOS, connect to a network share, and copy installation files to hard drive or install from a network share.

Use Regedt32 for security changes; use Regedit to search for keys and subkeys.

**Reset Spooler:** Start | Settings | Control Panel | Services | Spooler | Stop | Start

After new device driver, Windows NT boot fails. Use Last Known Good (spacebar); do not log in.

If *Users Must Log On In Order To Change Password* is selected, a user who does not change his password before the password expires requires assistance from the administrator to regain access to the network.